Moral Conscience through the Ages

Moral Conscience through the Ages

Fifth Century BCE to the Present

RICHARD SORABJI

The University of Chicago Press
Chicago

The University of Chicago Press, Chicago 60637
Oxford University Press, Oxford OX2 6DP

Paperback edition 2017
Printed in the United States of America

23 22 21 20 19 18 17 2 3 4 5 6
ISBN-13: 978-0-226-18272-8 (cloth)
ISBN-13: 978-0-226-52860-1 (paper)

Library of Congress Cataloging-in-Publication Data

Sorabji, Richard, author.
Moral conscience through the ages : fifth century BCE to the present / Richard Sorabji.
pages cm
Includes bibliographical references and index.
ISBN 978-0-226-18272-8 (cloth : alk. paper) 1. Conscience. 2. Conscience—Religious aspects. I. Title.
BJ1471.S64 2014
171'.6—dc23

2014017925

⊗ This paper meets the requirements of ANSI/NISO Z39.48-1992 (Permanence of Paper).

To Christopher and
Susan Bryan Brown

CONTENTS

ACKNOWLEDGMENTS

I am very grateful for excellent discussion in the seminars at which I tried these ideas out, first in the Philosophy Department at the Graduate Center of the City University of New York, and at the Classics Department of New York University, where Phillip Mitsis was kind enough to attend all the sessions. I then benefited very greatly from an interdisciplinary seminar put together by Richard Kraut in Philosophy at Northwestern University in 2011 and attended by students and faculty from many different departments from all of which I learned. I was also lucky to have among the anonymous referees obtained by Oxford University Press and University of Chicago Press readers whose expertise included in one case medieval philosophy and the later Aristotelian tradition and in another case political philosophy of the seventeenth to nineteenth centuries. They also made helpful suggestions on presentation. In a final set of four discussions at the University of Western Ontario, I was much benefited by their knowledge of the history of philosophy, and of contemporary political issues. Finally, I am very grateful to Dave Robertson for compiling the index locorum.

INTRODUCTION

This book starts with the question "what is moral conscience?" and seeks to identify a core concept established in the first five hundred years, to provide a framework that endured with variations for a further two thousand years until the present. It also seeks to trace a history of the treatment of conscience over that period, which encounters recurrent themes: the longing for different kinds of freedom of conscience, the proper limits of freedom, protests at conscience's being "terrorized," dilemmas of conscience, the value of conscience to human beings, its secularization, its reliability or unreliability, and ways to improve the values on which it draws. These historical issues are alive today, with fresh concerns about conscientious objection, the force of conscience, and the balance between freedoms of conscience, religion, and speech.

The original terminology for moral conscience,[1] found in the Greek playwrights of the fifth century BCE, and continued in Latin, has not been well understood in its Greek or Latin versions. Its meaning is indeed very surprising. But the original meaning coupled with the developments over the next five hundred years down to St. Paul established a framework and provides a thread that runs through the vicissitudes of the next two thousand years and helps us to understand them.

Etymologies are not merely a matter of grammar. They have often been offered in order to bolster one or another interpretation of moral conscience, and sometimes these interpretations had an ulterior motive. In chapter 1, I argue that the original meaning of the full Greek or Latin expressions was

1. I call conscience "moral," for the sake of French readers for whom "*conscience*" means consciousness, unless further qualified, as does the Latin *conscientia*, and the same may be true of yet other languages derived from Latin.

sharing knowledge with *oneself* of a defect, almost always a moral one of being in the *wrong*. This surprising metaphor suggests that each of us is split by bad conscience into two selves, one of which has the guilty knowledge but keeps it a secret and the other of which shares the secret. Conscience is a form of self-awareness that would always remain *personal*, and concerned with *particular* defects. Moreover, the idea of its *splitting* someone into two was to recur in Adam Smith, Immanuel Kant, and Sigmund Freud. More than that, it is a natural reaction to conscience to say, "I could not live with myself," as if, for another reason, one were two persons.

The idea of a moral defect looked to the past or present. But the forward-looking idea of *averting* future wrongdoing was also recognized by the fifth-century playwrights, and along with the forward-looking idea of *reform*, was connected by Epicurus to the terminology for moral conscience in the next century, the fourth century BCE.

The Greek terminology went over very easily into Latin. It has not always been recognized that the Latin represents no more than an attempt to preserve the etymology of the Greek. It thus preserves much of the original Greek implication of self-awareness and split personality, without imposing peculiarly Latin shades of meaning, however much Roman interests may have affected the concept over the course of time.

Christianity took over the concept and developed it differently for its own purposes, with St. Paul making very important innovations. He distinguished the *general* law of right and wrong written by God in our hearts from our *fallible* application of it to our own *particular* case. But he also emphasized non-Christians having a *bad* conscience, and Christians hoping to have a *clear* one. In both he retained the emphasis on believing oneself to be, or not be, in the *wrong*. I shall finish chapter 1 by offering a definition of the concept of moral conscience as it had developed up to Paul's time and by distinguishing features that were to persist.

So much for the original concept of moral conscience and its development. But there is also a history of how conscience was treated. A reversal in pagan-Christian interaction is described in chapter 2. Up to the third century CE, Christians borrowed Greek ideas about moral conscience. But after that they began to ignore interesting new treatments of conscience in Neoplatonism. By the sixth century the shoe was on the other foot, and one pagan Neoplatonist even had to bow to Christianity by explaining his concept of Socrates' guardian spirit in terms of Christian conscience.

During this period, as described in chapter 3, there were Christian debates on freedom of *religion* between 200 and 400 CE. The discussion anticipated many of the arguments for freedom of *conscience* that were to be offered in the seventeenth century, and even the refutation of one that Locke failed to foresee. When the terminology switched in the seventeenth century to freedom of *conscience*, we can see that freedom of religion is not quite the same thing, but the discussions remained close.[2] As regards freedom of religion in antiquity, there was different treatment for heretics, pagans, and Christian sinners. We move with alarming speed from pleas for freedom of *Christian* conscience to denial of freedom for *heretics*, and to Augustine's terrifying claim to have changed his mind about freedom, when he found that strictly limited persecution of heretics, falling well short of the death penalty, produced converts. *Pagans* fared by and large much better than heretics in a Roman Empire that long retained a pagan majority, and still needed the skills of Greco-Roman culture.

To skip for a moment to the twelfth century, there were important developments among Christians writing in Latin, as described in chapter 4. Reference to *synderesis* alongside conscience is recorded in manuscripts only then, and thirteenth-century thinkers looked for various roles for it to play. But these roles, both the motivational role suggested by Bonaventure and the general knowledge of right and wrong suggested by Thomas Aquinas and others, had already been covered by the accounts of conscience given by the Greco-Roman tradition and by St. Paul. The need to accommodate *synderesis* as well as conscience may possibly have arisen from a twelfth-century scribal error concerning a text of Jerome (ca. 347–419/420). Although Thomas connected *synderesis* with *general* knowledge, he usefully insisted that such knowledge had to be applied to one's own *particular* case and, as detailed in chapter 7, that stress on the particular case was taken to heart by the casuistry of the sixteenth to seventeenth centuries. Even if the distinction of *synderesis* was due to an error, it had significant consequences and traces survived even after Protestantism abandoned the concept.

Another aspect of conscience, recognized already by Greek tragedy, then, after hesitation, by Christians, especially from the twelfth century, was that sometimes we get into a moral *double* bind, so that whichever course of action we take is wrong. In some of these cases, it can be as wrong to follow our conscience as not to. Very different situations leading to a moral double bind were recognized by the sixth-century Christian Pope Gregory the Great, by Abelard, by Bonaventure and Thomas Aquinas in the twelfth to thirteenth centuries, by Pierre Bayle, and by Mahatma Gandhi. But the first of these, Gregory, was still anxious that if the moral double bind made sin inevitable, that should be through some earlier fault of the individual.

2. Ch. 8.

The later medievals dropped the requirement that the moral double bind must originate from personal fault, and Gandhi expanded the range of examples again.

Christian systems of penitence, discussed in chapter 5, ran continuously from 100 CE to beyond the Middle Ages. They were important, first because from the beginning they led Christians for centuries to examine their consciences, but later because by the twelfth and thirteenth centuries in the Western Church, they gave a greater role to the priest in absolving sins and obtaining eternal salvation. That greater role led in turn in the sixteenth century to Luther's complaint, the subject of chapter 6, that the systems *terrorized* conscience. He called for conscience to be freed from this "terrorization," and he claimed that another sort of freedom had already been offered to consciences by Christ, if only one had faith in his promise of mercy. His conscience accordingly turned from despair to joy, and he objected that the search for absolution had made conscience a burden. The earlier systems of penitence and absolution focused on *bad* conscience, the need to reveal it and atone, the need to examine conscience, to keep it watchful, sometimes the need to heal it. But the systems were at first designed to bring sinners *back* into the church community with conscience absolved. Even if the process of penance undertaken seems to us incredibly severe, priests were there to help, and it was clearly emphasized that absolution came from God. From the thirteenth century, the priest's role in obtaining absolution became greater. This may have encouraged the practice that sparked Luther's complaints, the selling of indulgences in return for absolution, although such practices were already condemned by Abelard in the twelfth century, and had their analogues in pagan Greece.

Luther and the Protestant Reformation had an unforeseen consequence discussed in chapter 7. Despite confession no longer being compulsory for Protestants, a new source of interest arose for Protestants and Catholics alike in *particular* dilemmas of conscience. In England, Catholics had had to hide their allegiance after 1559 and 1570. But oaths were demanded of others too every few years after that by the king, Parliament, the Model Army that defeated the king, and by those who supported the restoration of the monarchy. All those subjected to these conflicting oaths needed advice about dilemmas of conscience. The need was supplied from the mid-sixteenth to the mid-seventeenth century partly by the discipline of cases of conscience or casuistry as it was latterly known. The Jesuits, whose order was founded in 1540, were the leading practitioners, although a few English Protestant writers met Protestant needs. The criticism of casuistry, made famous by Pascal in the seventeenth century, was that it eased consciences through the development of lax evasions. But its strength was that it gave practical advice which recognized that universal rules have to be applied to particular circumstances.

The seventeenth century was above all the century of freedom of individual conscience, as described in chapter 8. The first English demands for freedom of individual conscience came from Baptists between 1612 and 1620, although they had to escape to Holland, or accept imprisonment. After two civil wars between 1642 and 1648, King Charles I was executed in 1649, Oliver Cromwell became the dominant figure and a commonwealth replaced the monarchy for a time. From 1643 John Milton called for freedom of conscience not only in religious adherence, within limits that excluded Catholicism, but also outside religion in the new areas of divorce and of publication. Thomas Hobbes, with whose views Oliver Cromwell identified, I believe, more closely than has been commonly recognized, wrote his case under the monarchy on the opposite side for surrendering individual conscience to a supreme sovereign. He published it in his *Leviathan* in 1651 under the Commonwealth, and had to re-explain his position at the restoration of the monarchy in 1660. In 1648–1649 the radical Levellers debated with Oliver Cromwell for three days on the subject of freedom of conscience, which they demanded both in religion, within limits that excluded both Catholicism and the Anglican system of bishops, and in military conscription. In these debates, Cromwell did not pull rank as the Levellers' senior in the victorious army, but himself spoke the very same language of conscience, appealing to the constraints on what his conscience would allow.

After the Restoration of the English monarchy in 1660, pleas for freedom of conscience became more dangerous. John Locke started off in 1660 decidedly intolerant of them and when he supported them, within limits, in 1667, he did not dare to publish. When new appeals for freedom of conscience were composed by John Locke, Pierre Bayle, and Benedict Spinoza, all three took refuge for a time in Holland: Locke from 1683 to 1688 as a refugee from England; Bayle as a refugee from Catholic persecution in France; and Spinoza as a native resident, but extruded from his Jewish community. After the tolerant William of Orange was invited from Holland to take the English throne, Locke was able to publish his famous *Letters Concerning Toleration* starting in 1689. His demand for freedom of conscience in religion was more restricted in certain ways than that of the other two, and did not include Catholics whom Bayle—strikingly—wanted well treated, at least as individual citizens, so long as they were not in a position to persecute others. What Locke called his *principal consideration* had been stated earlier in the century by the Baptist Thomas Helwys, and many of his other arguments had already been given in the ancient discussions of 197 to 408 CE, recorded in chapter 3. So had an objection to one of his arguments, which Augustine had made and which Bayle foresaw. Locke did not foresee it, and after it was pointed out to him, he had to revise his case in his second letter.

Pierre Bayle started by insisting on freedom equally for *erroneous* conscience, but came to recognize the necessary limits to freedom of conscience at least in relation to those whose consciences called for the suppression of other consciences—a real problem. His final position, supported by remarkable knowledge of ancient Greek thought, seems to have used the wider concept of toleration for erroneous religious beliefs, not so much to protect conscience, as to prevent irresoluble strife, because diversity of belief in religion is approved by God and makes erroneous doctrine inevitable.

Chapter 9 takes up the topic of the reliability of conscience. Unreliability had been stressed by the skeptic Montaigne, by Hobbes, and by Locke to the extent that he treated the moral principles on which conscience draws as often unreliable. The basis of one's conscience or principles might be mere custom, or the prejudices of those who brought one up. Locke did think that the measures of right and wrong might eventually be demonstrated with mathematical certainty. But his recommendations for gaining such certainty were very different from the steps for improving reliability to be advocated in chapters 10 and 12, and he did not think in any case that work had even started on his imagined demonstrative set of moral principles.

The eighteenth century saw several attempts to rehabilitate conscience, while acknowledging the influence of fellow humans on its content, and there were some retrenchments on the role of God. Bishop Butler and Adam Smith, though deeply religious themselves, explained the value of conscience with arguments that secularists could borrow. Butler pointed to the *function* of conscience as superintendent of all other psychological faculties. Adam Smith's idea of conscience as an imagined spectator, human or divine, was surely drawn from the Stoics and Epicurus, and he made the reliability of conscience depend on the impartiality of the imagined spectator. Kant's defense took a more secular step with his insistence that the ideal imagined spectator was only subjectively thought of as God, without any implication of God's objective presence. The very gradual secularization of the idea of conscience was, I believe, a *resecularization*, because the early Greek views of conscience were themselves comparatively secular. Rousseau allowed his Savoyard vicar to call conscience a much better guide than philosophy, because whatever had caused our being (on which he tried to avoid Church doctrine) had provided for our preservation by supplying us with innate *sentiments* suited to our nature. Kant's defense of conscience did not like the others consider how it might be reliable, so much as exempt it from the need for reliability by giving it a judicial role in which error was not a relevant liability. In Adam Smith and Rousseau, a new stress was placed on the connection of conscience with moral *sense* and with *sentiments*, such as disapproval, as opposed to *reason*, while in nineteenth-century England, J. S. Mill moved from sentiments to sensations and identified conscience with a sensation of pain. One can understand this shift, because painful bites and disapproval had in the original concept been seen rather as *consequences* of conscience—that is, of one's belief about what it had been or would be wrong for one to do.

The nineteenth and twentieth centuries included much more secular accounts of conscience, starting with Thoreau, some of them hostile as in Nietzsche, or concerned with the pathological as in Freud, who, drawing on Nietzsche, redirected attention from conscience to what he saw as its psychological basis in the superego. As discussed in chapter 10, Freud thought that his studies cast doubt on the role of God in conscience, but he seems, like Locke, to have been unaware that Christians had already denied the innateness or reliability of our *knowledge* of the law and the infallibility of conscience. Later Freudians needed to correct Freud's account of the development of conscience by drawing attention to important psychological influences which he had overlooked.

Nietzsche and Freud did not diminish the importance of conscience for others, and chapter 10 finishes with the nonsecular celebration of conscience in Tolstoy and Gandhi. Tolstoy's belief that conscience about violence would lead to a nonviolent future inspired Gandhi. Gandhi thought of conscience as the voice of God, and though he recognized that one has to learn how to listen, he treated what he heard from his *own* conscience as indubitable. In this he was like Socrates, whose account of his admonitory guardian spirit he paraphrased from an English translation into Gujarati. But Gandhi recognized that conscience can be mistaken, and also that that puts one in a moral double bind, wrong if one violates conscience and wrong if one follows it. His individualism and belief that different people have different duties gave conscience added importance in his eyes, because it speaks to the individual about individual duty.

I discuss also Gandhi's views on the reliability not of conscience, but of the values on which conscience draws. He gained his belief in nonviolence from reading Tolstoy. But he deepened the value he learned from Tolstoy by discussing with the communities he established how they should treat dangerous animals, and then by publishing his views in his own worldwide newspapers, along with objections to them. Each time he advanced the discussion by reflecting on the objections, until he came to a much fuller understanding, and brought some others to an understanding, of what the original value, nonviolence, amounted to.

There are many contemporary issues of conscience. Chapter 11 discusses the need for a balance in the law between freedom of conscience, of religion, and of speech. Conscientious objection is found in many areas including medicine and warfare. In Britain, conscientious objection to military conscription was widely accepted in the First World War of 1914–1918, not only on the ground of religion, but also on the ground of moral or socialistic objections. In the US, however, decisions were based on Madison's First Amendment of the Constitution in 1791, which had not spoken of conscience, so that only religious objection was accepted even as late as the Vietnam War in the 1970s. Some philosophers have recently argued that priority should be returned to freedom of conscience, and have discussed its *force*. This has been sought, I believe, in features *accidentally* related to conscience. The force urged in chapter 1 above as residing in the very *meaning* of conscience was due to conscience involving the idea of what it would be *wrong* for one to do.

Freedom of speech against groups was accepted by Madison in the First Amendment, but his modern interpreters have allowed the harassment of religious groups, arguably with implications for their religious freedom. Hate speech against worldwide religions can also imperil the safety of national property and personnel worldwide to an extent that Madison could not have foreseen. Hate speech arguably needs control, but balanced control, because an *unqualified* ban would license witch hunts for blasphemy. The Indian Constitution has a clever clause which requires *deliberate malice* to be proved in a prosecution for wounding or outraging religious feeling. This is a laudable attempt to strike a reasonable balance, but in practice implementation can go wrong. A further predicament recognized in Indian law concerns a potential conflict between protecting diversity of religious practice as against protecting individuals from unfair religious practice *within* their diverse religions.

In a retrospective chapter, chapter 12, I return to the question addressed at the end of chapter 1, what conscience is, and a more general recapitulation of what its nature has turned out to be. Of the variations over the centuries, only two of long duration were noticed. One was the introduction of *synderesis* alongside moral conscience as something that needed to be accommodated. The other was the eighteenth-century inclination to identify conscience with a sentiment like disapproval, rather than with belief about what had been or would be wrong, which *caused* that sentiment. These variations were not permanent, and others were more occasional, so that I believe there was a large measure of continuity. I describe the core of the idea of conscience, as I see it, over the ages. This provides a framework which makes it easy to understand the smaller deviations, but which also makes clear what has happened in the few cases where the original idea of conscience has been seriously violated. By and large, I think conscience remained a form of moral self-awareness concerning what in one's own case was or would be *wrong*, and it remained to a large extent the same as it had been in the early Christian period. Its resecularization I regard as no disadvantage and even as offering some advantages.

I return to the question of limits on freedom of conscience. Should it be offered to all erroneous consciences, however heinous their recommendations? Certainly, there should be limits. But nonetheless, Bayle's position stands that diversity of beliefs about God, and about right and wrong, may still need to be tolerated, not always for reasons of freedom of conscience, for consciences may be set on opposing each other, but because toleration may be the only means to keeping the peace.

I also return to the question of the *value* of conscience. Certainly, we need the *capacity* to think of our actual or potential actions as wrong. We would be inhuman without that. But how are we to improve the reliability of the values on which conscience draws, in response to the complaint that our moral principles are drawn from our local human contacts? Credible contributions toward an answer can be found in Bonaventure, Thomas Aquinas, Milton, Bayle, Adam Smith, Rousseau, and Kant. But I give a central role to two figures, first to J. S. Mill, even though his treatment of how to improve understanding, unlike the earlier treatment by Milton, made no reference to conscience, because of the reduced role he gave to it. I finish by returning to Mahatma Gandhi, as providing in his time a living example of the sort of practice that Mill recommended. In no case was conscience the *source* of his values, but reflection on his decisions of conscience helped to refine his values.

Among the difficulties of writing about a period of two and a half thousand years are the dangers of error, arising only partly from discussing centuries previously unfamiliar to the writer. There is the further problem that, although writing about the history of political philosophy would always call for knowledge of political events, that is only sometimes (it is sometimes) the case for the history of other branches of philosophy. One interest, but also one problem, about the present subject is that the idea of conscience became central to political events. It became central because views about conscience were propounded as part of a struggle in national, international, or church politics. This would be true of early Christian views about freedom of religion,[3] about the practice of penitence for bad conscience,[4] about the rise of Protestantism,[5] about the sixteenth- to seventeenth-century predicaments that called for professional advice on conscience,[6] and about the resulting calls for freedom of conscience.[7] Not only is it difficult to know enough about the politics, but with church politics, the danger remains strong of being misled by partisan interpretations. A further difficulty is the impossibility of taking up every element of the history. But I have nonetheless tried to trace a strand of overlapping threads. The chapters are arranged by topic, but a new topic may have special relevance to something that comes later, and yet go back in its origins to an earlier starting date. Even within a given chapter, a later view may need to be contrasted with a better-known earlier one, to avoid assimilation, or the trajectory of a topic may best be shown by starting with the two end points before those intervening. Nonetheless, there will be a gradual progression in time through the chapters, as brought out by the chapter headings. Each different topic tells a different story, but there should also be a gradual chronological progression, and the stories will interconnect. It should also be possible to trace a continuity through the successive stories, because they repeatedly refer back to the concept of conscience as developed in the first five hundred years of this account.

3. Ch. 3.
4. Ch. 5.
5. Ch. 6.
6. Ch. 7.
7. Ch. 8.

ONE

Sharing Knowledge with Oneself of a Defect: Five Centuries from the Greek Playwrights and Plato to St. Paul and First-Century Pagans

The Greeks and Romans played a vital role in the development of the concept of conscience, which Christianity took over and developed differently for its own purposes. Although the Hebrew Old Testament provides thrilling examples of what we should call conscience, notably in King David's remorse for acquiring Bathsheba by arranging the death of her husband, it used for conscience only the general word for heart, the seat of many different emotions. The few references to conscience in English versions of the Old Testament come from the ancient Greek translation of the Hebrew. This is not necessarily to say that the Hebrew writers lacked the concept. They could have had it without the word, and the Greeks may equally have supplied examples of moral conscience without the word. But it was the Greek word that stimulated Paul's discussions of conscience in the New Testament. It has been suggested that it may have been the Greek-speaking Corinthians, not Paul, who first raised the question of conscience in their correspondence.[1] Not only ancient Hebrew, but also medieval Arabic, lacked a word for moral conscience, and I have not been convinced that ancient Sanskrit had a word either. But modern Hebrew has introduced the word *matzpun*, and Arabic, which also spoke in the Middle Ages of the heart, has introduced the modern term *dameer*.

The Wording

The Greek expression which came to be the standard term for conscience began to appear with some of its eventual meaning in the playwrights of

1. C. A. Pierce, *Conscience in the New Testament*, SCM Press 1955.

the fifth century BCE. It involved a metaphor of one sharing knowledge with oneself, as if one were split into two. The shared knowledge is of a defect, and usually, except in Plato, of a moral defect. The metaphor was expressed by a particular form of the verb for knowing, *suneidenai*, to share (*sun*-) knowledge (*eidenai*), coupled with the reflexive pronoun in the dative (e.g., *heautôi* [oneself]). The metaphor is, but only rarely, expressed by other words starting with *sun*- (shared).[2] The magisterial work on the original meaning of the *Greek* terms was carried out by C. A. Pierce in his *Conscience in the New Testament*,[3] but he has seldom been followed. Moreover, he did not explain the force of *sun*- (sharing with), and the idea of one sharing knowledge with *oneself* is not obvious, but needs explaining. It treats us as if we were each composed of two people. One of them knows of the defect but is keeping it a secret; the other shares the secret—in cases of moral conscience, a guilty one. A different but analogous split, mentioned in the introduction, expresses moral conscience by saying, "I could not live with myself."[4] Since I first wrote about the split into two people, I have found the explanation in terms of a *secret* in two authors, Thomas Hobbes and C. S. Lewis, although neither recognizes this as the original meaning.[5] If the reflexive pronoun is absent, as it is bound to be when the noun or noun phrase is used (*suneidêsis, to suneidos*), instead of the verb, then one can tell only from the context whether the reference is to one sharing knowledge with oneself of a defect, for the root term, *suneid*-, can have quite a range of other meanings, though even here Pierce argues that the standard meaning involves one's own knowledge of one's own fault.[6] But in the particular grammatical construction specified, I believe the meaning is at first unambiguous.

2. *Sunhistorein* in Menander frag. 632, Koch, Teubner; *sunesis*, in Euripides' *Orestes* 396 and in Polybius 18.43.13 certainly refers to conscience, but might have the more general meaning of knowledge; *sungnôsis* in Philodemus, *De morte* 34. 35 (Kuyper), but probably not *xungnôsis* in Sophocles *Antigone* 926, the last two discussed below.

3. C. A. Pierce, *Conscience in the New Testament*, chs. 1–2, pp. 13–20, and *Analytical Index of Greek Sources*, pp. 132–47.

4. This expression is admirably discussed by James F. Childress, "Appeals to conscience," *Ethics* 89, 1979, 315–35, an article I read and agreed with only when my text was otherwise completed. Although appeals to conscience are a slightly different subject, I hope my account of the nature of conscience would support his excellent points.

5. Thomas Hobbes, *Leviathan*, ch. 7. The three stages are clearly distinguished by Mark Hanin, "Thomas Hobbes' theory of conscience," *History of Political Thought*, vol. 33, 2012, pp. 55–85; and C. S. Lewis, "Conscience and conscious," ch. 8 of his *Studies in Words*, 2nd ed., Cambridge University Press 1967.

6. C. A. Pierce, *Conscience in the New Testament*, ch. 3, p. 38.

Once we have this idea, the further idea of a *clear* conscience can then easily be expressed by simply inserting a negative: I do *not* share knowledge with myself of a defect. But the transition to the idea of sharing knowledge with oneself of *merit* comes a little later. It is rare in Greek and is not in the early playwrights or Plato, if I am right below about a truncated fragment of Sophocles.

It is usually thought that the original meaning of *suneidenai* must have been something less surprising—for example, sharing knowledge with *another* person. But I think that the sense of sharing knowledge with *another* person becomes common only later. There is one such use, we shall see, already in Plato in the fourth century. But it became common among lawyers, above all in Cicero in the first century BCE, to drop explicit reference to self, because lawyers are interested in the *other* party, in accomplices, witnesses, and confidants, who share the guilty knowledge of someone *else*.

Religious leaders, philosophers, and scholars have propounded many other etymologies in order to match their own theories of what the word for conscience means. Etymology may seem a specialist interest, but in fact fanciful etymologies have often been used with an agenda to support one or another conception of conscience.[7] In the thirteenth century St. Bonaventure understands the *con-* as meaning that conscience perfects our speculative capacity only insofar as that capacity is *joined* to desire and action.[8] Thomas Aquinas takes the *con-* to mean that conscience *applies* knowledge of right and wrong to some particular case.[9] Thomas Hobbes used the *con-* to support his view that conscience should not be mere private opinion, as he believes it has become, but must be the co-witnessed *public* law.[10] In their valuable book on casuistry,[11] Albert R. Jonsen and Stephen Toulmin take it that among casuists appeal to conscience was etymologically based on appeal to *shared community opinion*, and that appeal to unshared opinion is modern. It is not surprising that some of the best modern scholars and

7. On Calvin's definition of conscience, however, I suggest in ch. 9 that his reference to God as a witness of *others* does not exclude his recognition of conscience as *self*-awareness.

8. Bonaventure, *Commentary on the Sentences of Peter Lombard* 2.39, dist. 39a, article 1, question 1.

9. Thomas Aquinas, *Summa theologiae* 1, question 79, article 13; *On Truth*, question 17, article 1, reply; *Summa theologiae* 1, question 79, article 13, reply.

10. Thomas Hobbes, *Leviathan*, ch. 7, ed. Richard Tuck, p. 48.

11. Albert R. Jonsen and Stephen Toulmin, *The Abuse of Casuistry*, University of California Press 1988, 335.

historians have also offered their own alternatives.[12] But as regards the idea that conscience was until modern times based on shared community opinion, this does not fit with the interest in *erroneous* conscience as binding, to be discussed in chapter 4 as going back before the twelfth century, at least to Pope Gregory the Great in the sixth. Erroneous conscience tended not to reflect community opinion.

In Christian texts, Cicero's legal interest recedes. The central interest is in knowledge of one's *own* fault. But *alongside* this there sometimes comes to be an additional reference to *God* as witness. That idea is already prominent in the Stoic Seneca in the first century CE, who is congratulated by the Christian Lactantius for expressing the idea that one may try to avoid sharing one's guilty knowledge with one's fellow humans, but one cannot keep it hidden from *God*.[13] From this perspective, there is not much occasion for Christians to talk of one human sharing another *human's* guilty knowledge. The concern was that that would *not* be shared, which left God as the only one who could share it.

By strange good fortune, the special Greek idiom went over easily into Latin through the use of the adjective *conscius*, "sharing knowledge with." The Latin does not have an independent etymology of its own, but is a direct Latinization of the Greek participle *suneidôs*. One can say in Latin that a person is *sharing knowledge with* himself. The *con-* in the noun *conscientia* is simply a translation of the Greek *sun-* (shared with) and the *scientia* is a translation of Greek *eidêsis* (knowledge).[14] Because a literal translation, not a paraphrase, of the Greek term was used, Latin avoided importing its own presuppositions into the very choice of word, although obviously Latin-

12. One study of changes in meaning takes the original meaning of *conscientia* to have been sharing knowledge with someone *else*: Boris Hennig, "Cartesian Conscientia," *British Journal for the History of Philosophy* 15, 2007, 455–84 at 469. Another survey of important new ground sees the *con-* in *conscientia* as originally referring to *shared* values and public opinion: Paul Strohm, *Conscience, A Very Short Introduction*, Oxford University Press 2011, pp. 8, 10, 118. An important book on Luther treats the idea of conscience as starting with the Stoics, and takes from Lewis and Short's Latin dictionary that the root meaning of the Latin *conscientia* was knowledge shared with another, yielding a more exterior or public concept than the Greek: Michael Baylor, *Action and Person: Conscience in Late Scholasticism and the Young Luther*, Brill 1977, pp. 24–25. In his indispensible work, the foremost modern philosopher of war has conjectured that conscience came to mean a knowledge shared between God and man, although it also meant a knowledge shared among men: Michael Walzer, "Conscientious objection," in his *Obligations: Essays on Disobedience, War, and Citizenship*, Harvard University Press 1970, pp. 120–45, at 121–22 and 131.

13. Lactantius, *Divine Institutes*, 6.25.12–17.

14. The same is true of the Russian word for conscience, *so-vyestj*, as my one-time fellow student of Russian, Myles Burnyeat, has pointed out to me. The transliteration is my own attempt at capturing some of the pronunciation.

speaking society did less directly influence the meaning. Very early on, the Roman comic playwrights, Plautus in the third century BCE and Terence in the second, speak in Latin of sharing knowledge. Terence has a character say, "I am sharing knowledge with myself that this fault (*culpa*) is far from me." Plautus speaks of sharing knowledge of guilt with *another* person picked out by the reflexive pronoun: "Beware that they do not share knowledge with yourself (*ipsi*) of your wrongdoing."[15] The Latin tradition is continued by Cicero in the first century BCE and by the Stoic Seneca in the first century CE. Each speaks of sharing knowledge with oneself of a fault or of its absence, although the reflexive pronoun is not always explicit. Each also speaks of sharing knowledge of guilt with *another* party, and here they do not use the reflexive pronoun, except insofar as they are discussing the original guilty party. The sharers of guilty knowledge may be gods or humans, and even inanimate room walls are imagined as being witnesses.[16]

An increasingly common element in the Roman writers, Cicero and Seneca, is the interest in a conscience that shares knowledge of one's own *merit*. For the Greek term Pierce finds but one occurrence of this in Plato's contemporary, Xenophon, who speaks of us as sharing knowledge with ourselves of being practitioners of noble and good works. But otherwise, apart from the ambiguous fragment of Sophocles to be discussed, he finds only one example (sharing knowledge with oneself of patriotism) in a letter dubiously attributed to Demosthenes, fifty years the junior of Xenophon.[17]

The Fifth-Century Greek Playwrights

In the Greek playwrights of the fifth century BCE, the term *suneidenai* is used by the comic playwright Aristophanes (ca. 448–ca. 380 BCE) three times, with the reference to oneself explicit, and by the tragedian Euripides (c. 480–406 BCE) twice, with the reference to self understood.[18] In Aristophanes, people share knowledge with themselves of infidelity after three days of marriage, and of having set a defendant free by giving the wrong vote, and an ironical suggestion is made that someone will not succeed in politics if he shares knowledge with himself of having done anything good. In Euripides the knowledge shared with oneself is Orestes' self-knowledge

15. Plautus, *Rudens* 1247; Terence, *Adolphae* 348.

16. Cicero, *Pro Caelio* 60.

17. Xenophon, *Cyropaedia* 1.5.11; Demosthenes, *Epistulae* 2.20.

18. Aristoph., *Wasps* 999–1002; *Thesmophoriazousae* 477; *Knights* 184 (where "good" is ironical for "bad"); Eurip., *Medea* 495; *Orestes* 395–96.

of murder, and Jason's (insisted on by Medea) of his breaking his marriage oath to her. Orestes' self-knowledge is initially called *sunesis*, which might have the more general meaning of knowledge, but in this and another text refers to conscience, being clarified here in terms of sharing knowledge with oneself. The examples of sharing knowledge with oneself given by these playwrights, unlike many of those in Plato, all involve a *moral* failing. It may also be the meaning of an ambiguous one-line fragment in the still earlier fifth-century playwright Sophocles (496–406 BCE), that it is a terrible thing (*deinon*) for one who is (normally) virtuous (*esthlos*) when he shares knowledge with himself of fault (*hênik' hautôi suneidêi*).[19]

In another passage,[20] Sophocles uses a different word for shared knowledge, omitting the dative ("with ourselves"), when he has Antigone speak of her punishment by King Creon for burying her brother in accordance with what she has earlier in the play called a "law higher than the king's."[21] If our punishment, she says, is well with the gods, then after our sufferings we might share knowledge (*xungnoimen*, a form of *sungnoimen*) of having erred. But it is ambiguous with whom she thinks of this posthumous knowledge as being shared. It might be simply that she may share the knowledge of *others*, like King Creon, that she has erred. There will have been no previous guilty knowledge of her *own* for her to share with *herself.*

Euripides also distinguishes good and bad shame (*aidôs*). The good shame should avert one's wrongdoing, the bad torments one for it. But Phaedra, who fancied her stepson, is made to lament that the occasion for acting on the good shame is not clear.[22] The good shame, we might imagine, should have stopped her even thinking of him that way. Good shame (*aidôs*) and the virtue of heeding good shame (*aidêmosynê*) become a prominent subject in the Stoic Epictetus in the first century CE.[23]

19. The contextless fragment of Sophocles at 669 Dindorf is taken from Stobaeus, and Pierce plausibly suggests that at least Stobaeus understood it to refer to a fault. But Pierce (less plausibly, I think) allows it to be just possible that Jebb's less obvious rendering of *deinon* is right, which would mean that Sophocles himself originally meant the opposite: "It is a powerful aid (*deinon*) when a virtuous person shares knowledge with himself of his merit."

20. Sophocles, *Antigone* 926. I am grateful to Christopher Strachan for pointing out the passage to me.

21. Sophocles, *Antigone* 450–57, discussed below.

22. Euripides, *Hippolytus* 380–87, as analyzed by Bernard Williams, *Shame and Necessity*, University of California 1993, p. 95.

23. Rachana Kamtekar, "*Aidôs* in Epictetus," *Classical Philology* 93, 1998, 136–60; Epictetus, *Discourses* 1.5.3–5; 2.8.23; 3.7.27; 4.5.22–23; frag. 14, with Diogenes Laertius, *Lives* 7.116; Stobaeus, *Eclogae* 2.61 (Wachsmuth), lines 10–11; Ps.-Andronicus, *On Emotions*, in H. Von Arnim (ed.), *Stoicorum veterum fragmenta* 3.432.

It has often been said that early Greek culture is a culture of shame, not of guilt. Werner Jaeger added that the conscience of a Greek was entirely public and that the early Greeks never conceived anything like the personal conscience of modern times.[24] But whatever may be the case in Homer, I do not think that shame can be separated off from guilt so easily in all the examples given by the later dramatists. Even in the guilt culture which Christianity is said to be, shame and guilt can very well accompany each other. The difference between shame and guilt has been explained in one account by saying[25] that the person who is ashamed is thinking about what sort of person he is, typically in relation to the imagined contempt of others concerning his deficiencies, but sometimes, as I think the account agrees, in relation to his own self-image. The deficiencies include nonmoral ones like poverty. The person who feels guilt, by contrast, is typically thinking more narrowly about a victim and justified recrimination. So far this account in terms of a victim omits the idea of violating the requirements of an authority such as God. But another source of guilt, I believe, is thinking about violation of the requirements of an accepted, possibly divine, authority and about that authority's disapproval, whether or not there is a victim. I agree with a further claim in this account that, although the Greeks do not distinguish guilt from shame, the situations which provoke shame in the Greek portrayals in some cases provoke also the attitudes which *we* distinguish as guilt, even though the Greeks and Romans did not make the distinction.

This sort of phenomenon is common. King David clearly showed tormented conscience, despite there not being a Hebrew word to distinguish this from other affections of the heart. May not moral guilt be included along with shame in the idea of Jason's breaking his marital oath, of Orestes murdering his mother, and of Aristophanes' case of marital infidelity after three days? For these all involve a victim, and one at least invites divine disapproval. Jason has violated his oath to the gods, who side with Medea. There are complications about assigning feelings of guilt. Orestes' feelings are bound up with ideas of pollution, but E. R. Dodds has argued that this does not prevent him from feeling guilt rather than shame.[26] Another complication is that the divine Furies who in Aeschylus' earlier dramatization pursue the matricide Orestes are replaced in Euripides' account, cited above,

24. W. Jaeger, *Paideia*, 2nd ed., Oxford 1945, vol. 1, p. 9. I thank J. Zachuber for the reference.

25. Bernard Williams, *Shame and Necessity*, 88–94 and appendix 1.

26. E. R. Dodds, *The Greeks and the Irrational*, University of California Press, 1956, ch. 2, "From shame culture to guilt culture."

by Orestes' self-shared knowledge of his misdeed, treated by his *interlocutor* not as guilt, but as a mere sickness (*nosos*). But what matters is that Orestes *himself* believes he has violated divine authority.

Guilt does seem to be discussed in a philosophical fragment ascribed to the fifth-century philosopher Democritus (flourished 435 BCE) which says: "Some people, through not recognizing the dissolution of human nature (at death) and through sharing knowledge (*suneidêsis*) with themselves of wrongdoing in life, make the time in which they have life miserable with anxieties and fears, inventing falsehoods about the time after death."[27]

Plato

Whether or not there is a sense of guilt, the knowledge shared with oneself in cases of conscience is of a moral defect, whereas the defect is not always moral in Plato's examples, to which I shall now turn. It is because the defect in Plato's examples is often intellectual that I have spoken of the full expression, "sharing knowledge with oneself," as one that *came to be* the standard term for conscience. But in the earlier playwrights and after Plato, the defect was standardly moral, and so I shall not keep repeating the caveat.

In all nine cases where Plato (ca. 427–348 BCE) uses the full expression "to share knowledge with oneself," he is referring to knowledge of one's own defect or weakness, or once of its absence.[28] Socrates shares knowledge with himself of his own ignorance, Alcibiades of self-neglect and unjustifiably disobeying Socrates, Cephalus of faultlessness—of *not* having committed injustice, others of being seduced by poetry, of being unduly hasty or precipitate, of speaking well only of Homer and so lacking any art of literary criticism, and of their feeble attempts in childhood to distinguish letters from each other—admittedly a trivial defect in this case. In one last case in *The Laws*, Plato speaks of people not wanting anyone *else* to share their *own*

27. Democritus fr. 297 in Diels, Kranz.

28. Plato, *Apology* 21B 4 and 22D 1 (Socrates' claim to know nothing in the second passage supports my interpretation of the first as expressing awareness of not being wise, rather than mere nonawareness of being wise. I thank Christopher Taylor for the query); *Phaedrus* 235C 7 (aware of own ignorance in all three passages so far); *Symposium* 216A 3; B 3 (aware of self-neglect and mistaken disobedience to Socrates); *Republic* 331A 2 (aware of no injustice in self); *Republic* 607C 6 (aware that seduced by poetry [reading: *hautois*]); *Laws* 773B 1 (aware that unduly hasty and precipitate); *Ion* 553C 5 (aware that others say I speak well only about Homer, in which case I may lack the art of literary criticism); *Theaetetus* 206A 2 (aware of youthful attempts to distinguish letters [a weakness, not a fault]); *Laws* 870D 2 (sharing someone else's guilty knowledge, which he also shares with himself, of cowardice or injustice).

guilty knowledge of their cowardice or injustice. He uses the reflexive pronoun "themselves" (*sphisin*), evidently to emphasize that the people share the guilty knowledge with themselves. These nine cases make it particularly clear what is meant when the verb is used with the reflexive pronoun. That leaves four cases in which Plato speaks of sharing knowledge with *another* person, *without* using the reflexive pronoun. In these cases the knowledge is usually about their bad actions, but once about their talents, and once about whether they will take the course of action that has just been praised as the only acceptable one.[29]

Divine or Natural Law in Pagan Greeks

The idea of divine law, which the Christian Paul would later connect with conscience, was not missing from Greece of the fifth century BCE. It was merely not explicitly associated with the words that were used for conscience. Already in the fifth century BCE, the philosopher Heraclitus said that all human laws are fed by the one divine law.[30] Aristotle drew attention to two other examples from the same century. Antigone, in Sophocles' play of that name, accepts that the king's law (*nomos*) forbids her to bury her brother, and claims no exemption from punishment. But she insists that there is a more important law (*nomimon*) not of today or yesterday but of all times which requires her to bury him.[31] Aristotle calls it a natural law (*nomos kata physin*) and naturally just (*physei*). His second example is the philosopher Empedocles, who spoke in the same century of a law (*nomimon*) that, unlike human laws, obtained everywhere that one should not kill sentient beings, animal or human.[32] Aristotle gives a third example from the next century, his own, of Alcidamas, who declared, contrary to Aristotle's own view, that no slavery is natural. Cicero ascribes to Zeno who founded Stoicism in 300 BCE the belief that natural law (*naturalis lex*) is divine and commands what is right and forbids the opposite.[33] Elsewhere he describes the law more fully.[34] God gave the law, but it also comes from nature, and it holds at all times and places. The bold step that is found already in Plato is

29. Plato, *Apology* 34B 5; *Euthyphro* 4C; *Symposium* 193E 4; *Protagoras* 348B 7.
30. Heraclitus, *frg*. 114 (Diels-Kranz).
31. Sophocles, *Antigone* 450–57.
32. Aristotle, *Rhetoric* 1.13, 1373b 4–17.
33. Cicero, *On the Nature of the Gods* 1.14. 36.
34. Cicero, *On Laws* 1.6.18, 1.7.23, 1.12.33, 2.4.8; *On the Republic* 3.22.33.

the internalization of natural law, which is identified with reason or intellect. In Plato's *Laws*, it is said that we should identify the administration of intellect (*dianomê nou*) as law.[35] Cicero, as a Platonist, says that the internal law is the same as reason, that is, correct reason not wrong reason, in the human mind, and we all have right reason—even those who go against it. We shall see a similarly Platonist idea in Philo of Alexandria, that right reason is a *law* (*nomos*) imprinted by immortal nature in the immortal *mind*.[36]

Stoic law does not consist of specific rules like the Ten Commandments of Moses or his dietary laws. An example of Stoic law is given by Cicero five times in book 3 of his *On Duties*. He uses four expressions for it: "law of nature" four times (*naturae lex*), "law of nativity" (to paraphrase "born with a law"—*lege natus*), "law of nations" twice (*ius gentium*), and "formula" three times (*formula* also in Latin). On each of these occasions he gives the same example of a law. There are common bonds of humanity and certain behavior would break them. In giving the formulation of the Stoic Antipater, Cicero puts the point more positively: the common interest of human society should be yours and vice versa.[37] The Stoic Seneca comes out with just the same example, when he looks for a *formula*. After describing the natural bonds of human society, he thinks the *formula* is best summed up in the verse of the comic playwright Terence: "I am a human; nothing human do I think to be alien from me."[38]

It has been held that the idea of conscience presupposes the idea of law,[39] and that the idea of moral right and wrong presupposes the idea of a lawgiver.[40] It is true that conscience presupposes some knowledge of wrong on which it draws. But that knowledge need not take the form of a law. When the words for conscience about wrongdoing are used as early as the fifth-century BCE playwrights, the wrong done includes an element that we would call moral, without any invocation of divine or natural law, despite the idea's availability. Until St. Paul, sharing knowledge with oneself about wrongdoing and divine law remained separate ideas.

35. Plato, *Laws* 713E–714A.

36. Philo, *Every Good Man Is Free* 46, included in *Stoicorum veterum fragmenta* 3.360 (von Arnim).

37. Cicero, *On Duties* 3.19–21; 23; 27–28; 52–53, 169.

38. Seneca, *Letter* 95.51–53.

39. M. Waldemann, "Synteresis oder syneidesis?," *Theologische Quartalschrift* 119, 1938, 332–71.

40. G. E. M. Anscombe, "Modern moral philosophy," *Philosophy* 33, 1958, 1–19.

Socrates' Guardian Spirit

There was another idea which, like divine law, remained as yet separate from that of sharing knowledge with oneself of wrongdoing, but which had some analogy with the idea of conscience, and which was later to become more closely identified with it. Plato presents his mentor Socrates (469–399 BCE) as frequently being warned by a daemon (*daimôn*, spirit; or *daimonion*, spiritual being) acting as a guardian spirit. According to Plato, the daemon is a voice which opposes some of Socrates' intentions, but never proposes.[41] The point is not a *grammatical* one that the daemon prefers the negative form of words. On the contrary, Xenophon's slightly later account of Socrates allows that the daemon may tell Socrates to do things as well as not to do them.[42] The idea is that the daemon tells Socrates to change some of his *intentions*. Whether such an instruction is formulated in terms of staying or not going, it can equally *countermand* an intention to leave.

There are analogies with conscience, for that too was often to be heard as a voice and as forbidding conduct. But in contrast with St. Paul's treatment of conscience, Socrates treats as *indubitable* the warnings of the daemon, and it is made explicit by Xenophon that they are indubitable.[43] St. Paul's conscience was not indubitable, and not the voice of God. Rather, it was to bear witness on the day of judgment, accusing or excusing one, while God would be not the witness, but the judge.

In Plato's *Apology*, Socrates is accused of not believing in any gods (*theoi*), but in new-fangled spiritual beings (*daemonia*). Plato gives him the merely dialectical reply that a spirit or daemon is thought to be a god or the child of a god by a nymph or such like, and so they should think that, in believing in daemons, he believes also in gods.[44] In Plato's *Timaeus* he identifies Socrates' daemon with the most authoritative type of soul which is placed in the head and is intellectual (*katanooun*)—in other words, his intellect. If Socrates' daemon is his intellect, this does not initially seem to fit with the dialectical claim that the daemon is a god or child of a god. But the daemon is recognized as in some broad sense the divine (*theion*) type of soul, though

41. Plato, *Apology* 31D–32A (a voice, only opposes); *Apology* 40A–C; *Phaedrus* 242B–C (opposition).

42. Xenophon, *Recollections of Socrates* 1.1.4 (orders to do or not to do). Gregory Vlastos sees Xenophon's account as differing in this from Plato's, in his *Socrates, Ironist and Moral Philosopher*, Cornell University Press 1991.

43. Xenophon, *Recollections* 1.3.4.

44. Plato, *Apology* 26 C–E; 27 C–E.

not as a god, merely as given to us by God (*theos*). It is said to suspend (*anakremmannunai*) the body from the heavens and keep it upright.[45]

There are advantages in taking Socrates' daemon to be his intellect. For this will imply that what it says is something that he already had available to himself in his intellect, but failed to recognize, and that has been argued to be exactly Plato's view.[46] It would also fit with the idea, not here expressed, that he shares knowledge with himself, or at least with his intellect.

Four centuries later than Plato, a Platonist contemporary of St. Paul, Plutarch (ca. 46–120 CE), wrote a treatise on Socrates' daemon, and included a speech which reminds us both of Plato's *Timaeus* and of conscience. The speech claims to be reporting what had been learned from an oracle about Socrates' daemon or guardian spirit. In apparent contrast with Plato's *Timaeus*, Plutarch says that people are wrong to call it intellect (*nous*) as if it were internal (*entos*). It is really a daemon and external (*ektos*) to the body and to the irrational parts of the soul, which are sunk in the body. It is compared with a buoy floating above the water. But though external, it is in contact (*epipsauein*) with the head, and it holds up with a tether the irrational parts of the soul submerged in the water, just as it was said in the *Timaeus* to suspend (*anakremmannunai*) the body from the heavens and keep it upright. Through this tether it inflicts on the irrational parts of the soul repentance and shame (*metameleia, aiskhunê*),[47] reminding us still further of conscience. But Plutarch will have diverged from Plato when he added to the function of warning the further functions of causing repentance and shame. In Plato, Socrates' daemon does not shame him.[48]

Aristotle

After Plato there arose in Athens the schools of his pupil Aristotle (founded 335 BCE), of Epicurus (founded about 307 BCE), and of the Stoics (founded 300 BCE), while the Roman Cicero concentrated his philosophical writings between 45 and 43 BCE. I have so far left out Aristotle except for his references to natural law, and this may seem surprising since Thomas Aquinas was in the thirteenth century to use Aristotle's practical syllogism to expli-

45. Plato, *Timaeus* 90 A–D.

46. Roslyn Weiss, *Socrates Dissatisfied: An Analysis of Plato's* Crito, Oxford University Press 1998, 17–23.

47. Plutarch, *On the Daemon of Socrates* 591E–592B.

48. Nor for that matter is it described as refuting him—*elenkhein*, the word later used for one's conscience *convicting* one. It is Socrates and his intellect which do the refuting of *other* people.

cate the workings of conscience. However, Aristotle's practical syllogism did not happen to use examples of conscience, but chiefly of virtue or of healthy living. Aristotle nonetheless uses in two places the terminology of sharing knowledge with oneself of a moral fault: in one knowledge of an intellectual fault; and the *Magna Moralia*, whether by him, as recently argued, or by his school, reflects the later idea of sharing with oneself knowledge of merit.[49] In his account of self-love, without using the terms for conscience, he describes bad people as not amicably disposed toward, but at variance with, themselves. Some go against their better judgment about their own welfare. Others who are hated for their terrible deeds commit suicide.[50] Cicero tells us that the Aristotelians thought that the guilty were better off being "bitten" (*morderi*) by conscience, which is a pain provided by nature.[51] Aristotle thus illustrates tendencies familiar from elsewhere, but on this subject more innovations are to be found in his successors, the Epicureans, Stoics, and Cicero.

Epicureans

Cicero and Seneca ascribe to Epicurus a view of conscience as *fear* of detection and punishment.[52] Seneca disagrees that fear is the only motive for justice, but agrees that it is an effect of injustice. Cicero finds this an unsettling form of conscience and complains that Epicurus rejects the steady conscience that he believes in.[53] The Epicurean Lucretius in the first century BCE uses the standard Latin term for conscience, when he says that the mind which shares knowledge with itself (*sibi conscia*) of bad deeds torments itself with *fears* about the Furies and punishment after death in Tartarus, even though punishment cannot come from supernatural sources, nor after death, when our atoms will have dispersed.[54] We have already seen Euripides in the fifth century BCE replacing the Furies with the sickness of a bad conscience, and the same reinterpretation of supernatural punishment as bad conscience is found in a good many authors, Greek and Latin, and repeated by the

49. Aristotle, *Rhetoric* 2.5, 1382b6; *History of Animals* 9.29, 618a26 (of a cuckoo); *Nicomachean Ethics* 1.4, 1095a25 (intellectual fault); *Magna moralia* (now argued authentic by Peter Simpson, *The Great Ethics of Aristotle*, Transaction Publishers 2014), 1.25, 1192a26.

50. Aristotle, *Nicomachean Ethics* 9.4, 1166b5–29.

51. Cicero, *Tusculan Disputations* 4.45.

52. Seneca, *Letters* 97.15–16; Cicero, *On Ends* 2.16.53.

53. Cicero, *On Ends* 2.22.71.

54. Lucretius, *On the Nature of Things*, bk. 3, lines 1011–1024.

Christian Origen for the fires of hell.[55] Conscience cannot consist merely of fear, and we shall see in chapter 5 that the Christian Clement of Alexandria has something to say about this. In Christianity conscience can coexist with fear of punishment, so long as it is not swamped by it.

But Cicero ascribes to Epicurus a more fruitful idea, closer to our own idea of conscience: that of being *watched*. People believe (wrongly according to Epicurus) that even if they escape human eyes, they are watched by the gods, and so they are troubled in conscience (*conscientia*).[56] Epicurus held that members of the school should *imagine* that *he* was watching them as a witness to avert wrongdoing.[57] As well as imagining a watcher as witness, Epicurus is credited by Seneca with the idea of imagining an admired philosopher as an example (*exemplum*). This moves from one function of conscience, averting wrongdoing, to another, directing toward doing right. Both ideas are credited to Epicurus in a single passage.[58] Imagination was facilitated by the bust of Epicurus in the Athenian school and by the seal rings of his image which ancient Epicureans wore according to Cicero *On Ends*, of which examples have been found and impressions made.[59] Epicurus' imagined philosophical watcher, endorsed also by the Stoics, foreshadows the conscience as imagined impartial spectator in Adam Smith.[60]

Another function of conscience is reform, and Seneca credits Epicurus with interest in that, when he reports him as saying that recognition of sin (*notitia peccati*) is the beginning of salvation.[61] Still more surprising is the connection made by the Epicurean Philodemus around 100 BCE between conscience and the practice of *confession*. Philodemus' *Rhetoric* describes people who because of a guilty conscience (*syneidêsis*) engage in lawsuits until they are convicted and ruined.[62] His *On Death* uses a rarer Greek word for conscience when it speaks of a (good) conscience (*sungnôsis*) and irre-

55. Ps.-Democritus, *frag.* 297; Cicero, *Pro Roscio Amerino* 24.67; Diodorus Siculus (Greek historian of first century BCE), *Bibliotheca historica* 4.65; Origen, *De Princ.* II 10.4.

56. Cicero, *On Ends* 1.16.51.

57. Seneca, *Letters* 25.5.

58. Seneca, *Letters* 11.8–10.

59. Cicero, *On Ends* 5.3: impression of finger ring from British Museum reproduced in Peter Green, *Alexander to Actium: The Historic Evolution of the Hellenistic Age*, University of California Press 1990, p. 629. I am grateful to Nathan Gilbert at the University of Toronto Classics Dept. for showing me this. Busts of Epicurus are illustrated in Bernard Frischer, *The Sculpted Word, Epicureanism and Philosophical Recruitment in Ancient Greece*, University of California Press 1982.

60. Adam Smith, *Theory of Moral Sentiments*, pt. 3, ch. 1.

61. Seneca, *Letters* 28.9–10.

62. Philodemus, *Rhetoric* 2, frg. 11, lines 1–9 (Sudhaus), 139–40.

proachable life,[63] the word used in Sophocles' *Antigone*, line 926, but not probably in the same sense. But most striking for our purposes is the treatise *On Frank Criticism* about the practices in the residential school in Athens two hundred years after Epicurus, which included confession by students and even teachers more than a hundred years before the birth of Christ.[64] One fragment declares: "Even the servants share his (guilty) knowledge (*synoidasin*)."[65] Another fragment, on the standard reading, says that if the professor quickly turns away from assisting the student who is slipping up, the student's swelling (*synoidêsis*) will subside.[66] Why should professorial neglect make a *swelling* subside? This makes no sense, and an emendation suggested a long time ago by C. J. Vooys should be accepted. *Syneidêsis* (conscience) differs from *synoidêsis* (swelling) by only the one letter "e," which, in Greek as in English, looks very like an "o," so that the words are easily confused. Moreover, four short lines later the related verb *syneidenai* appears. It makes perfect sense that the student's conscience will become less intense, if the professor does not attend to criticism and help of the right sort, and this gives us a picture of the Epicurean school in Athens at the time of Philodemus' teacher, Zeno of Tarsus, in the second century BCE. Confession is concerned with the past, but the school is concerned with the future-looking functions of conscience and wants to develop the consciences of its students through a process of confession of misdemeanors and carefully tailored, but frank, criticism.

The Stoics

The Stoics, especially Seneca (ca. 4 BCE—65 CE), inherited Epicurus' interest in *watchers* and in *reform*, though not his rejection of a role for God. Seneca's conscience is open to God, and one has God within as an observer of bad and good.[67] In two different letters, Seneca asks us to live as if someone (presumably someone human) were observing us, then points out that in fact nothing is hidden from God, and as a result he determines that he

63. Philodemus, *De morte* 34. 35 (Kuyper). I thank David Armstrong and Benjamin Henry for showing me this text and the latest emendations of it. The verb is used by Herodotus for admitting something, as Henry Chadwick points out in his comprehensive survey, "Conscience in ancient thought," in his *Studies on Ancient Christianity*, Ashgate 2006, ch. 20, at p. 7.

64. Philodemus, *On Frank Criticism*, frg. 41.

65. Philodemus, *On Frank Criticism*, col. 12a, line 5.

66. Philodemus, *On Frank Criticism*, frg. 67. I thank David Sider for showing me the emendation.

67. Seneca, frg. 24 Haase (=Vottero 89) from Lactantius, *Divine Institutes* 6.24.12; *Letters* 41.1–2.

will watch himself. Thus, he brings in three different types of watcher.[68] His younger Stoic contemporary, Epictetus (ca. 50–ca. 125 CE), also brings in God, and gives his reference to watching a Socratic turn when he says that God (Zeus) has installed a daemon within us to watch us and is within us himself.[69]

Seneca approves Epicurus' further idea, when he repeatedly advises you to have a philosopher as companion and mentor,[70] or to imagine an admired philosopher simply watching you.[71] Seneca and Epictetus also recommend imagining a past philosopher to serve as a model and example (*exemplum*).[72]

We saw Seneca approving Epicurus' interest in reform when he reported him as saying that recognition of sin is the beginning of salvation. He himself regards such recognition as leading to a desire for *correction* and *reform* (*emendare*).[73] Epictetus, we have noticed, made use of the idea of good shame, *aidôs*, earlier highlighted by Euripides.

But the Stoics also introduced differences. As already remarked, the Romans Cicero and Seneca, writing in Latin, speak much more than the Greeks of sharing knowledge with oneself of one's own *merit*, and of a correspondingly *joyful* conscience. Seneca had particular occasion to refer to merit in discussing the ethics of benefactors in his treatise *On Benefits*.[74] In the second century CE, the Stoic Roman Emperor Marcus Aurelius has a special word, *eusyneidêtos*, for having a good conscience.[75] But the idea of sharing awareness of *merit* was largely dropped by Christianity,[76] and references to a joyful conscience are scarce. At most, Origen cites St. Paul's Second Letter to the Corinthians: "Our boast (*kaukhêsis*, Latin *glorificatio*) is this: the testimony of our conscience that we have behaved in the world, and still more toward you, with holiness and godly sincerity." Origen glosses this claim, in Rufinus' Latin paraphrase, by saying that conscience rejoices and exults

68. Seneca, *Letters* 83.1–2; 23.1–2. See on this Shadi Bartsch, *The Mirror of the Self: Sexuality, Self-Knowledge, and the Gaze in the Early Roman Empire*, University of Chicago Press 2006.

69. Epictetus, *Discourses* 1.14.11–15.

70. Seneca, *Letters* 6.5–6; 52,1–4.

71. Seneca, *Letters* 11. 8–10; 25.5–6; cf. 32.1; 83.1–2.

72. Seneca, *Letters* 95.72; 104,21–2; *On Leisure* 1.1, *On the Shortness of Life* 14.5; Epictetus, *Handbook* 33.12.

73. Seneca, *Letters* 28.9–10.

74. See Cicero, *Tusculan Disputations* 2.64; Seneca, *On Benefits* 2.33.2–3, 4.11.3, 4.12.4, *Letters* 71.76, and on his wife's approval of his interrogating himself on his conduct at the end of the day, *On Anger* 3.36.

75. Marcus Aurelius, *Meditations* 6.30.

76. Paul's claim in Acts 23:1 under interrogation to have a good conscience and the appeal in 1. Peter 3.21 for a good conscience probably mean a clear conscience.

(*gaudere, exsultare*) in good deeds.[77] The idea of a *joyful* Christian conscience can also be used in John Chrysostom (347–407 CE) in connection with the martyr, whose conscience makes him joyful in adversity.[78] However, a joyful conscience was the very antithesis of the repentance for which the Christian Church often called and of the despairing conscience of Luther. It was only by shifting to an entirely different view that Luther acquired a joyful conscience when he found merciful redemption in the promise of Christ's Gospel.[79]

A valuable contribution of the Stoics was their interest in self-interrogation. This took several forms and one was of only indirect relevance to conscience: mistaken judgment might be avoided, they thought, if we questioned appearances before assenting to them. This was applied by them not particularly to matters of conscience, but to other types of value. When situations initially appeared harmful or beneficial and such and such a reaction appeared appropriate, we were to *question* these appearances before reacting. By withholding assent until satisfied, we could avoid misguided emotions, since they depended on *assent* to appearances.[80] This would prevent emotionalism rather than serving conscience, even if the practice of self-interrogation might encourage the questioning of conscience as a *side effect*. Joseph Butler's definition of conscience as "an approbation of some principles or actions and disapprobation of others" has been thought to derive from the Stoic Epictetus, even though Epictetus was referring to the approbation and disapprobation of these other values, not those of conscience.[81]

A more directly relevant form of self-interrogation, practiced every evening, was learned by Seneca from a contemporary Pythagorean, Sextius, and it is found in a later Pythagorean text, the *Golden Verses*.[82] Seneca tells us

77. Second Letter to Corinthians 1.12, cited by Origen in Rufinus' Latin paraphrase, Commentary on Romans (2.15), bk. 2, ch. 9, *Patrologia Graeca* 14, 893B.

78. H. Chadwick cites four of his texts in "Conscience in ancient thought," in his *Studies on Ancient Christianity*, Ashgate, Aldershot 2006, ch. 20 = the original English text, with revisions, of "Gewissen," *Reallexikon für Antike und Christentum* 7 (Bonn 1969), cols. 663–711, at col. 1091 = 55 of the English.

79. Luther, *A Sermon on the Sacrament of Penance*, second, third, and eleventh points, *Luthers Werke*, Weimar edition vol. 2.

80. Seneca, *On Anger* 2.2–4. More generally, impulsion to action depended on assent to appearances, as reported by Plutarch, *On Stoic Self-Contradictions* 1057A.

81. Bishop Butler, *Fifteen Sermons Preached at the Rolls Chapel*, 2nd ed. 1729, Preface 19; cf. Epictetus, *Discourses* 1.1.1, as pointed out by A. A.Long, "Stoicism in the philosophical tradition: Spinoza, Lipsius, Butler," in Jon Miller and Brad Inwood, eds., *Hellenistic and Early Modern Philosophy*, Cambridge University Press 2003, ch. 1, pp. 7–29, at 22.

82. Seneca, *On Anger* 3.36; cf. *Letters* 28.9–10; 41.1–2; 83.1–2; *The Golden Verses*, lines 40–44.

that Sextius summoned his mind (*animus*) every day to give an account of itself: "What defect of yours have you cured today? What vice have you resisted? In what respect are you better?" Anger recedes if it knows it will have to appear before a judge every day. Seneca himself used the practice with the ambitious aim of making progress toward virtue, rather than correcting wrongdoing, and he was rather self-congratulatory. So for him the self-interrogation was not quite a matter of conscience. But his younger Stoic contemporary Epictetus used it both morning and evening with a stress on wrongdoing closely relevant to conscience.[83] From Seneca's account, we get a picture of his and his wife's domestic life. He finds the practice calming, perhaps because he is a little lenient with himself. We may recall his belief in joyful conscience:

> What sleep follows this self-examination, how tranquil, deep and free, when the mind is either praised or admonished and the self-investigator and secret critic has recognized its own habits. I use this facility and every day I render an account to myself. When the light is removed from sight and my wife, conscious (*conscia*) in advance of my habit, has fallen silent, I scrutinise the whole of my day and I reassess everything I did and said. I hide nothing from myself and I pass over nothing, for why should I be afraid of any of my mistakes when I can say: "See that you do not do that again. For now I pardon you. In that dispute you spoke too aggressively. In future do not engage with inexperienced people. Those who have never learnt do not want to learn. Him you admonished more freely than you ought, so that you did not reform, but offended him. For the future, see not only whether what you say is true, but whether the man to whom it is said can take the truth. A good person rejoices in being admonished. All the worst people take their corrector very badly."

The Stoics introduced something else relevant to conscience, or rather to the natural law within us, with their idea that we have natural preconceptions (*emphytoi prolêpseis*) of good and evil.[84] And Cicero makes his Stoic spokesman, Balbus, describe as natural (*innatum*) and, as it were, engraved in the mind the belief that there are gods as innate. But there is evidence that the early Stoics are unlikely to have meant the word translated "natural" to carry the more obvious meaning of *innate*, because another text tells us that we are born with our reason like a blank sheet of paper and our conceptions (*ennoiai*) are written onto it. The preconceptions (*prolêpseis*) are the

83. Epictetus, *Discourses* 4.6.35.
84. Plutarch, *On Stoic Self-Contradictions* 1041E.

ones that get written in by nature without further thought on our part,[85] but evidently not from birth. However, evidence has been offered that in non-Stoic texts *innatus* can mean innate,[86] and, further, it does look as if at least in the later Stoic Epictetus that certain moral preconceptions have become innate.[87] The Stoic Epictetus stresses the difficulty of applying preconceptions of good and evil.[88] This makes it all the more surprising that Seneca thinks that our conscience is never deceived about us (*numquam fallitur*), and there may be an example cited by Philo from Platonism.[89] I have not found this said elsewhere in ancient Greco-Roman thought, unless there is an example to be found in Olympiodorus in the next chapter, which I rather doubt.[90] Phaedra in Euripides' *Hippolytus* says that it is difficult to know the right time to heed shame, and Ps.?-Aristotle's *Magna moralia* and Galen both talk about the difficulty of knowing one's own faults.[91]

Cicero

Cicero (106–43 BCE), the Roman lawyer and statesman, makes hundreds of references to conscience (*conscientia*) in his speeches and philosophical texts. The latter were written in his last years, when under Julius Caesar he had lost political influence. We have seen that in his earlier speeches he often refers to accomplices, witnesses, and confidants as sharing the guilty or innocent knowledge of *another* party. In this, Pierce's records suggest that he is unlike the earlier Greek orators, Demosthenes and Isocrates. We have

85. Aëtius, 4.11.1–4; *Doxographici Graeci* (Diels).

86. David Konstan has supplied clear examples from Plautus and Terence where the meaning of *innatus* can hardly be "innate." On the meaning of *innata* as applied to preconceptions in Epicureanism at Cicero, *On the Nature of the Gods* 1.44–45, see the controversy between David Sedley "Epicurus' theological innatism" and David Konstan, "Epicurus on the gods," both in "Epicurus' theological innatism," in Geoffrey Fish and Kirk Sanders, eds, *Epicurus and the Epicurean Tradition*, Cambridge University Press 2003, ch. 4.

87. Epictetus, *Discourses* 2.11.1–15 and Ps.-Epictetus, *frag.* 97.

88. Epictetus, *Discourses* 2. 11.1–15.

89. The example in Philo, the Jewish thinker of the first century CE, in *Every Good Man Is Free* 46, should, I think, be ascribed to Platonism, not as in Von Arnim's *Stoicorum veterum fragmenta* 3.360, to Stoicism, because it speaks of the human mind as *immortal*. Philo treats right reason as a *law* (*nomos*) that is never wrong (*apseudês*) imprinted by immortal nature in the *immortal mind*.

90. Seneca, *On the Shortness of Life* 10.3; Olympiodorus, *On Plato's First Alcibiades* 23.2–7, Westerink.

91. Euripides, *Hippolytus* 380–87, as analyzed by Bernard Williams, *Shame and Necessity*, University of California Press 1993, 95; Galen, *On the Errors and Passions of the Soul*, *Scripta minora* vol. 1 (Marquardt), ch. 2, 4.11–5.2; ch. 3, 6.17–7.1, Ps.?-Aristotle, *Magna moralia* 2.15, 1213a13–26.

also noticed that he often speaks of sharing knowledge of *merit*, and of a correspondingly *joyful* conscience.

Cicero appears to have neglected the forward-looking functions of conscience, even though the forward-looking function of shame (*aidôs*)—aversion as opposed to remorse—was distinguished in Greek as early as the cited passage of Euripides' *Hippolytus* in the fifth century BCE. Cicero is quoted by the Christian Lactantius, writing in the early fourth century CE in his *Divine Institutes*,[92] as taking the lawyer's view that repentance (*paenitere*) is not an effective route to reform (*corrigere errorem*). It has further been claimed[93] that there is only one example of aversion in Cicero and none in Seneca. But whatever may be true of Cicero, Seneca treats conscience as averting wrong conduct quite a few times[94] and also sees it as producing reform,[95] and he thinks the same about the practice of self-interrogation.[96]

Cicero's idea of the conceptions of good and evil derives from Plato, not from the Stoics. He explains that for Plato these conceptions are *pre*-nate, existing *before* birth as inheritances from an earlier life.[97] As a follower of Plato himself, Cicero can in his own person speak of certain ideas as innate. He describes us as having formed from the very first shadowy understandings (*adumbratae intelligentiae*) that we get from the God-given divine element within us. Again in one of his forensic speeches, he claims that the right to self-defense is a law not written but born (*nata*) with us, for which we are not instructed but made, with which we are not indoctrinated but imbued.[98] But in this last text he is fighting an uphill battle to make out a legal defense and is not expressing his philosophical opinions.

St. Paul on the Relation of Conscience to the Law in Our Hearts

I now come to Christianity and Paul, the convert from Judaism and the great proselytizer of non-Jewish communities to whom he wrote letters. These are preserved, along with some others wrongly ascribed, in the New

92. Lactantius, *Divine Institutes* 6.24.1–10.

93. J. Hebing, "Ueber conscientia und conservatio im philosophischen Sinne bei den Römern von Cicero bis Hieronymus, *Philosophisches Jahrbuch* 35, 1922, pp. 136–52, 215–31, 298–326.

94. Seneca, *Letters* 105.7–8; 117.1; *frag*. 14 Haase (=81 Vottero) from Lactantius *Divine Institutes* 6.24.16–17 (a guardian: *custos*, cf. Epictetus *phulakê, phulassein, Discourses* 1.14.11–15 and uncertain frag. 97).

95. Seneca, *Letters* 28.9–10.

96. Seneca, *On Anger* 3.36; *Letters* 41.1–2; 83.1–2.

97. Cicero, *Tusculan Disputations* 1.24.57.

98. Cicero, *On Laws* 1.22.59; *On the Nature of the Gods* 2.4.12; *Pro milone* 10.

Testament. In his Letter to the Romans he has something new and important to say about conscience. He refers to the written law of God by which the Jews distinguished themselves, and which would include the Ten Commandments delivered by God to Moses, and he contrasts the written law with the law written in men's hearts. This latter law he connects closely, although he does not identify it, with conscience:[99]

> When Gentiles who have not the law do by nature what the law requires, they are a law to themselves, even though they do not have the law. They show that what the law requires is written in their hearts, while their conscience also bears witness and their conflicting thoughts accuse or perhaps excuse them on that day when, according to my gospel, God judges the secrets of men by Christ Jesus.

The law written in men's hearts was already referred to in the Hebrew scriptures.[100] What is new is to connect it so closely with conscience. Paul describes it as something that co-witnesses (*symmartyrei*). On one interpretation, the conscience of Gentiles on the Day of Judgment, even if ignorant of the Jewish *written* law, co-witnesses that they possessed the *inner* law which they have violated. As with the original Greek concept, conscience in Paul is not the ultimate source of our knowledge of right and wrong. For him, the law in our hearts is the source. But conscience reveals our possession of that law. This makes the relationship between conscience and the inner law close, but not *identity*. The only Church Father I am aware of who may assert an actual identity is John of Damascus in the seventh to eighth centuries CE, and even his remark is ambiguous when he speaks of conscience *or* the law of my intellect.[101] Thomas Aquinas finds the identification uncomfortably close and glosses John as intending something looser, such as that conscience is a judgment of reason *derived from* natural law.[102]

As for the relation between the *written* law of God and the law written in men's *hearts*, two major ancient Christians offered an interpretation. We find in Origen (185–253/254) and ascribed to Augustine (354–430CE) by his opponent Bishop Julian of Eclanum the explanation that the law was written in men's hearts at the time of the Fall of Adam in the Garden of

99. Romans 2:14–15.

100. *Is.* 51:7a; *Jer.* 38:33 (70); cf. Deuteronomy 30:14, the word of commandment in your heart for you to observe. I thank Josef Lössl and Yohanan Petrovsky-Shtern for the references.

101. John of Damascus, *On Orthodox Faith* 4.22.

102. Thomas Aquinas, *On Truth*, question 17, answer 1, first difficulties to the contrary, 1, and answers to them 1.

Eden, when he ate of the tree of the knowledge of good and evil. The written law was given by God to Moses at a much later date.[103] Before the Fall, Adam presumably felt that he should not eat the apple from the tree because of his filial relation to God who had forbidden it, but this will have fallen short of a knowledge of good and evil.

Insofar as the law in our hearts covers the same ground as the written Ten Commandments of the Jewish Old Testament, it will offer a general knowledge of what is right as well as wrong. But Paul's connection of it with our thoughts accusing or excusing us on the Day of Judgment returns the emphasis to violations or the absence of violations, and hence to individual wrongdoing. Divine judgment was perfectly familiar to the Greek playwrights, and was invoked by such philosophers as Empedocles and Plato. But a more central emphasis in the ethics of Greek and Roman philosophy was on virtue or good character. Wrongdoing is certainly relevant to this as being hard to square with good character, and we have seen that conscience is repeatedly invoked. But the philosophers' search for virtue created a different emphasis. Christianity introduced other changes too. Discarded are the consciousness of one's own merit from Cicero and Seneca and the consciousness of nonmoral faults and weaknesses from Plato and others. Further, the lawyers' concern with sharing the guilty secrets of others receded, except insofar as God shares all secrets.

Paul had earlier made another very important point in discussion with Greeks from Corinth, that one's conscience is *not infallible*. Of course the inner law is faultless, but one's reading of it is fallible. It is a great mercy that this became the main Christian tradition, since human claims of infallibility are dangerously wrong. Paul makes the point in his first letter to the Corinthians. This addresses Greek Christians who claim to have a clear conscience in eating meat sacrificed to idols, because they are sophisticated people who know that the belief in idols is a delusion. Paul replies that if they are seen eating sacrificed meat they may corrupt the conscience (*suneidêsis*) of their less sophisticated brethren.[104] The message is that a clear conscience is not a sure guide, and this is reaffirmed in the same letter when Paul says that his own clear conscience (*ouden emautôi sunoida*) does not acquit him, since God is the judge.[105] Paul does not regard *knowledge* of the law written in our hearts as available to us from birth, since he says in his Letter to the Romans

103. Origen, *Commentary on Romans* 6.8 (PG 14, 1080A–81A); Augustine, *Incomplete Work against Julian*, ch. 228 (PL 45, 1244).

104. 1 Corinthians 8:7–13.

105. 1 Corinthians 4:4.

7:9 that he was once alive without the law, and was then sinless.[106] Paul's belief in fallibility was confirmed by two major Christian thinkers who went on to discuss whether *knowledge* of the law written in men's hearts was innate. The view of Origen (ca. 185–253/254) seems to be that it is sown by God into the hearts of men, but that when we are still growing up, we do not *hear* it.[107] The metaphor of sowing may suggest that the seed is there from birth, even though not yet heard. The remark of Augustine (354–430) almost two centuries later is ambiguous, that the natural law in our hearts only *appears* (*apparet*) at the age of reason, but he has the same idea as Origen, that people may have the law in their hearts and in their conscience but be unwilling to *read* it.[108] The fallibility—not of the law, but—of conscience remained the normal Christian view. Even in pagan texts I found above at most two claims of infallibility.

A final point has been put to me,[109] that in St. Paul, and in letters in the New Testament by others, some wrongly ascribed to Paul, the idea of a *bad* conscience is largely confined to non-Christians, whereas Christians can hope for a good conscience. That is not a self-congratulatory conscience, but a clear one, the negation of a bad conscience, so that the idea of awareness or unawareness of fault is still central. Paul claims to have a clear conscience, as does the Letter to Hebrews, no longer ascribed to Paul, and the Letter to Timothy of disputed authorship.[110] He and Peter exhort others to have a clear conscience.[111] Peter says that baptism is a request to God for a clear conscience.[112] By contrast, in the Letter to the Hebrews Jewish sacrifices fail to secure a clear conscience.[113] Moreover, in the Letter to Timothy false teachings come from people seared in conscience, and in the Letter to Titus of disputed authorship, the consciences of unbelievers are corrupted.[114]

Conscience Does Not at First Necessarily Refer to God

In the five hundred years reviewed, the references in the fifth-century Greek playwrights to conscience as sharing knowledge with oneself of a defect do

106. S. Origen, *On Romans* 6.8 (PG 14, 1080A–81A).
107. Origen, *Against Celsus* 1.4; *On Romans* 6.8 (PG 14, 1080A–81A).
108. Augustine, *Letters* 157.15 (PL 33, 681); *Enarratio in Psalmos* 57.1 (PL 36, 673).
109. I owe this important point to Martyas Havrda.
110. Acts 23:1; 24:16; 2 Corinthians 1.12; 2 Timothy 1:3; Hebrews 13:18.
111. 1 Timothy 1:5; 1:19; 3:9; 1 Peter 3.16.
112. 1 Peter 3.21.
113. Hebrews 9:9 and 14; 10:2 and 22.
114. 1 Timothy 4:2; Titus 1:15.

not necessarily refer to God. We have already seen that that early idea of conscience did not invoke a lawgiver, as Elizabeth Anscombe would have expected. Admittedly, the crime of which Jason is accused involved breaking his oath to the gods, and the juryman who cast a mistaken vote asked the gods' pardon. But even in those examples, God played no part in accusing them. Euripides even got rid of the supernatural Furies from the story of Orestes, and replaced them with a self-shared knowledge that, in the mouth of Orestes' interlocutor, is treated naturalistically as a sickness. Epicurus too thought it was a mistake if conscience took the form of fearing punishment from the gods instead of from fellow humans. Plato's nine uses of the idea of sharing knowledge with oneself of a defect did not invoke God. We have above seen that Plato did not feel able to commit himself to Socrates' daemon being a god, or child of a god, although it is a type of soul given to us by God and is in some very broad sense divine (*theion*).[115] The idea that one's conscience is inspected by God, and that, in agreement with Plato, God installed the guardian spirit within, is most clearly articulated and stressed by the Stoics. In St. Paul, the connection with God is firm, but even here it is subtle. Conscience, I have said, is not for him the voice of God, but the agency that will give witness to God, as to whether one has lived by the inner law provided by God. Of course, insofar as conscience involves guilt, it was suggested above that one source of guilt is the sense of going against an authority, and God is one relevant authority. But he is not the only authority, and another source of guilt is in any case the idea of a victim. In sum, it can be said that if conscience has now become for many a secular idea, it also started at some remove from the idea of God. One of our tasks will be to see if it can retain its force when it is resecularized.

What Is Conscience?

We have found very different conceptions of what conscience is. It started off as a *knowledge* of faults or faultlessness, at first of past faults, but soon of what would in the *future* put one at fault. Some Romans came to connect it with knowledge of one's *merit*. St. Paul connected it with a more *general* law in our hearts of right and wrong. Paul's law, however, was not *identical* with conscience, but something on which conscience *drew* in accusing or excusing oneself. A very useful point made in the thirteenth century is that knowledge is an ambiguous term, since it can be applied to the possession of knowledge or to the thing known. Application to the thing known will

115. Plato, *Apology* 26 C–E; 27 C–E; *Timaeus* 90 A–D.

make it possible then to talk of revealing one's conscience, as if it were a ledger of the sins of which one was aware.[116] The recognition of knowledge as both possession of knowledge and thing known may help us to capture what many people in antiquity thought conscience to be. It was often seen as a knowledge, in one sense or the other, of what it was *wrong* or not wrong for one to have done, and/or of what it would be *wrong* for one to do or not to do in an expected situation calling for decision.

However, because conscience is normally seen as fallible (despite infallibility later being assigned to the related disposition called *synderesis*), we should describe the majority view as being that conscience is a *belief*, which may or may not amount to knowledge. Conscience is, then, a belief about what it was, or would be, wrong or not wrong for one to do or not to do. One can also have a conscience about one's past or future *attitudes*. The term can further be used to speak of one's *capacity* for such beliefs. I shall ask about the capacity as well as about the beliefs when I ask about the value of conscience in the final chapter, chapter 12. When one consults one's conscience in a perplexing situation, one may feel the need to revise the values on which it draws, but the conscience which one consults is not different from one's belief about what it would be wrong to do in the present case.

The stress on anything as *rational* as knowledge or belief might seem to leave out the motivating power of conscience. But rational knowledge of evaluative propositions about what is or is not wrong can itself be motivating, for example, if I know that some action to which I am tempted or which I have performed is *wrong*. There was to be a movement at its strongest in the eighteenth century, but starting earlier and finishing later, to equate conscience with *sentiment* or *feeling*. But this cannot be said to have been the majority view over time, and it is unnecessary to bring in feeling in this *particular* way. It comes in anyhow because such motivating knowledge or belief directly *gives rise* to feeling. The connection of conscience with rationality is not ubiquitous, but is already found in the Greco-Roman period, since the Stoics identify most psychological functions with reason, and we saw in Plato the Socratic daemon being identified with human reason. In chapter 4 we shall encounter an attempt by Jerome to place conscience, or its spark, still higher *above* reason. At intervals, it was also to be placed, as by Olympiodorus and by Bishop Butler, at the very summit of reason.

116. Alexander of Hales (ca. 1185–245), *Summa theologica*, ed. Quaracchi, vol. 2, 1928, n. 418, p. 493; Bonaventure (ca. 1217–1274), *Commentary on the Sentences of Peter Lombard*, bk. 2, dist. 39, article 1, question 1, both quoted in Latin by O. Lottin, *Psychologie et morale aux XII et XIII siècles*, vol. 2, pp. 179; 203, note 1. Also Thomas Aquinas (ca. 1225–1274), *On Truth*, question 17, article 1, reply.

Attributes of Moral Conscience Persisting from the First Six Hundred Years

The first six hundred years of the development of the idea of moral conscience identified some attributes which remained comparatively stable features over the next two thousand years. I shall mention eight of them.

1. Conscience as a form of *personal self-awareness* is not invariably an awareness of *others*.
2. It draws on values not necessarily shared by others.
3. It originally involved the idea of a person split into two, with one self hiding a guilty secret, and the other self sharing it. The idea of conscience as involving a split person was to recur in different forms and with different rationales in Adam Smith, in Kant, and in Freud, and is found in the expression "I could not live with myself."
4. Its original function was retrospective, but very soon prospective functions developed and all of these were retained.
5. Although conscience drew on general values it was very much concerned with what was or would be wrong for the *particular* individual in a *particular* context.
6. The concept of conscience started off secular and remains capable of being secular.
7. It was traditionally viewed in Christianity as fallible.
8. Though a belief and hence cognitive in character, conscience nonetheless had motivating force.

TWO

Christian Appropriation and Platonist Developments, Third to Sixth Centuries CE

St. Paul's statements about conscience were innovative but few, and the early church fathers appropriated further ideas from the Greco-Roman tradition partly in order to fill out what Paul had said, but also partly to show that Christianity was happy to use pagan ideas, so that there was no need for the pagans to engage in dispute.

Early Christian Appropriations: Origen

Origen (ca. 185–253/254) was one of the ablest of all Christian thinkers, especially in using his vast knowledge of Greek philosophy, in the school he headed in Alexandria, for adaptation to Christian purposes. Writing in Greek, he borrowed from the Pythagoreans the practice of interrogating himself every night and morning on whether he had spent the day aright.[1] The fullest surviving account of this practice conducted at bedtime had been given by Seneca, who also took it from the Pythagoreans. But we saw that in Seneca the atmosphere is quite different. He is seeking moral progress and is on the whole rather pleased with himself. He finds the practice calming.[2] His younger Stoic contemporary Epictetus returned to the attitude of self-reproach closer to that of the Pythagoreans themselves, when he advocated the same practice conducted every morning as well as evening.[3] When Origen took the practice over, he connected it, *unlike* Seneca, with a shameful recital (*aoidêmon rhêseidion*), "bites" (*dakneisthai*) of *conscience* and

1. Origen, *Commentary on Romans* 6.8 (PG 14, 1080A–81A).
2. Seneca, *On Anger* 3.36, *cf. Letters* 28.9–10; 41.1–2; 83.1–2.
3. Epictetus, *Discourses* 4.6.35.

compunction (*katanussein*). Origen and Epictetus cited the very same questions to ask, drawn from the Pythagorean book *Golden Verses*: "Where did I go astray? What have I done? What duty has been left undone?"[4] Origen's change of mood goes along with the rejection of the Roman consciousness of one's own moral *merit*.

This example illustrates, I think, how differently various individuals can feel about matters of conscience, when encouraged, but not determined, by different cultures. For Seneca, the Roman Stoic aristocrat, self-interrogation was not a matter of conscience at all. Roman *conscientia sui* was in his case consciousness of his own moral progress. But the Pythagoreans we hear about from later sources went through an ascetic five-year testing period of silence without money, after which their money would be returned if they had failed the course.[5] Origen, the Christian, is reputed to have engaged in self-castration. The very reputation reflects a concern with sin, which the system of penitence to be described in chapter 5 would intensify for many Christians, not of course for all, since individuals differ.

Origen's reference to the "bites" of conscience had a long tradition. In the first century BCE, Cicero had described the Aristotelian school as valuing conscience because of the "bites" by which it averts bad conduct, and the "bites" of conscience had been discussed in the next century by the Platonist Plutarch, although in a more severe form for someone who has already done wrong.[6] Bites of conscience were repeatedly taken up by Christians, and entered into the title of the early fourteenth-century English text of Dan Michel, *Ayenbite of Inwit*, or repeated bites of conscience, and are still mentioned by Kant.[7] In English, the term "remorse" comes from *morsus*, the Latin word for bite.

Origen also took the Stoic idea of common conceptions, among which some, the Stoic "preconceptions," are *written* into us (the same writing metaphor as in Paul) by nature without special thought on our part. According to the Stoic Epictetus in the first century CE, we have preconceptions of good and evil supplied by nature, but they are hard to apply (the theme

4. Origen, frg. *On Psalms* 6 from René Cadiou, *Commentaires inédits des Psaumes* (Paris, 1936), 74; Origen, *Selections on the Psalms* 4 (PG 12, 1144B–45B), drawing on the Pythagorean *Golden Verses*, lines 40–44.

5. Iamblichus, *Pythagorean Life*, ch. 17.

6. Cicero, *Tusc.* 4.45; Plutarch, *On Tranquillity* 476F–477A.

7. Kant, *Lectures Recorded by Vigilantius on Metaphysics of Morals*, Works of Kant, Academy of Sciences, Berlin, vol. 27.618.

of fallibility again).[8] Origen went on to compare with these Stoic common conceptions St. Paul's law written in our hearts.[9]

Lactantius' Appropriations and View on God's Anger

If we turn now to the slightly later Christian, Lactantius (ca. 240–ca. 320), writing in Latin, he may be not so much filling out the Christian picture as sometimes appropriating and sometimes correcting the pagan picture, available to him in Latin, so as to transcend the pagan alternative. He appropriates Cicero and Seneca by praising their appeal to God and our conscience as both watching us, without any possibility of our closing our conscience to God.[10] He appropriates another pagan source when he seeks the sacrifice not of animals but of a pure heart. For he goes on to find the sacrifice of purity advocated in the corpus of Hermes Trismegistus, a compilation in Greek of Egyptian wisdom from the early centuries CE.[11] This may involve a further convergence with pagans, because Hermes Trismegistus was very possibly drawn on also by the pagan Neoplatonist Porphyry, when he too advocated the sacrifice of a pure intellect and heart.[12]

While Origen had identified St. Paul's law in our hearts with Stoic common conceptions, Lactantius made a different identification of the internal law, although he was speaking of the internal law derived from the Stoics by Cicero in book 3 of his *On the Republic*.[13] In referring to Cicero's law, he distorts it in an interesting way by connecting law, like St. Paul, with conscience, which he has just been discussing. Cicero had cited as the Stoics' favorite example of the internal law: preserving the bonds of human fellowship.[14] Lactantius changes this to a Christian conception, when he says that Cicero's law is making the sacrifice of a pure *conscience*.[15]

In another work, *On the Anger of God* (*De ira dei*), Lactantius describes the way in which God is angry (*irascitur*). His is not a temporary boiling or commotion like ours. Against unrepentant sinners his anger is eternal,

8. Epictetus, *Discourses* 2.11.1–15.

9. Origen, *Against Celsus* 1.4. Origen was further seen in chapter 1 to think that Paul's law is sown by God into the hearts of men, but that it is *not heard*, when we are growing up before the age of reason.

10. Lactantius, *Divine Institutes* 6.24.11–20.

11. Lactantius, *Divine Institutes* 6.24.27–29; 25.10–11.

12. Porphyry, *On Abstinence from Killing Animals* 2.61.1.

13. Quoted earlier by Lactantius at *Divine Institutes* 6.8.6–9.

14. Cicero, *On Duties* 3.19–21; 23; 27–28; 52–53; 69.

15. Lactantius, *Divine Institutes* 6.24.20–29.

but he moderates it as he wills, and so we can give him satisfaction (*satisfactio*) and he can be appeased (*placabilis, placatur*) by a reformed way of life (*morum emendatione*).[16] Repentance is therefore appropriate. In chapter 1, we saw Lactantius in *Divine Institutes* criticizing Cicero for not agreeing that repentance (*paenitere*) was an effective route to reform. Lactantius goes further when he says that in bringing about reform, repentance can also lead to something else: God's forgiveness. Indeed, it can lead to something different again from forgiveness: God's *remission* of sins.[17] Remission is unlike forgiveness, in that it erases sins from the ledger, instead of continuing to acknowledge them. Humans can remit human punishments, but they cannot remit guilt (*culpa*). Remission of sins may seem more suitable than forgiveness to Lactantius' unemotional God, and it calls only for mercy or clemency, which the Stoics insisted was not an emotion. God, he says, with his great indulgence (*indulgentissimus*) and mercy (*clementia*), will remit, obliterate, and condone sins and abolish the stain (*remittere, obliterare, condonare, labem abolere*). This part of Lactantius' language suggests remission.[18]

The Neoplatonists Iamblichus and Simplicius: An Alternative View of God's Anger

Starting immediately after Lactantius, the Greek Neoplatonists Iamblichus (ca. 250 to before 325 CE), Simplicius (wrote after 529 CE), and Olympiodorus (495/505 to after 565) reinterpreted God's anger even more extensively. They would not have read the Latin of Lactantius, but if they had, they would have seen him as still conceding too much when he made God's anger unemotional. Neither forgiveness nor remission is in the least relevant, in their view, to God. Iamblichus, staunch supporter of Egyptian religion and the power of priests, had made God entirely unemotional. This was in riposte to his own Neoplatonist teacher, Porphyry (232–309 CE), who had raised a criticism of Egyptian religion: do not invocations (*klêseis*) to the gods imply that they can be swayed by *emotion* (*empatheis*)? Iamblichus in response allows that the gods are benevolent, loving, and solicitous (*eumeneis, philia, kêdemonia*), but he replies that invocations work by allowing priests, like himself, to gain union with the gods and that the divine nature has so little to do with emotion that the union actually purifies the

16. Lactantius, *On the Anger of God* 21.

17. Lactantius, *Divine Institutes* 6.24.1–5. I thank David Konstan for pointing out to me the difference between forgiveness and remission in connection with his book, *Before Forgiveness*, Cambridge University Press 2010.

18. Lactantius, *Divine Institutes* 6.24.1–5.

priests from emotion (*katharsis pathôn*). What, then, is his account of our appeasing (*exhilasis*) God's wrath (*mênis*)? Iamblichus uses the analogy of our stepping out of the light.[19] Appeasement is not to be seen in a conventional way. It is our stepping back into the light. Simplicius, the last of the Athenian Neoplatonists of the sixth century CE, goes even further. He asks why it is thought that God is persuaded to change his mind (*metapeithesthai*) and to pardon those who go astray (*sunginôskein hamartanousin*) by means of gifts, votive offerings, prayers, benefactions, and supplications. Simplicius denies that this is what happens. God is not even angry (*orgizetai*), nor does he turn away from us when we go astray, or turn back when we repent (*metamelomenôn*). Rather, it is we who have turned away. The analogy is with a man who allows his boat to slip away from the rock to which it had been tethered. Acts of repentance help to bring him back again to the rock, and assimilation to God (ideally even union) was the Platonist ideal. But the rock is meanwhile unmoved. The goal of our repentance is to be purified (*katharsis*) and embrace virtue. Those who are genuinely repentant are corrected more quickly because of the sharp wounds of *conscience* (*to suneidos*).[20]

The third Neoplatonist, Olympiodorus, the last pagan professor in the philosophy school at Alexandria, makes God more involved when he explains Plato's views in the *Gorgias* on punishment after death. But even then he says that the soul's punishment in Tartarus is not due to the *wrath* of the divine (*mênis tou theiou*), but for the sake of curing it.[21]

Platonists on Socrates' Guardian Spirit and Conscience

Socrates' guardian spirit was reinterpreted both by Platonists of the first two centuries CE and by the Neoplatonists. To start with, Plutarch of Chaeronea (ca. 46–120 CE) went beyond Plato when he represented Socrates' daemon as causing *repentance* and *shame*, functions typically associated with conscience. Apuleius, the Platonist of the second century AD (b. 123/125), said that Socrates' daemon resided in the very depths of the mind in place of conscience (*vice conscientiae*) and four hundred years later the Neoplatonist

19. Iamblichus, *Mysteries of the Egyptians* 1.12–13, pp. 40.16–43.15 Des Places, replying to Porphyry's fragmentary *Letter to Anebo* (quoted here and ed. Sodano).

20. Simplicius, *Commentary on Epictetus' Handbook*, ch. 38, lines 674–703 in I. Hadot = Ch. 31, 107, 15–22, Dübner.

21. Olympiodorus, *Commentary on Aristotle's Meteorology* 146.10–11.

Olympiodorus, speaking for the benefit of his Christian pupils, actually identifies Socrates' daemon with conscience (*to suneidos*).[22]

Socrates' guardian spirit was further discussed by Platonists and Neoplatonists over the same period, in order to work out how it communicated with Socrates, and this discussion may have influenced the Christian Augustine. Although Plato calls the spirit a voice, Plutarch, in the treatise mentioned, ascribes to Simmias the interpretation that there is no speech, or voice, or striking of the air (*phthongos, phônê, plêgê*). Rather, as in sleep, the thought of the statement (*logou noêsis*) contacts one, and one grasps the beliefs and thoughts (*doxai, noêseis*) in the statements, merely *thinking* that one hears them. The statement contacts one simply through what is indicated (*to dêloumenon*) by the thinker and by what is thought (*to noêthen*). Again, the air signals (*ensêmainetai*) the statement by means of what is thought (*to noêthen*). These thoughts do not need verbs or nouns. Rather, like light, they produce a reflection in the receiver.[23] Later Platonists agree. Calcidius, the Christian author of a Latin commentary on Plato in the fourth century CE, says that in dreams, when we think we hear voice and speech, there is in fact only meaning (*significatio*) performing the office of voice, and that is how, when awake, Socrates divined the presence of the daemon, by the token of a vivid sign.[24] Both authors suggest that the daemon communicates pure meaning (*to dêloumenon, to noêthen, significatio*), although the meaning is not yet said itself to be a language. Proclus (ca. 411–485), head of the Athenian Neoplatonist school, returns to the analogy of light, saying that light is received in the tenuous material (not flesh) that provides a vehicle for our souls, and by that route reaches the fleshly sense organs and is recognized by self-perception (*sunaisthêsis*).[25]

Augustine (354–430), Bishop of Hippo, could have had access to Calcidius' Latin. At any rate, he discussed how *God* speaks to us and denied that the process involves figures appearing (this is all he meant by denying the comparison with dreams). On the other hand, there is no ordinary hearing, either. Rather, God speaks to those who can hear with the mind (*mens*) by means of the truth itself (*ipsa veritate*).[26] Truth here does the work of meaning in Plutarch and Calcidius. Augustine, however, is not referring

22. Plutarch, *On the Daemon of Socrates* 592B; Apuleius, *On Socrates' Daemon* 16; Olympiodorus, *On Plato's First Alcibiades*, p. 23, lines 2–7 (p.17 Westerink).

23. Plutarch, *On the Daemon* 588B–589D.

24. Calcidius, *Commentary on Plato's Timaeus*, ch. 255, p.288.

25. Proclus, *Commentary on Plato's First Alcibiades* 80.

26. Augustine, *City of God* 11.2. I thank David Robertson for first drawing my attention to this discussion.

to conscience, which in the tradition of St. Paul is not God's speech, but something that speaks about us in the *presence* of God as judge.

Three Neoplatonists on Conscience as Belonging to a Special "Attentive" Faculty of the Soul

The most interesting Neoplatonist development was a fifth-century view, recorded in a text ascribed to the Christian Neoplatonist Philoponus (490s–570s CE),[27] that moral conscience (*to suneidos*) is one species of a faculty of self-awareness or *attention* (*to prosektikon*). This fits with the original idea of *suneidêsis* as a form of self-awareness. What is new is the recognition that a special faculty of self-awareness is needed (attention) that transcends any of the psychological faculties of which it is aware, whether cognition or desire. There had been no word like the English "consciousness" bridging both perception and thought,[28] much less one bridging *awareness* of perception, thought, and desire. Under the new faculty of *attention*, it is now said that moral conscience is directed only to *some* faculties, the *vital* (*zôtikai*) ones, and the other species of attention to the *cognitive* faculties. The vital faculties turn out to be faculties for different types of *desire*. For the term *suneidos* is used earlier and later in the sixth century by the Neoplatonists Damascius (last head of Athenian Neoplatonist school up to 529) and Olympiodorus in Alexandria, in the very same context to say that one and the same faculty is aware of the cognitive faculties and, as conscience (*suneidos*), of the *desiring* faculties (*orektikai*), with the difference that Olympiodorus uses the term *suneidos* additionally as the generic term for both forms of self-awareness.[29] That *suneidos* refers to *moral conscience* is clear from the fact that in Olympiodorus this same *suneidos* is identified with Socrates' guardian spirit, which,

27. "Philoponus," *On Aristotle on the Soul,* bk. 3, 464.24–465.31 and 466.18–29. The case for and against Philoponus' authorship of the bk. 3 commentary was very well assembled by William Charlton, but the case for has now been strongly supported by Pantelis Golitsis, to be published in a successor volume in preparation to Richard Sorabji's (ed.) *Aristotle Transformed.*

28. Charles Kahn, "Sensation and consciousness in Aristotle's psychology," *Archiv für Geschichte der Philosophie* 48, 1966, pp. 43–81, repr in Jonathan Barnes, Malcolm Schofield, and Richard Sorabji, eds, *Articles on Aristotle,* vol. 4, Duckworth 1979, pp. 1–31.

29. Damascius, *Lectures on Plato's Phaedo* 1, para. 271, Westerink, pp. 162–63; Olympiodorus, *Commentary of Plato's First Alcibiades,* 22.14–23.18, Westerink. Although I gave accounts in *The Philosophy of the Commentators 200–600 AD,* vol. 1 *Psychology* (Cornell University Press 2005), p. 152, and in "Moral conscience: contributions to the idea in Plato and Platonism," in Vassilis Karasmanis and Eliza Tutellier, eds, *Presocratics and Plato, A Festschrift in Honour of Charles Kahn,* Parmenides Publishing, Las Vegas 2012, the nomenclature has been made very much clearer by Jed W. Atkins, "Euripides' *Orestes* and the concept of conscience in Greek Philosophy," *Journal of the History of Ideas,* 75, 2014, 1–22.

as just seen, had been treated like conscience or said to take the place of conscience.[30]

In some modern philosophy of the last century, the importance of attention was sometimes neglected at least in the view that our actions were a function of our beliefs and desires, without reference to which ones we were motivated to *attend* to. The Greeks, by contrast, were duly conscious of attention; for example, in Aristotle's account of why, through motivated inattention, we do *not* abide by our better judgment.[31] However, the idea of a single attentive capacity of the mind for awareness of cognition and desire was a new one. The background to the new idea was a discussion in Aristotle, who, following Plato, had been considering our awareness of different sensory modes, seeing and tasting. Plato had already urged that when we recognize that sweet is different from white, the different senses must converge (*sunteinein*) on something unitary (*mia*), the soul. Aristotle had substituted for soul a certain capacity of the soul, a *perceptual* capacity common to all the five senses. Otherwise, he added, it would be as if *I* perceived sweet and *you* perceived white.[32] It is by this same common perceptual capacity, according to Aristotle, that we are aware of using our senses,[33] and he even makes the same claim once about awareness of *thinking*, that we *perceive* that we think.[34] This had been accepted by some, but seemed strange to others. The new theory agrees that the human being is unitary, so there ought to be one single faculty apprehending all faculties. But an inferior faculty cannot apprehend a superior one. Moreover, sense perception is too bodily a faculty to be able to turn in on itself, *epistrephesthai*, as self-awareness requires, since body cannot penetrate body. The attentive faculty must therefore be a rational one.[35] This idea was introduced by "newer interpreters." The reference may well be to one of the three discussants already mentioned, Philoponus' older contemporary, Damascius, in Athens.

The third discussant, Philoponus' younger contemporary, Olympiodorus, in Alexandria, in explaining the Platonist idea of moral conscience to his Christian students, used the original terminology of *suneidos*, sharing knowledge with oneself, and connected conscience both with Socrates'

30. Atkins further confirms by pointing to Olympiodorus' reference, quoted below, to Orestes' conscience at having killed his mother in Euripides' play.

31. Aristotle, *Nicomachean Ethics* 7.3.

32. Plato, *Theaetetus* 184D; Aristotle, *On the Soul* 3.2, 426b17–23.

33. Aristotle, *On Sleep* 455a12–20.

34. Aristotle, *Nicomachean Ethics* 9.9, 1170a25ff.

35. "Philoponus' *On Aristotle on the Soul*, bk. 3, 464.24–465.31; 466.18–29.

guardian spirit, and with his Christian students' own beliefs ("things as they are nowadays"), as follows:

> But we shall try to expound this compatibly with things as they are nowadays. For hemlock was indeed the sentence against Socrates on the charge of introducing new spiritual beings (*daimonia*) to the young and believing in gods whom the city did not believe in. So it should be said that conscience (*to suneidos*) was Socrates' allotted daemon, which is the supreme flower of the soul, and sinless [or possibly infallible: *anhamartêton*] in us, and an unswayable judge and witness before [the divine judges] Minos and Rhadamanthus of what is being done down here. It also comes to be the cause of our salvation, as always remaining sinless [or infallible] in us, and not being sentenced along with the soul's misdeeds, but rather shrinking back at these and turning the soul to what is right (*to deon*). Conscience lifts the soul back up from its faults, just as a child starts crying at some image from its sleep, when one says [and here is quoted one of our opening texts from Euripides, *Orestes*, 395–396], "What are you distraught about? What illness is destroying you?" and the other replies, "Conscience (*sunesis*). For I share knowledge with myself (*sunoida*) of having done terrible things."[36]

I doubt if Olympiodorus is calling conscience infallible rather than sinless. But what he is doing is explaining Socrates' guardian spirit to his Christian students as something that they themselves believe in: conscience.[37] At the close of antiquity, the tables have been turned, and a Platonist is trying to accommodate a Christian way of thinking, instead of the other way round.

36. Olympiodorus, *Commentary on Plato's 1st Alcibiades*, pp. 22,14–23,13 (p. 17 Westerink).

37. The point is made by L. G. Westerink in "The Alexandrian commentators and the introductions to their commentaries," in Richard Sorabji, ed., *Aristotle Transformed: The Ancient Commentators and Their Influence*, Cornell University Press 1990, ch. 14, pp. 325–48, at 334, revised from Westerink's *Anonymous Prolegomena to Platonic Philosophy*, Amsterdam 1962, introduction.

THREE

Early Christianity and Freedom of Religion, 200–400 CE

Freedom of conscience is freedom not only of belief, but also freedom, within limits, to act on that belief. Thomas Hobbes, as will turn out in chapter 8, seems to have ignored this, as did his then model Oliver Cromwell, when he claimed that he allowed freedom of conscience on the grounds that in compelling conformity of *behavior*, the ruler would not attempt to change inner *belief*. It is true that conscience draws on beliefs about right and wrong, and is itself a belief about how right and wrong applies to one's own case. But this application includes deciding how it was or would be *wrong* or not wrong for one to act or not. It thus concerns *action* as well as belief, and there are *two* ways in which conscience can be oppressed, *either* by punishing belief, *or* by punishing action.

In the early centuries CE, freedom of conscience was discussed particularly in connection with freedom of religion—that is, in connection with the persecution first of Christians, then of Christian heretics, and more slowly, as Christianity grew stronger, of pagans. In the two hundred years from 200 to 400 CE, many of the arguments for freedom of conscience of the seventeenth century were formulated and at least one already refuted. A difference was that the first Christian author to be mentioned below spoke of freedom of *religion* (*libertas religionis*), and the expression "freedom of conscience" was not typically used, as it would be in seventeenth-century England. It will emerge when the seventeenth century is discussed,[1] that there is a considerable overlap between freedom of religion and freedom of conscience and that many of the arguments for them are the same, with small transpositions, but that they are not the same concept.

1. In ch. 8.

An important text for Christians was Christ's parable of the tares or weeds in the field. They were not to be picked out prematurely, for fear of harming the wheat.[2] Christians regarded as tares a wide range of *sinners*, including perpetrators of apostasy, blasphemy, unchastity, and homicide. That might call for *penance*, and so will be the subject of chapter 5. But tares were sometimes also equated with *heretics*, and that equation was relevant to freedom of conscience. Was Christ requiring that heretics be tolerated, and not prematurely eradicated?

Tertullian: Persecution Cannot Convert Christians, but Heretics?

The Christian convert Tertullian (ca. 160–220 CE), writing in Latin, composed his *Apology*, in the sense of a *defense* of Christianity, perhaps around 197 CE, before he joined the puritanical Montanist sect, which was regarded as heretical. Addressing the rulers of the Roman Empire, he argues that it would be irreligious if they took away "freedom of religion," and that no being, not even a human—a reference presumably to the emperor—would want to be worshipped involuntarily. This is an appeal to the *ineffectiveness* of compelling worship. He adds that this is why Rome has allowed very varied worship of non-Roman gods in its provinces. So it is Christians alone who are prevented from having their own religion. By applying the argument from ineffectiveness to *worship*, and not only (like some in the seventeenth century) to conscientious *belief*, Tertullian makes it clearer that the freedom required is freedom of *action*, not only of belief.

In 212 CE, even if now in a sect seen as heretical, the Montanists, he was still defending Christianity from persecution in writing to the Proconsul of Africa, in his *To Scapula*, using the same argument, along with others, that involuntary worship has no value:

> But it is a matter of human justice (*humanum ius*) and natural liberty (*naturalis potestas*) that each should worship as he thinks. Nor does one person's religion hinder or help another's. But neither is it for religion to compel religion, which has to be undertaken by choice (*sponte*), not by force (*vi*), since even sacrifices are required from a willing mind. So even if you have compelled us to sacrifice, you will not help your gods, since they will not desire sacrifices from the unwilling.[3]

2. Matthew 13:24–43.
3. Tertullian, *Ad Scapulam* 2.2.

Despite this powerful argument, Tertullian's Montanist period included an ominous remark in his *Scorpiace*, or *Against the Scorpion's Bite*: "Heretics deserve to be compelled (*compelli*) to duty, not enticed (*inclini*)."[4]

Augustine, 408 CE: Compel Donatist Heretics with a Little Bit of Persecution?

This omen was terrifyingly fulfilled, though in a brilliant way, by the change of mind to which Augustine laid claim in 408 CE. In order to see how, I shall briefly skip forward two hundred years, before returning to chronological sequence. Augustine was reflecting on his experience since 405 with Donatists, a heresy with which the Catholic Church was contending.[5] The word "Catholic" here meant *universal*, and Augustine was concerned that the Church should be universal, not divided. The Universal Church then still included the Eastern Church, and there was no lasting split between the Western and Eastern Churches until 1054. In his reflections of 408 on the Donatists, Augustine says he had earlier thought that one must convince, not compel, since that would be ineffective—ineffective as producing only hypocrites. That objection to persecution, we shall see, had been repeatedly used in the two hundred years before Augustine's letter. But in actual experience, he said, he found that compulsion, introduced in 405 by the Western Emperor Honorius, on the basis of the laws of his father, Theodosius I, had wonderfully opened eyes and led to mass conversion to the Catholic Church. In this, Augustine anticipated an alarming finding that was to be overlooked by John Locke in his first *Letter Concerning Toleration* of 1689. We shall see in chapter 8 that Locke's main argument for toleration was answered by Jonas Proast making Augustine's point that a little persecution can open eyes, and Locke had in the same year to write *A Second Letter Concerning Toleration*, withdrawing his argument from *ineffectiveness* and relying on others. Augustine had already put the point as follows in his *Letter* 93.17:

> For my opinion originally was simply that no one should be compelled to the unity of Christ, that one must act with words, fight by argument, conquer by reason, so as not to have as feigned Catholics people we knew to be openly heretical. But this opinion of mine kept being overcome not by words of

4. Tertullian, *Scorpiace* 2, *Corpus Selectorum Ecclesiasticorum Latinorum* (CSEL) vol. 20, 147, 3–8.

5. Further described in ch. 5.

> disagreement, but by examples that were pointed out. First my own city was being made a counter-example. Whereas it had been wholly on the side of Donatus, it was converted to catholic unity by fear of imperial laws. We now see it so abhorring the destructiveness of this vehemence of yours, that it would be thought never to have been on that side. . . . How many, as we know with certainty, already wanted to be Catholics, moved by the most evident truth, and kept delaying every day, for fear of offending their own people. How many were bound not by the truth—for you made no presumption about that—but by the heavy chain of hardened custom. . . . How many thought that the side of Donatus was the true church because security was making them too sluggish, disdainful and apathetic to recognize the Catholic truth. For how many was the approach to entry barred by the rumours of slanderers who bandied it about that we placed I know not what alternatives on God's altar. How many remained on the side of Donatus in the belief that it made no difference on which side a Christian was, because they had been born there and no one was compelling them (*cogere*) to leave and transfer to the Catholic side.

In fact, we shall see, Augustine had already taken this approach in 401–405, even though he here implies that actual experience after 405 led him to change his mind. After the supposed change, he nonetheless still insisted on important limits to the degree of persecution to be allowed, but I shall come back to that. I will add only that Augustine also introduced in this letter a quotation from a different context that was to prove surprisingly influential. On the subject of compelling, Christ told the parable of guests who made excuses when invited to a banquet, and of a host who sent his servants into the streets to bring in instead the poor, maimed, blind, and lame. The host told them finally to go into the highways and hedges and *compel* them to come in.[6] Augustine surprisingly compares the compelled hedge dwellers with the heretics who were to be compelled to come in. I return now to the preceding two hundred years from the point where I left off with Tertullian's plea for tolerance of Christians but threat to heretics.

Origen and Heretics: Admonition, Not Hate

In the century after Tertullian, Origen (ca. 185–253/254 CE), head of the Christian catechetical school in Alexandria, had expressed the opposite view on heretics. Writing in Greek some time after 245 CE, he cited the Letter to

6. Luke 14:15–24.

Titus ascribed to Paul for the claim that a heretic should first be admonished (*paraitein*) twice and then excluded. But he added that one should not hate (*apostugein*) those who so err (*planâsthai*).[7] This is compatible with his further idea that heretics cannot be excused for the sincerity of their conviction or faith (*fides*), because what they have is credulity (*credulitas*) rather than faith, the implication being that their error is sin.[8]

Lactantius: Christians, Not Pagans, Know that Persecution Cannot Convert

Lactantius (ca. 240–ca. 320), another convert to Christianity, wrote his *Divine Institutes*, already mentioned, in Latin probably between 304 and 313 CE, a period of major persecution for Christians under the emperors of the eastern part of the empire, where Lactantius had gone to work. At some stage, Constantine I, the first Christian emperor, as yet ruling only in the West, hired Lactantius there as tutor to his son. Familiar with the persecution of Christians, Lactantius repeated some of Tertullian's arguments against it, and added his own.[9] Pagans should not try to force compliance. For religion cannot be compelled (*religio cogi non potest*), since nothing is more voluntary (*voluntarius*). If the mind is averse to sacrifice or is unwilling, there is neither religion nor sacrifice. Unless offered by choice (*sponte*), sacrifice is rather a curse. Christians did not try to force converts, or detain anyone involuntarily, he said, because anyone who lacks devotion and faith is useless to God. Nor did Christians entice converts (*inclinare*), as alleged. Rather they *proved* their beliefs, and pagans should attempt the same.

Christian Emperor Constantine and Successor: Pagans Freer than Heretics

Constantine's imperial rule in the West had been disputed since 306. But his Western rule and his Christian sympathies were confirmed in 312. He then in 313 put out a joint declaration with Licinius, emperor in the East, in the Edict of Milan, allowing religious freedom to Christians and pagans alike. This brought the persecution of Christians by pagans virtually to an end, all the more when Constantine took over the East as well from Licinius in 324.

7. Origen, *Against Celsus* bk. 5, ch. 23.

8. Origen, *Commentary on Romans* 14:23, in *Patrologia Graeca* vol. 14. col. 1256A, explained in ch. 4 below.

9. Lactantius, *Divine Institutes* bk. 5, ch. 19, secs. 11–13, 23; ch. 20, sec. 7.

He then reiterated that pagans should have their "temples of falsehood," but prayed that they might be converted.[10] But heretics did not all fare so well, because of the danger they posed to Christian unity. Constantine persecuted the Donatists, but appeared to have gained agreement against the Arian heresy without persecution at the Council of Nicaea in 325, when it declared Christ not created (*genêtos*) in the Arian manner by God the Father, but begotten (*gennêtos*, with double "n"), and so of the same substance as the Father (*homousios*).

Constantine's son, Constantius II, emperor from 337–361 at first only of the East, restricted only a few pagan practices, such as animal sacrifice. But he was led to persecute holders of the Nicaean formula, when it failed to retain unity against other formulae, which again sometimes differed by little more than one letter. Christ might be merely of *like* substance with the father (*homoiousios*), or merely like (*homoios*), or on the other hand unlike (*anhomoios*), or not even distinct. In attempts at unity, the supporters of his father's Nicaean formula were persecuted, and the leading Nicaean figure, Athanasius (295–373 CE), suffered two of his five exiles from Alexandria. He wrote in his Greek *History of the Arians* about his Arian opponents as being ungodly, because it is godly to persuade, not to drag by force, and his Nicaean view eventually prevailed.[11] After Constantine, it was for quite some time heretics who were persecuted on any considerable scale, rather than pagans. Pagans, by contrast, were able to speak up in favor of freedom of religion, and I shall take three examples.

Themistius and Two Other Pagans Speak Up for Freedom

The pagan Themistius (317–ca. 390 CE) was both philosopher and orator. Constantius II involved him in politics, appointing him to the Senate, where he remained, putting him on its selection committee, and sending him on embassies, as well as paying for part of his role as teacher of philosophy in Constantinople. He managed to remain on good terms with six emperors, five Christian and one pagan, of very different views. In sequence they were Constantius II, the pagan Julian the apostate, the restorer of Christianity Jovian, Valens, Gratian, and Theodosius I. The last increased the restrictions on paganism from 391 CE, perhaps under the influence of his Christian priest, Ambrose, whose penitential requirements of 390 will be described in

10. See Peter Garnsey, "Religious toleration in classical antiquity" in W. J. Sheils, ed., *Persecution and Toleration*, Blackwell 1984, pp. 1–27, at p. 18.

11. Athanasius, *History of the Arians*, ch. 67, secs. 1–3.

chapter 5. He was nonetheless happy to appoint Themistius as city prefect of Constantinople, a post Themistius had declined under Valens.

Themistius addressed the subject of freedom of religion in writing to Jovian, whom he praised for practicing religious toleration of pagans at the start of his eight-month reign in 363–364 CE, and he used a range of arguments, old and new. We find already here the argument later questioned by Augustine that reverence for the divine cannot be compelled through fear, since this only leads to hypocritical pretense. Secondly, God did not provide only one road leading to him, because the difficulty of finding him makes us more energetic in seeking him, and also makes us feel awe (*sebometha, tethêpamen*) and astonishment at him. Although this argument appeals to the difficulty of knowledge, it is quite different from the argument that there *is* one right road, but we do not know it. Thirdly, God himself has allowed diversity of belief among and within the different races of the empire.[12] In chapter 8 we shall see this last argument of Themistius being taken up by Pierre Bayle.

Themistius' political success as a pagan philosopher in a Christian regime is the easier to understand, given that pagan Platonism was not a single thing. Of Themistius' six emperors he was on the *least* close terms with his fellow pagan and one-time pupil, Julian (Emperor, 361–363 CE), who wrote a reply, *Letter to Themistius*, somewhat distancing himself from Themistius' lost letter of encomium.[13] This was not as surprising as it may seem, because the Platonist philosopher whom Julian most admired, Iamblichus, handled Platonism in a manner utterly contrasted with Themistius' treatment. Iamblichus was the high priest of Neoplatonism whose memory Julian reverenced by installing symbolic mosaics in his former school.[14] Iamblichus, though writing commentaries on Aristotle like Themistius, offered an "intellective interpretation," relating the words of Plato and Aristotle to Neoplatonist higher theology. In a separate essay on the speech of Zeus in Plato's *Timaeus*, Iamblichus divided the world of Intellect into many triads of gods.[15] Themistius' commentaries on Aristotle, also by

12. *Themistii orationes*, ed. H. Schenkel, Teubner vol. 1, Leipzig 1965, 67b–70c; Oration 5, translated: Peter Heather and David Moncur, *Politics, Philosophy and Empire in the Fourth Century: Select Orations of Themistius*, Liverpool University Press 2001, ch. 3, pp. 159–73.

13. Julian's letter is translated by Wilmer C. Wright in *Julian II*, Loeb Classical Library 1913 and, with Themistius' second thoughts by Simon Swain, *Themistius, Julian and Greek Political Theory under Rome*, Cambridge 2013.

14. Richard Sorabji, *Aristotle Transformed*, Duckworth, London 1990, ch. 1, pp. 9–10, offers a reinterpretation of these mosaics.

15. John Dillon, *Iamblichi Chalcidensis in Platonis dialogos commentariorum fragmenta*, Brill 1973, appendix 3, pp. 417–19.

contrast used Plato and Aristotle equally and displayed a certain simplicity, being partly paraphrases of Aristotle, but at the same time Themistius provided original and stimulating ideas in physics about the views of Aristotle and Galen on space, time, motion, vacuum, and change.[16] Further, two commentaries included a detailed philosophical reinterpretation of Aristotle's Active Intellect, that was to prove extremely influential.[17] He will further have been the less congenial to Julian, in that he was not committed, like Iamblichus, to the preeminence of Neoplatonic priestly powers, and his engagement in politics would also not have commended itself to committed Neoplatonists, like Iamblichus, because political virtue for them was the very lowest level of virtue, with priestly virtue at the top. Conversely, it has been argued that so eloquent a pagan orator and philosopher would have been particularly useful to *Christian* emperors in an empire not yet predominantly Christian.[18] The paraphrase format of his commentaries on Aristotle may have been suited to Constantinople's students of rhetoric, preparing for careers in politics or law, who wanted only a limited grounding in the philosophy of Plato and Aristotle. Nonetheless, they would have found original ideas in physics and a detailed psychology of the intellect.

The other major pagan Greek orator of the age was Libanius (ca. 314–394 CE), also in the East, teaching rhetoric successively at Constantinople, Nicomedia and, from 354, his birthplace, Antioch. He was also a teacher

16. For his ingenuity in physics, see, e.g., prefaces by Richard Sorabji to *Themistius on Aristotle Physics 4*, translated by Robert Todd, Duckworth, London 2003, and *Themistius on Aristotle Physics 5–8*, translated by Robert Todd, Duckworth, London 2008; the paragraph on Themistius in the introduction to all three volumes of Sorabji, *Philosophy of the Commentators, 200–600 AD: A Sourcebook*, Duckworth, London 2004, and the fact that the *Physics* commentary of Philoponus has been thought by its editor, Vitelli, to draw on Themistius six hundred times.

17. In his commentaries on Aristotle *On the Soul*, and on Aristotle *Metaphysics* bk. 12, a detailed analysis of Aristotle's account of Intellect replaces paraphrase. But the identification of Aristotle's Active Intellect with God is rejected, and the discussion remains throughout philosophical, not priestly. Thomas Aquinas reinterpreted the first commentary as implying that Aristotle ascribed immortality to the individual rational souls of humans, although Themistius did not say so. See the translation and notes of F. M. Schroeder and Robert B. Todd, *Two Greek Aristotelian Commentators on the Intellect*, Toronto 1990, Mediaeval Sources in Translation 33; and *Themistius On Aristotle On the Soul*, translated by Robert Todd, Duckworth, London 1996; Bloomsbury 2012. The second commentary is being translated into English from the surviving Hebrew and Arabic by Carlos Fraenkel and Yoav Meyrav. See also Shlomo Pines, "Some distinctive metaphysical conceptions in Themistius' commentary on Book Lambda and their place in the history of philosophy," in J. Wiesner, ed., *Aristoteles Werk und Wirkung* 2, de Gruyter 1987, pp. 177–204.

18. For these political roles, see Peter Heather and David Moncur, *Politics, Philosophy and Empire in the Fourth Century*, esp. chs. 1 and 3.

at one time of Julian, and of notable Christians, and a recipient of political office from Theodosius I. He particularly admired Themistius as an orator successful with the emperor in Constantinople, from where he himself was exiled through the jealousy of rivals. But he was more fully supported by Julian, and his letters to Julian and funeral oration on him survive. Libanius' Oration 30, *For the Temples*, was addressed to Theodosius I (Emperor, 379–395, at first only in the East), and protested the smashing of pagan temples in the East, allowed, though not ordered, by Theodosius. It used the argument that persecution is ineffective in producing change of faith because victims only *pretend* to be redirecting their worship, and is in any case against the Christians' own laws.[19]

Better known is the unsuccessful plea in 384 CE of the urban prefect of Rome, Symmachus, to Valentinian II (Emperor in the West at Milan, 375–387, until he required Theodosius' protection), to restore the Altar of Victory removed by Gratian from the Senate in Rome. Symmachus used the earlier argument of Themistius, saying that it is not possible to reach so great a secret as God by a single route, but his case was answered in a letter by Ambrose to Valentinian.[20]

John Chrysostom: Mild Correction of Heretics

Returning to heretics, and their treatment by Christians, I shall take one last example before returning to Augustine's subtleties on the subject. Although there were imperial persecutions of heretics, it is somewhat more encouraging to see the example of John Chrysostom (347/349–407) as priest in Antioch. He was a pupil of Libanius of Antioch in this thoroughly interactive pagan and Christian empire, and he repeatedly advocated gentle persuasion, not persecution, for heretics; but, on the other hand, he added qualifications. In one of his homilies on Matthew, he applied to heretics rather than sinners Christ's command not to uproot tares prematurely, and very clearly stated two current interpretations. Premature uprooting would either damage the existing wheat, or prevent tares (a type of pulse) turning into good wheat. The second interpretation invoked the possibility of a change of mind. Chrysostom understands that heretics are not to be killed; but he allows that they may be silenced.[21] He offers a milder verdict in a

19. *Oration* 30, secs. 28–29; *Libanii opera*, ed. Foerster, Teubner, Leipzig 1903–8.

20. Symmachus, relatio 3 to Valentinian, para. 10; reply by Ambrose, Letter 73 (Maur. 18) to Valentinian.

21. John Chrysostom, *Homily 47* (sometimes 46) *on Matthew 13*, *Patrologia Graeca* vol. 58, cols. 477–78.

homily on Genesis. Heretics are like sick men with weak eyes. Gentle correction and teaching may bring a change of mind (*metanoia*) and knowledge of the truth. Here only the change of mind is mentioned.[22] In *On the Priesthood*, after discussing sinners, he turns briefly to heretics—the severed limbs of the church—and again says that they cannot be dragged by force (*bia*), or the necessity of fear, but can be brought back only by persuasion (*peithein*).[23] Another homily on Matthew discusses not heretics but those who, having heard the word, commit the sin of blasphemy by denying the divinity of Christ. Force (*bia*) is ineffective, since fear will be followed by relapse. Such people are wounded and need sorrowing and gentle admonition for a change of mind (*metanoia*). The parable of the tares, he says, was borne out by the Apostle Paul, who was converted from earlier persecution of Christians, and by the thief who repented on the cross, as well as by other sinners. Late repentance is possible because our will (*prohairesis*) is privileged with freedom (*eleutheria*). As good doctors of the soul, we should try out a succession of psychological remedies.[24]

Augustine and the Donatist Heresy Again: Penalties, but Not Death

In another interaction between paganism and Christianity, Augustine (354–430 CE), originally a Manichaean, says in his *Confessions* that he was led to Christianity through the "books of the Platonists." He heard of Platonist ideas through Ambrose in Milan, and certainly his conversion from one pagan faith via pagan Platonism was due not to force, but to persuasion. But as regards Donatist heretics, we have seen his claim to have been persuaded of the value of a certain level of force. It is not clear that what he presented in 408 as a change of mind since 405 was after all such a change. Already in 400 CE, talking admittedly of sin (*peccatum*), not of heresy, he inferred from the parable of the tares something that is not actually said—that if the wheat happened to be safe, then discipline should not sleep.[25] He was also worried by the charge of the Donatist Petilian, to whom he wrote a long reply between 401 and 405. Petilian complained that God only *drew* (*attrahere*) people to Christ, according to the Gospel of John 6:44. Petilian added, "Far be it from *our* conscience (*conscientia*) to compel (*compellere*)." Why, he

22. John Chrysostom, *Homily 8 on Genesis 1*, sec. 3, *Patrologia Graeca* vol. 53, col. 72.

23. John Chrysostom, *On the Priesthood* 2, sec. 4, *Patrologia Graeca* vol. 48, col. 635, *Sources Chrétiennes* vol. 272.

24. Homily 29 (sometimes 30) *on Matthew*, sec. 3, *Patrologia Graeca* vol. 57, cols 361–62.

25. Augustine, *Against the Letter of Parmenian* bk. 3, ch. 2, para. 13, CSEL 51.

asks, are the Donatists not allowed to follow the free choice (*liberum arbitrium*) that God has given? Augustine provides the alarming answer: "How does God *draw*, if he leaves everyone to choose what he wants? . . . What is threatened by the coercion of the law does not take away free choice. For whatever hard trouble a man suffers, he is being warned to think why he is suffering, in order that . . . he may change his will in a better direction."[26] This is the same view as that of the supposedly later change of mind. In 407–408, Augustine argues that his "drawing" people to Christ does not violate their will: only *physically* moving them would do that. So he does not use violence (*violentia*) rather than will (*voluntas*). No one can believe except willingly (*credere non potest nisi volens*). Belief is not produced in the unwilling through some movement of the body, but through the willing of the heart.[27]

Augustine still insisted against the death penalty, because what he hoped for was repentance. Writing in 409 to the Proconsul of Africa, coincidentally called Donatus, he says that he is seeking correction (*corrigi*) and repentance (*paenitere*) through fear of judges and laws, not death. Donatists should be taught (*doceri*), not compelled (*cogi*).[28] In 412, he wrote to the imperial commissioner, Marcellinus, in Carthage that he should not execute even Donatists guilty of assault on a Catholic priest and murder but should have them flogged, as might a parent, schoolmaster or bishop, and should have their liberty restricted.[29] Further in 417, he wrote *Letter* 185, also called *On the Correction of the Donatists*, saying that he had wished to confine punishment to a substantial fine for Donatists in places where violence had been committed, so that Catholicism could be freely taught, without compulsion (*cogere*), so as to avoid false and hypocritical converts (*falsi, simulatores*). As it turned out, however, the imperial course that prevailed was salutary: a fine and exile for all Donatist clergy, but without capital punishment.[30]

Augustine Applied by Thomas Aquinas to Nonbelievers, Apostates, and Heretics

Augustine's view on Donatist heretics was still exerting influence on the greatest compendium of reasoned Catholic views, the *Summa theologiae*

26. Augustine, *Against the Letters of Petilian the Donatist*, bk. 2, chs. 84–85, CSEL, vol. 52.
27. Augustine, *Tractate 26 on John*, paras. 2–3, *Corpus Christianorum Series Latina* (CCSL), vol. 36.
28. Augustine, *Letter* 100, paras. 1–2.
29. Augustine, *Letter* 133, paras. 1–2.
30. Augustine, *Letter* 185; *On the Correction of the Donatists*, ch. 7, CSEL, vol. 57.

of Thomas Aquinas (ca. 1225–1274) over eight hundred years later in the thirteenth century. But by then the Church had abandoned Augustine's opposition to capital punishment for heretics. He discussed first "whether *unbelievers* (*infideles*) are to be compelled to the faith," including under that head those who never believed, like Gentiles and Jews, apostates (whom Augustine tended to count as sinners at a time when apostasy, though not Julian's, had often been due to persecution) and heretics. Thomas cited Augustine's change of mind about *heretics* in Letter 93, and his earlier inference about *sinners* of 400 CE that tares may be picked out *if the wheat happens to be safe*. He concluded that the first group of unbelievers may be compelled (e.g., by war) not to impede the faith, but not in order to convert them to it. The other two groups are to be physically compelled (*corporaliter compellendi*)—contrary to Augustine's earlier protestations—to fulfill their earlier promises, or be excommunicated, though, in agreement with Augustine, they may not be killed.[31] Under the question "whether heretics are to be tolerated," he again takes up the case Augustine applied to *sinners*, in which the wheat is not in danger of being eradicated with the tares. Applying it to heretics, Thomas abandons Augustine's prohibition and says that if the heretics will be totally eradicated by death, that is not contrary to Christ's command about the tares.[32]

Relation to Freedom of Conscience

Freedom of religion for Christians, heretics, and pagans foreshadows the overlapping, but different, concept of freedom of *conscience*, which will be discussed in chapter 8. The two hundred years just surveyed anticipated many seventeenth-century arguments for freedom of conscience, as already remarked, as well as Proast's objection to one of those arguments. Freedom of conscience, like freedom of religion, is not just freedom to hold beliefs, but freedom, within limits, to *act* on those beliefs, since beliefs of conscience are beliefs about what it would be *wrong* for one to do or not to do.

31. Thomas Aquinas, *Summa theologiae* IIa IIae question 10, article 8, "I answer" and *ad* 1.
32. Thomas Aquinas, *Summa theologiae* IIa IIae question 11, article 3, *ad* 3.

FOUR

Doubled Conscience and Dilemmas of Double Bind: A Medieval Insight and a Twelfth-Century Misconstrual?

Moving to the Middle Ages, I shall take first one of the best-known developments, the distinction of *synderesis*. If the idea was due to a mistake, as I think it may have been, it was a mistake with important consequences.

Conscience and *Synderesis*

Origen was by accident the indirect source of the idea of *synderesis*. He describes Ezekiel's vision of an animal made up of four living creatures: a human, a lion, a calf, and an eagle.[1] The first three remind Origen of Plato's human, lion, and many-headed beast, which in Plato's *Republic* represent the three parts of the soul, reason, irascibility, and appetite.[2] But what is the fourth part, the eagle? It is the human's spirit (*spiritus*) presiding over the other three, according to a fragment of his lost twenty-five-book commentary on Ezechiel, and Origen elsewhere, in Rufinus' Latin translation of him, says that conscience (*conscientia*) is also spirit.[3]

This may have been enough to motivate Jerome, writing in Latin in the late fourth century CE. He is probably drawing on Origen and those who followed him, when he says that "most people" refer the three parts to Plato's three parts of the soul, but refer the eagle to a fourth part, for which the Greeks have a name, and which is the "spark of conscience" by which we recognize that we are sinning. The Greek word was read in the twelfth to fourteenth centuries as *suntêrêsis*, or in Latin *synteresis* or *synderesis*. The

1. Ezekiel 1:10.

2. Plato, *Republic* 9, 588C–589A.

3. Origen, *On Ezechiel*, homily 1.16, Fragment, *Patrologia Graeca* 13.681; Rufinus' Latin of Origen's commentary on Romans 2.15 at *Patrologia Graeca* 14, 893A–B.

Greek word, usually the related verb, is used by post-Aristotelian philosophers most commonly to mean to preserve, or to safeguard, and of laws to observe, or concerning choice of friends to watch carefully.[4] Closer to the relevant meaning, I should add, is *paratêrêsis*, a word used by the Stoic Epictetus for the watchful *self*-inspection which he recommends,[5] and of which Origen may well have known. But Epictetus' watchful self-inspection is not exactly conscience, but an examination of one's thoughts about what matters in a situation, and it is carried out by reason, not by something higher.

Since Jerome went on later in the passage to use the standard word for conscience, in Latin *conscientia*, theologians for several centuries from the twelfth believed that there were two different things to discuss, conscience and the spark of conscience (*sunderesis*). Because of this doubling of conscience, they had to divide into two all such questions as whether conscience can be mistaken and whether that is what Jerome meant by its "falling." This now had to be asked separately for conscience and for *synderesis*. However, in an arresting article, a French scholar, Jacques de Blic, claimed that the new word (and all the subsequent distinctions based on it) was first introduced in the twelfth century CE.[6] The Greek word in twenty-six manuscripts of Jerome—twenty-four of them earlier than the twelfth century, and in a parallel passage of Gregory of Nazianzus—is the standard Greek word for conscience, *suneidêsis*. Before the twelfth century no manuscripts of Jerome, nor (except for that of Raban Maur in the ninth century) of Latin commentaries on Ezechiel, give the other word. Nor do the extant works of Origen ever use it, whereas they do speak of *suneidêsis* and *to suneidos*. Admittedly, Origen's twenty-five-book commentary on Ezechiel is lost, even though we have the fragment that calls the eagle spirit (*pneuma*). Whether the word was introduced simply by a scribal error, which would not be difficult,[7] or deliberately, it seems to have caused a diversion, though a momentous one, for many centuries in theological thought. If it was introduced deliberately,

4. Preserve: Diogenes Laertius *Lives* 8.61; Plutarch, *Precepts on Keeping Well* 130A; *Against Colotes* 1125 C; Athenaeus, *Philosophers at Dinner* bk. 13, para. 28, line 1; Porphyry, *Letter to Marcella*, sec. 10; *Cave of the Nymphs*, sec. 15; similarly Gospel of Matthew 9:17. Safeguard: Porphyry, *On Abstinence* 4.13.3. Observe (laws): Stobaeus, *Eclogae* bk. 3, ch. 39 sec. 36. Watch carefully: Diogenes Laertius, *Lives* 4.51.

5. Epictetus, *Discourses* 3.6.15.

6. Jacques de Blic, "Conscience ou syndérèse?," *Revue d'ascétique et de mystique* 25, 1949, 146–57.

7. The divergent four letters "*-dere-*" and "*eide-*" have a "*de*" and an extra "*e*" in common, as Elizabeth Sawyer has pointed out to me.

one suggestion has been that the word referred to the *safeguarding* function of conscience, but this has been convincingly criticized.[8] I think the case for a scribal error is strengthened by the variation in roles suggested for *synderesis* by the ablest thirteenth-century thinkers, and the absence of a clear need for a special agency to play those roles. Whether or not de Blic is right about the origin of the reference to *syntêrêsis,* it had big consequences for future discussion of the subject.

In the thirteenth century, Bonaventure (ca. 1217–1274), who became head of the Franciscans, distinguished *synderesis* in one way, the Aristotelian tradition in another. It is as if they had to search, without guidance, for an extra function. *Conscientia* for Bonaventure has a cognitive role. It is the light possessed by the intellect which is its natural court of justice (*iudicatorium*) and directs it concerning what needs to be known (*in cognoscendis*) toward moral action. The role of *synderesis* is motivational. It is the natural weight (*pondus*) of the will (*voluntas*), a weight possessed by feeling (*affectus*). Or it is the will with that weight. It directs feeling concerning what should be wanted (*in appetendis*). It is on the side of the capacity for feeling rather than for cognition (*non . . . ex parte cognitivae, immo potius . . . ex parte affectivae*).[9] This is the earliest attempt I have noticed to make a connection with *feeling,* here understood as the weight of the will. The connection of *conscience* with feeling and sentiment was to come into its own in the eighteenth century. But here it is *synderesis* that is connected with feeling and will, whereas *conscientia* is still connected with knowledge and intellect. The division of labor is, I believe, not needed for the purpose of explaining motivation. For knowledge or belief is itself motivating, provided it is the knowledge or belief that some action would, or would not, be wrong for one to perform in an expected situation calling for decision. Bonaventure has found a task for *synderesis* to perform, but if I am right, the task could have been performed without it.

8. So J. Hebing, "Ueber conscientia und conservatio im philosophischen Sinne bei den Römern von Cicero bis Hieronymus, *Philosophisches Jahrbuch* 35, 1922, pp. (136–52, 215–31, 298–326) who is answered by M. M. Waldemann, "Synteresis oder syneidesis?," *Theologische Quartalschrift* 119, 1938, 332–71.

9. Bonaventure, *Commentary on the Sentences of Peter Lombard,* bk. 2, distinctio. 39, article 2, question 1, reply and *ad* 3, 910, ed. Quaracchi, vol. 2, quoted in Latin by O. Lottin, *Psychologie et morale aux XII et XIII siècles,* vol. 2, p. 207. O. Lottin gives the major account of discussions of *synderesis* and *conscientia* in the twelfth to thirteenth centuries, pp. 105–349. Further discussion is provided by Timothy Potts, "Conscience," in Norman Ktetzmann, Anthony Kenny and Jan Pinborg, eds., *The Cambridge History of Later Medieval Philosophy,* Cambridge University Press 1982, and with English translations of some passages in his *Conscience in Medieval Philosophy,* Cambridge University Press 1980.

Earlier in the same text, before he reaches *synderesis*, Bonaventure asks whether conscience is an innate or an acquired disposition (*habitus*). He replies that it is in a way innate and in a way acquired. Conscience is an innate disposition concerning moral first principles and what comes from the first dictates (*dictamina*) of nature. Examples of first principles include that parents are to be honored; neighbors are not to be harmed; God is to be obeyed; and you should not do to another what you do not want done to yourself. Even here we do not at first have the concepts of mother and father, but must acquire them from sense perception. But the disposition to recognize the first principles is innate in the sense that once the concepts are acquired, nothing more is needed. Derived moral principles, by contrast, will not be understood without further instruction, and our disposition to recognize these is acquired. Thomas Aquinas agrees with this part of Bonaventure's account, except that he gives *synderesis* a cognitive as well as a motivational role, as the disposition to embrace moral first principles. He says that practical reason has to make deductions from self-evident principles, such as that evil is not to be done and God's commandments are to be obeyed. The disposition of *synderesis* to obey these principles is in a way innate, in that the principles are known in the light of active intellect, as soon as the concepts are known; whereas practical reason can make mistakes in drawing its conclusions, which are not innate in us.[10] The belief in the innateness of very general moral principles goes beyond St. Paul's idea that we have a law of right and wrong written by God in our hearts. But it was seen in chapter 1 that Origen and Augustine did not think that the inner law appeared in childhood. And I think it is healthier to believe that our general values may or may not have reliable sources and may or may not need revision.

At least three thinkers deserve to be mentioned who found a role for *synderesis* by adapting Aristotle's treatment of the practical syllogism, his practical reasoning based on two premisses. Philip, chancellor of the diocese of Paris (d. 1236), writing before Bonaventure, included a treatise on conscience in his *Summa de bono*, of 1235. He gives to *synderesis* not Bonaventure's motivational role, but the cognitive role of apprehending principles. He constructs an illustrative Aristotelian syllogism: "If it is written in *synderesis* that everyone should die the death who has made himself out to

10. Bonaventure, *Commentary on the Sentences of Peter Lombard*, bk. 2, dist. 39, article 1, question 2, reply. Thomas Aquinas, *Commentary on the Sentences of Peter Lombard*, bk. 2, dist 24, question 2, article 3, both discussed in O. Lottin, *Psychologie* vol. 2, pp. 205 and 223, with Bonaventure partly translated in Potts, "Conscience," 697.

be the son of God and is not, but[11] this man (indicating Christ, as accused by the Jewish community) is making himself out to be the son of God, and is not; thus the opinion is formed: therefore he should die the death." *Conscientia* apprehends the conclusion and in this case is mistaken, because the second premise is mistaken, but he wants *synderesis* to be never mistaken, in effect infallible, citing Geoffrey of Poitiers earlier in the thirteenth century.[12] Hence he connects the possibility of error with *conscientia*.

Albert the Great (ca. 1200–1280), mentor of Thomas Aquinas, continues the Aristotelian interpretation. He says that conscience (*conscientia*) is the *conclusion* (*conclusio*) of a practical syllogism. He sees the premises and the conclusion as *acts* (*actus*). The conclusion is an act that infers the conclusion as a judgment (*infert per modum sententiae*). The conclusion, that this must be done or not be done, is a command (*imperare*), and that is why Paul can say in his Letter to the Romans 2:15 that conscience excuses or accuses one, according to whether or not one follows it.[13] By contrast, the first premise is *synderesis*, whose job it is to incline us to good through universal reasons relating to good, and it does not yet concern the particular. The second premise is the work of reason applying the particular to the universal, and saying that this is good. It does not yet command that something should be done or not done, but gives the *reason* why something should be done. Thus the first two premises are acts of *synderesis* and reason, respectively, a multiplication of agencies not found in Aristotle himself.

Thomas Aquinas (ca. 1225–1274) develops the Aristotelian interpretations. *Synderesis* is a disposition (*habitus*) within the power of reason. It supplies the universal premise, for example that worship should be offered to God. Such principles are the general principles of natural law.[14] Once again *synderesis* is never mistaken, but in effect infallible.[15] Because it is a disposition, it has motivational force: it warns, inclines, incites, and deters.[16] Conscience (*conscientia*), by contrast, is an *act* of applying the universal premise

11. I omit here the "that" in Potts's translation, because *synderesis* does not make the mistaken and changeable judgment, as is further indicated by the change of verbal mood in the Latin.

12. Philip the Chancellor, *Summa de bono,* Treatise on conscience, question 3 on *synderesis,* Latin quoted in O. Lottin, vol. 2, pp. 151–52, at lines 61–69; English translation in Timothy Potts, *Conscience in Medieval Philosophy,* 104.

13. Albert the Great, *Summa de homine*. question 72, article 1, ed. Borgnet, vol. 35, 599, quoted in Latin by O. Lottin, vol. 2, pp. 217–18.

14. Thomas Aquinas, *On Truth,* question 16, article 1.

15. Ibid., question 16, articles 1 and 2

16. Ibid., question 16, article 1, ad 12; *Summa theologiae* 1, question 79, article 12.

to a particular situation.[17] Unlike *synderesis*, which is said to be infallible in itself, conscience can make mistakes. There is a danger, however, that the infallibility of *synderesis* depends on its supplying premises so general as to carry very little information, especially in a Christian world. Besides the example already given, that worship should be offered to God, others are that we should love God, evil should not be done, and we must not do anything that is forbidden by the law of God.[18] Conscience can introduce mistakes in two ways, either through invalid inference,[19] or through introducing a mistaken premise. An example would be the mistaken premise that it is pleasing to God to kill the apostles, or that the law of God forbids me to swear oaths,[20] as was believed by the Waldensians, followers of Peter Valdez, long before the Quakers. Conscience's concluding act of judgment will then be false, despite the truth of the premise supplied by *synderesis* that worship should be offered to God, or that I must not do anything that is forbidden by the law of God.

That conscience is an *application* of values is clarifying, but that it is an *act* is somewhat counterintuitive, as emerges when Thomas brings out the implications, and draws the startling conclusion that conscience is not found in someone who is asleep.[21] The main tradition was to think of conscience as knowledge or belief, not interrupted by sleep, about right and wrong in oneself. In English we might be misled into thinking conscience an act by shorthand turns of phrase like "forcing someone's conscience." But that is only shorthand for forcing the *exercise* of conscience.

Aquinas gives conscience, no less than *synderesis* motivational force, so motivation does not form the basis, as it does in Bonaventure, of the distinction between the two. Conscience can prospectively prod, urge, or bind, and retrospectively accuse or cause remorse.[22] The biggest difference lies in *synderesis* being a disposition disposing us to values so universal as to ensure its infallibility, and conscience being a fallible act of applying *synderesis*.

It may be asked why the Aristotelian tradition of the thirteenth century needed to split off some of the functions associated with conscience and assign them to a separate disposition, *synderesis*. For Aristotle's own

17. Thomas Aquinas, *On Truth*, question 17, article 9; *Summa theologiae* 1, question 79, article 13, reply.

18. Thomas Aquinas, *On Truth*, question 17, article 2, reply.

19. Ibid., question 16, article 2, ad 2; question 17, article 2, reply.

20. Ibid., question 16, article 2, ad 2; question 17, article 2, reply.

21. Ibid., question 17, article 1, *ad* 9.

22. Ibid., question 17, article 1, reply; similarly *Summa theologiae* 1, question 79, article 13: witness, incite, accuse.

account of practical reasoning, which admittedly does not particularly focus on conscience, is content to distinguish two *premises*. As to what dispositions or faculties may be needed for apprehending these premises, he gives different answers for different types of practical reasoning, some of it prudential and some concerning ethical virtue, rather than conscience. To turn to his account for a moment, in an admittedly difficult passage of his *Nicomachean Ethics*, book 6, which I have interpreted elsewhere,[23] he says of the two premises in a certain piece of practical reasoning that it is the very *same* thing that apprehends them, *nous*, which he repeatedly explains in book 6 of this treatise as a kind of intellectual perceptivity or spotting. For this context, I offered the example that the first premise tells us that various ethical virtues are desirable for their own sake, while the second premise, the particular one, tells us that *this* action is what virtue requires of us now. In book 7, with a different type of example, I took Aristotle to say that the first premise affirmed one of our carefully thought-out policy decisions (*prohaireseis*) in life, such as the desirability of a particular diet. The second premise, by contrast, being more particular, might declare that *this* food would violate the determined diet, and could become the subject of inattention through the presence of temptation. Had we attended, it would have been sense perception, the sense of taste, that alerted us that this food was too sweet,[24] while it was step-by-step deliberation that had revealed to us the best dietary policy.[25]

When this Aristotelian tradition was used in the thirteenth century to provide a role for *synderesis*, there was an incentive to go beyond Aristotle and distinguish not merely two premises and a conclusion, but also two agencies in the soul distinctly connected with the first premise and the conclusion. I believe, however, that St. Paul's simpler distinction had supplied all that was needed. He had already distinguished the law in our hearts with its *general* knowledge of right and wrong from the conscience that accused or excused us as *individuals*. St. Thomas Aquinas's idea that conscience *applies* values to the individual's particular situation, rather than being the original source of values, seems to me to be in the spirit of that distinction. But it is not true to St. Paul, nor to fact, to add that we have a disposition to recognize the law infallibly, and Origen and Augustine denied that we

23. Aristotle, *Nicomachean Ethics* 6.11, 1143a35–b5, interpreted in my "Aristotle on the role of intellect in virtue," in Amélie Rorty, ed., *Essays on Aristotle's Ethics*, University of California Press 1980, ch. 12, pp. 201–19, repr. from *Proceedings of the Aristotelian Society*, new series 74, 1973–1974, pp. 107–29.

24. Aristotle, *Nicomachean Ethics* 7.3, 1147b13–17.

25. Aristotle, *Nicomachean Ethics* 6.2, 1139a23.

could at first, or would necessarily ever, read or hear that law. None of them thought that conscience made us infallible, and humans are not infallible. So I am not sure that the right role has been found for *synderesis*. On the other hand, it is useful, and in accordance with St. Paul's distinction, to distinguish a *general* knowledge or opinion concerning values, on which conscience may *draw*, from what conscience says to the *individual* about right and wrong in his or her own particular conduct and thought. I shall explain in the final chapter why I prefer to speak of values rather than of law, but Paul needed to refer to law in order to make his point about the Jewish insistence on law.

As it turned out, William of Ockham (ca. 1285–1347/1349) in the fourteenth century CE dispensed with *synderesis*, on the basis of his famous principle that distinctions should not be multiplied beyond necessity. In fact, he applied his ban on multiplication far more widely than I should myself, and on the subject of *synderesis* he did not convince all his contemporaries or successors. But it is interesting to see that in the fifteenth century, although Gabriel Biel accepted *synderesis*, Martin Luther (1483–1546) only started by accepting it, but later dropped the idea and did not mention it after 1519. Nor did Calvin mention it in his *Institutes*.

So far it might seem that the idea of *synderesis* died out in the Protestant tradition. But Robert A. Greene has argued that ideas clustering around *synderesis* were still felt as needed.[26] Calvin was anxious to stress that the human mind was perverted by the fall of Adam. But he still wished to allow that the human soul is so illumined by God's light as never to be without at least a *spark* of it. "Spark" is the term originally applied by Jerome perhaps only to conscience, but which was taken to apply instead to *synderesis* and is now reduced to meaning a *mere* spark. Greene finds this application of "spark" made explicit in the sixteenth century by a Protestant author who distinguished himself from the theologians or "divines," Pierre de la Primaudaye, who summarized scientific, moral and philosophical understanding of the time. The second part of his *French Academie* was published in English translation in London in 1594, and there he argued that despite sin, there remain in our mind some mere *sparks* of the knowledge of good and evil which the divines call *synteresis*, or the *preservation* of the *light and law of nature*. In 1605 Francis Bacon, the champion of scientific method,

26. Robert A. Greene, "Synderesis, the spark of conscience in the English Renaissance," *Journal of the History of Ideas* 52, 1991, pp.195–219; "Instinct of nature: natural law, synderesis and the moral sense," *Journal of the History of Ideas* 58, 1997, pp. 173–98.

said in his *Advancement of Learning* that mankind has by the *light and law of nature* some notions and conceits of good and evil, imprinted by an inward *instinct,* which is a *spark* of the purity of the first estate (before Adam's fall). The reference to illumination and to the "light of nature" has a different origin[27] and we shall find it in chapter 8 used by Ireton in the seventeenth century in debates between Cromwell and the Levellers and by John Locke and Pierre Bayle. It may not be so distinctive of *synderesis,* since conscience also was called a light by Bonaventure. But Greene traces a history both of the "spark" and of Bacon's other term, "instinct." In the thirteenth century Bonaventure applied the term *instinctus* directly to *synderesis,* treating it as an instinct that operates independently of ratiocination.

Moral Double Bind

I turn now to the subject of moral double bind that was much clarified in medieval discussions of erroneous conscience. The idea of a moral double bind had been recognized earlier separately from that of erroneous conscience. Greek tragedy was conscious of it. Orestes, in the example mentioned in chapter 1 and illustrated on the book cover, would be in the wrong if he did not avenge his father, but also in the wrong if he killed the murderer, his mother. It is not that one duty is merely prima facie, and that it is canceled out by the other. In the case of this moral double bind, his conscience was not considered to be in error. Orestes is mentioned as an example of bad conscience not only by Euripides in the text cited in chapter 1, but also, as J. W. Atkins has brought out, in texts by Plutarch of Chaeronea, Philostratus, "Philoponus," and Olympiodorus, some of them cited in chapter 2.[28] In Sophocles' *Antigone,* the double bind is alleviated, because Antigone believes she has a divine duty to bury her brother which overrides the civic duty to obey the king's forbiddance. In line 962, we saw in chapter 1, she is aware that she may after death find that she was in error, but that was not the source of her dilemma.

Christians may have been slower to take up the subject. But discussion of moral double bind (without *explicit* reference to conscience) has been

27. Stephen Menn, *Descartes and Augustine,* Cambridge University Press 1998, ch. 4, traces back the metaphor of the light of nature to Augustine's assimilation of God as the source of truth in our minds to the divine Intellect of Plotinus, e.g. in his claim in *Confessions* 4.15.25 that our minds need to be illuminated by that divine truth.

28. Jed W. Atkins, "Euripides' Orestes and the concept of conscience in Greek Philosophy," *Journal of the History of Ideas* 75, 2014, 1–22.

found in Pope Gregory the Great (540–604).[29] The source of these moral dilemmas is a different one, some *earlier wrongdoing* on the part of the one who gets into the double bind. This source avoids a problem uncomfortable for Christians, because eventual divine punishment needs no special justification, if the inevitable wrongdoing in a case of double bind is always due to one's *own* earlier wrongdoing. Gregory's advice to do the *lesser* evil interestingly admits that it is still evil. The wrongdoing in one story is keeping company with an evildoer and swearing to conceal his secrets. The double bind arises if the oath taker finds that the evildoer is planning murder. In a second case, a man seeking to forsake worldly things takes insufficient care in submitting himself to the authority of someone he wrongly believes to be godly. The chosen authority then gives him ungodly commands. A third man uses bribery in order to gain a position of pastoral authority over others. But then, repenting of the bribery, he has to choose between abandoning his pastoral duties and continuing to retain the privileges of office.

In the twelfth to thirteenth centuries, cases of moral double bind were discussed that arose from a different source: *erroneous* conscience. This was a less comfortable source, because no one could be faulted for getting into a moral double bind, if the error was faultless. The subject was arrived at slowly. Erroneous conscience had been discussed by Origen in the third century CE. Paul's Letter to the Romans, 14:23, had said that that if weaker bretheren eat meat sacrificed to idols, while entertaining doubts, they sin, because "whatever is not from conviction (or faith, *pistis*) is sin." This implies that it is a sin to go against one's beliefs. In that case, Origen imagined someone asking, when heretics act according to their erroneous beliefs (*credere*), are they then acting as required by *pistis* (or *fides* in Rufinus' Latin translation of Origen)? He seeks to escape the problem by saying that they act not from *fides*, but from credulity (*credulitas* in Rufinus' Latin).[30] In the twelfth century Peter Abelard (1079–1172) in France addressed erroneous belief in his interesting treatise *Ethics*, or *Know Thyself*. Under the heading "That there is no sin except against conscience," Abelard considers the example of those who persecuted the martyrs or crucified Christ, and he said that they were not sinning if they believed that what they did was pleasing to God. But under the next heading, "In how many ways may sin be spoken of?," he says that they performed an unjust action and sinned in deed (*per*

29. Pope Gregory I, *Moralium Libri* 32, secs. 36–39, translated as *Morals on the Book of Job*, by S. Gregory the Great, Oxford and London 1850, vol. 3, pt. 2, pp. 539–41, cited by Albert R. Jonsen and Stephen Toulmin, *The Abuse of Casuistry*, University of California Press 1988, p. 95, following Alan Donagan, *The Theory of Morality*, University of Chicago Press 1977, p. 144.

30. Origen, *Commentary on Letter to Romans* 10, PG vol. 14, col. 1256A.

operationem), but would have sinned more gravely if they had spared Christ against their conscience.[31] This second approach admits a moral double bind, but with a solution in terms of a less bad course of action. A different solution was offered by St. Bonaventure in the thirteenth century in a text on *synderesis* already cited above. Erroneous conscience, he said, does not bind us to act or not to act. Instead, it binds us to *get rid of it*. For it puts us in a moral dilemma. If the erroneous conscience directs one against the law of God, then to follow it is a mortal sin. But if one goes against conscience, that too is a mortal sin, because one does it in the belief that it displeases God.[32] It may look as if Bonaventure is saying that erroneous conscience puts us in a moral double bind. But in fact, he seems to be trying to escape that conclusion by saying that we are bound to neither, but to a third course: getting rid of the erroneous belief.

For a clear statement that erroneous conscience puts us in a moral double bind we may look to Bonaventure's contemporary, Thomas Aquinas. Thomas discusses erroneous conscience, in several places, and clearly confirms that it can put one in a double bind. In one text he raises an example not unlike Abelard's, but drawn from the Gospel of John. Those who killed apostles in accordance with erroneous conscience were sinning, unless the ignorance was unavoidable or involuntary, something he had defined a little earlier.[33] This is clearer than Thomas's earlier attempt to qualify the double bind by saying that erroneous conscience binds only conditionally upon error not being laid aside, and only accidentally because it is an accident of the conscience that it is mistaken.[34]

In three texts, Thomas seeks to qualify the double bind by citing Aristotle's discussion of a case which he admits to be only virtually (quasi) the same.[35] Aristotle takes a situation in which one cancels out an erroneous policy decision (*prohairesis*) by failing to live up to it.[36] If we imagine an erroneous policy of taking a medicine mistakenly believed to be a means to

31. Peter Abelard, *Ethics* or *Know Thyself*, not sin pp. 54–57; unjust action, p. 62, line 6; sinned in deed but less gravely, p. 66, lines 30–34 in the edition and translation of David Luscombe.

32. Bonaventure, *Commentary on the Sentences of Peter Lombard*, bk. 2, dist. 39, article 1, question 3, partly quoted and translated by Timothy Potts, "Conscience," 698–99.

33. Thomas Aquinas, *Summa theologiae*, first of the second part, question19, article 6, citing John 16:2, and referring back to question 6, article 8.

34. Thomas Aquinas, *On Truth*, question 17, article 4.

35. Thomas Aquinas, *Commentary on the Sentences of Peter Lombard*, bk. 2, distinctio 39, question 3, article 3; *On Truth*, question 17, article 4; *Summa theologiae*, first of the second Part, question 19, article 5.

36. Aristotle, *Nicomachean Ethics* 7.9, 1151a29–b4.

health, the medicine will not be chosen for itself (*kath' hauto*), but only for the supposed coincidental connection with health (*kata sumbebêkos*), and hence a lapse of self-control (*akrasia*) in not taking it will be coincidental and not unqualified (not *haplôs*). Thomas repeatedly bases one half of the double bind, the bindingness of conscience, on Paul's Letter to the Romans 14:23, "Whatever is not from *pistis, fides*, is sin," which had earlier been cited in Origen's discussion of erroneous conscience. But the double bind arises from the fact that going *with* one's conscience may be wrong too. Cases of moral double bind became particularly pressing in the wake of the sixteenth-century Reformation, in which allegiance was required in turn by different religious persuasions. Advice on cases of moral double bind was a specialty of the casuistry of the sixteenth to seventeenth centuries, but that will be the subject of chapter 7.

The dilemma of erroneous conscience raises a question about the extent to which freedom of conscience should be allowed. Many errors are harmless, but in the case of conscience requiring the killing of Christ or the apostles, the resulting harm would be great. We shall find in chapter 8 other cases of moral double bind raised in the seventeenth century by Pierre Bayle, a Protestant victim of an intolerant Catholic French king. In defending tolerance, he thought at first that even erroneous conscience always overrides other considerations. But, faced with paradoxes, he later rested his case on the need to keep the peace. We shall see him from the first answering almost universal Protestant doubts about the toleration of Catholics in matters of conscience, doubts which were justified on the grounds that once Catholics prevailed, they would be intolerant in matters of conscience. The unusual plea by a Protestant for toleration of Catholics in a Protestant country required only limited restrictions against the risk of their exercising intolerance, and left them freedom of conscience in their life as individual citizens.

I will finish with a figure of the twentieth century with a distinctive view on moral double bind: Mahatma Gandhi. Gandhi's examples of moral double bind illustrated various different problems. Only some arose from what Gandhi would consider erroneous values, or wrongly believing that retaliation was morally superior to nonviolence. Only a few examples arose from earlier misguided decisions, as when an Indian, having inadvisably accepted a post from the British Raj, found himself required to maintain law and order by firing on a mob. But there would be no earlier wrong decisions nor erroneous conscience in a number of Gandhi's cases. For example, he would be prepared to violate his principle of nonviolence by using tear gas to prevent an assault or riot. Or a believer in nonviolence might chair a municipal council with a duty to preserve public health, but with a majority which did not share his belief in nonviolence to animals. He might then be required, to have stray dogs destroyed for possibly carrying rabies, in violation of his belief in nonviolence.[37] Gandhi differs in other ways too. Unlike Gregory, he often specifies which would be the less bad course. In the case of people who believe that violent retaliation is the virtuous course, he thinks it better that they should follow their consciences despite their grievous error of judgment. But there are other cases in which conscience does not help, because it points in two directions. At least one of Gregory's cases was like this, and so is Gandhi's insistence to some Christian pacifists that he would have recourse to tear gas, if he "could not save a helpless girl from violation or prevent an infuriated crowd from indulging in madness except by its use. . . . God would not forgive me if, on the Judgment Day, I were to plead before him that I could not prevent these things from happening because I was held back by my creed of non-violence."[38]

In this chapter, I have focused on two developments of the Middle Ages, the distinction of *synderesis* and the recognition of moral double bind. Both issues went back to antiquity—the first stemming from an interpretation of Jerome, the second being anticipated at much earlier dates. Both outlasted the Middle Ages, and the second is found in Gandhi in the twentieth century. In the next chapter, I shall turn to a Christian penitential practice that also started in antiquity and lasted beyond the Middle Ages, although, like the idea of *synderesis*, it was not to be widely accepted by the Protestant Reformation.

37. Richard Sorabji, *Gandhi and the Stoics: Modern Experiments on Ancient Values*, Oxford University Press and University of Chicago Press 2012.

38. M. K. Gandhi, *Harijan*, March 9, 1940, *Collected Works*, vol. 71, p. 225.

FIVE

Penitence for Bad Conscience in Pagans and Christians, First to Thirteenth Centuries

Christian practices of penitence are relevant for two reasons. They started very early, and from the beginning played the important role of making Christians think about their consciences. Their beginnings sound strange to us, but had the innocent aim of bringing sinners back into the church. Absolution of sin was already a crucial part of the system. But very much later, priests were credited with increased powers of securing absolution and hence of making the difference between eternal salvation and eternal damnation. Although ideas about how priests can or cannot influence our eternal fate may not attract the widespread sympathy they once had, the topic is historically essential for understanding the protests of the Protestant Reformation, which split the Western Church, and in particular Luther's complaint in the sixteenth century that consciences were being terrorized, and the contrast of that lack of free conscience with his own view of how Christ had long since allowed for Christian consciences to be free, if only Christians would understand his message. That recognition changed his conscience from despair to joy. Greater power for priests may also have encouraged the practice that initiated Luther's complaints, the selling of priestly indulgences to provide eternal salvation, although that practice had already been criticized in the twelfth century and had its ancient Greek parallels.

From 100 CE for over five hundred years the Christian Church provided absolution for bad conscience with systems of penitence for lay people, which differed at different places and times. The Christian systems of penitence often involved a *bad* conscience that needed *healing*, as reflected in

Hippolytus in Rome (ca. 160–236),[1] Tertullian (ca. 150–230)[2] and Cyprian (Bishop 248–258)[3] both in Carthage, or that needed *revealing* to God, as in John Chrysostom of Antioch.[4] Sometimes a *watching* conscience was called for, as in Pope Leo the Great, to be discussed in what follows. Sometimes the idea of conscience was invoked instead, as in accounts of early Constantinople, to suggest that engaging in the holy sacraments should be a *voluntary matter of conscience*, rather than policed by confessors.[5]

The pagan systems of penitence are less well known. We have already noticed confession being used in the Epicurean school in the second century BCE.[6] What has hitherto remained largely unknown are the systems of confession, satisfaction, and penalty in pagan temples in the first three centuries CE. I will try to reinterpret two pagan inscriptions, drawn to my attention by Angelos Chaniotis, which both mention consciousness or unconsciousness of a fault (*suneidêsis*).[7]

Conscience in Pagan Temples

The consciousness or unconsciousness turn out to be connected respectively with punishment or *sparing*. But this has been concealed because of two difficulties with the word *êlêsa*. One difficulty arose through the attempt to derive it from the word *aleein*, "to grind or mill," which makes no sense, and was tentatively suggested to be explicable as *adikein*, "to do wrong." But I think it is exactly the word wanted in its *standard* meaning, which is from *eleô*, "I pity," and this helps to reveal how to overcome the second difficulty. I take a further cue from an article of Chaniotis in which he explains that in

1. The penitentiary system of his successful rival, Callistus, for the bishopric of Rome pandered to those smitten in conscience (*suneidêsis*); Hippolytus, *Refutation of all Heresies* 9.7, *Patrologia Graeca* vol. 17.

2. Proof of penitence for apostasy under persecution should be revealed not only in conscience, but also in deeds; Tertullian, *On Penitence* 9.

3. Eucharistic communion might not be offered to those guilty of apostasy induced by persecution, before the sin had been expiated (*expiare*) and the conscience (*conscientia*) purged by the hand of the bishop; Cyprian, *On the Lapsed* (apostates) 16, *Patrologia Latina* vol. 4, col. 493. Some apostates had polluted their conscience (*conscientia*) by buying certificates falsely attesting that they had performed pagan sacrifice; Cyprian, *Letter* 14, Migne, *Patrologia Latina* vol. 4, col. 269. Some had merely contemplated apostasy, and should confess a sin of conscience, rather than of deed; Cyprian, *On the Lapsed* 28, *Patrologia Latina* vol. 4, col. 503.

4. John Chrysostom, *Homilies against the Anomoeans* 5; *On the Incomprehensible Nature of God*, unfold your conscience (*to suneidos*) before God—discussed below.

5. Reports on Constantinople: Socrates, *Historia ecclesiastica* 5.19; Sozomen, *Historia ecclesiastica* 7.19—discussed below.

6. Ch. 1, above.

7. *Tituli Asiae Minoris* vols 5, 1, numbers 261 and 318.

these inscriptions, the person of the verb can change when the priest moves from reporting the charge or confession to conveying the god's sentence.[8] The first person of *êlêsa* has been wrongly taken to represent the culprit's words. I think it makes sense, if it is the *priest* reporting the god's verdict, in this case absolution because her *conscience* was clear: "I pitied/ had mercy on/ spared her, because she did not recognize any fault in her own consciousness—*egô oun êlêsa, ep<e>i mê idia sunei [dêsei* . . . (lacuna)]." The ambiguity as to whether the god or the priest is absolving is nicely matched in the history of Christian absolution.

The other pagan inscription is not about a confession, but rather about a denial of accusations under oath, in a failed attempt at self-exculpation. It results in the gods punishing the culprit because of her guilty *conscience*: "Tatias set up [the oath-maker's] staff and placed oaths in the temple by way of satisfaction (*hikanopoiousa*) for having been the subject of rumour. The gods put her under punishment (*kolasis*), which she did not escape, being in such a state of consciousness [of her fault] (*en suneidêsi toiautê*)."

Penitence for Lay Christians

In describing *Christianity*, I shall discuss the systems of confession and discipline for *lay* people, not those for monks and nuns, which differed, except for rapprochements in the later Celtic treatment of lay people to which I shall come. For many centuries, the systems were conducted not out of self-serving motives, but by and large in good faith, although it takes historical imagination to appreciate how Christians can have accepted them. Some will now seem bizarre, some unbelievably severe. But only later did the abuses become widespread that led to the protests of reformers. Penalties for sin, including excommunication—that is, exclusion from the communal sacrament—were to a large extent designed to keep Christian sinners *within* the Church, not to drive them out. For, with the exception of heresy, and at first of certain capital sins, the system of penitence was designed to lead to reconciliation with the Church.

The system of penitence also served a general social function of keeping the peace and resolving disputes. There was no overall criminal prosecution

8. Angelos Chaniotis, "Under the watchful eyes of the gods: divine justice in Hellenistic and Roman Asia Minor," in *The Greco-Roman East*, vol. 31, 2007, pp. 1–41. I have not seen his "Ritual performances of divine justice: the epigraphy of confession, atonement, and exaltation in Roman Asia Minor," in Hannah M. Cotton, Robert G. Hoyland, Jonathan J. Price, and David J. Wasserstein, eds., *From Hellenism to Islam: Cultural and Linguistic Change in the Roman Near East*, Cambridge University Press 2009, pp. 115–53.

service run by the civil authorities. It was to a large extent up to individuals to initiate legal proceedings, and they could take them either to the State or to bishops, whose influence the State welcomed.[9] But the system of penitence was not a court system. Offences might become known to the Church through a civil or ecclesiastical sentence. But if the offence had not become public knowledge, it was up to the Christian perpetrator whether he or she chose to confess to the Church. Augustine comments that confession, or sentence, whether civil or ecclesiastical, were the only two routes by which excommunication could be imposed.[10] The situation was to change in the twelfth century with the creation of canon law for ecclesiastical courts, as will be described in chapter 7.

In tracing the development of Christian systems of penitence, I shall inevitably follow the accounts of specialist historians, and one in particular for the period up to 950 CE, which has the great advantage of supplying the Greek and Latin texts.[11] I shall start with Christ and his disciples.

Christ and His Disciples

Some of Christ's statements to his twelve disciples seem to offer a religion of forgiveness. When he teaches them how to pray, he gives them the Lord's prayer, in which they are to say to God, "Forgive (*aphienai*) us our debts (*opheilêmata*, or in the Gospel of Luke sins, *hamartiai*), as we forgive them who are in debt to us."[12] Christ also said to them that one should forgive

9. I am grateful to Caroline Humfress for answering my questions about the relation of the system of penitence to courts, and for kindly showing me an early draft of her article, "Bishops and lawcourts in Late Antiquity: how not to make sense of the legal evidence," *Journal of Early Christian Studies*, special issue, ed. Kate Cooper, 2011. See also Peter Brown, "A tale of two bishops and a brilliant saint," *New York Review of Books*, vol. 59, March 8, 2012, p. 30.

10. Augustine, *Sermon* 351, *Patrologia Latina* vol. 39, col. 1546.

11. For the period 100 to 950 CE, I have closely followed the magisterial work of Oscar D. Watkins, *A History of Penance*, Longman, Green and Co., London 1920, in two volumes and 775 pages. Many of the texts I refer to for that period can be found there in Greek or Latin with translations. Vol. 1, which reaches 450 CE in 496 pages, is out of print. The scanned 2009 reprint by General Books covers only the shorter vol. 2, which goes up to 1215 CE. There is an account in French under "Pénitence," in *Dictionnaire de théologie catholique*, vol. 12, with a good condensed review covering the same centuries up to 1215 by E. Amman, columns 722–945, and a review of the period from 1215 to the sixteenth century by A. Michel, cols. 948–1127. I have also used Mark Boda and Gordon Smith, eds, *Repentance in Christian Theology*, Liturgical Press, St John's Abbey, Collegeville, MN 2006, and for the period immediately before Luther's Reformation, Thomas Tentler, *Sin and Confession on the Eve of the Reformation*, Princeton University Press 1977.

12. Matthew 6:9–15; Luke 11:2–4.

(*aphienai*) a brother who sinned and repented (*metanoein*) seven times a day, or seventy times seven.[13] But there were complications. It was thought by some that the forgiveness described here was for small sins against each other, not against God.[14] For these sins it was better not to involve the Church and in another passage Christ recommends appeal to the Church community only as a *later* step *after* one has tried to gain one's brother by reproaching (*elengkhein*) him in private for his sin (*hamartanein*).[15] In the first letter attributed to the disciple John, mortal (*pros thanaton*) sins are distinguished from nonmortal sins, and for the nonmortal sins of one's brother one should ask God to give him life, but the text declines to say that one should ask that in connection with mortal sins.[16] Christ himself said that blasphemy (*blasphêmein*) against the Holy Spirit would not be forgiven (*aphienai*).[17] A text in the Acts of the Apostles was differently transcribed and understood in the Western and Eastern Churches. In the West, the apostles (or emissaries), who included the disciples, were understood to tell the Gentiles to abstain from the pollution of idols and sacrifice to idols, from unchastity, and from bloodshed, and these came to be regarded as three capital sins. But in the East, the message was thought to be mainly about dietary, not capital, sins. Gentiles were to abstain from eating meat sacrificed to idols, from eating animals killed the wrong way, whether by the wrong bleeding or by strangling, and from unchastity.[18]

Crucial for the role of the Church in absolution were three statements by Christ to his disciples, in which he was later taken to be offering to the Church the keys to the Kingdom of Heaven. In the Gospel of Matthew, he was represented as talking in one case to Peter, telling him, "On this rock (*petra*) I shall build my church," but adding, "I will give you the keys of the kingdom of heaven, and whatever you bind (*dein*) on earth shall be bound in heaven, and whatever you loose (*luein*) on earth shall be loosed in heaven."[19] A little later, Matthew describes Christ as speaking to the disciples generally in similar words about binding and loosing, though without the reference to Peter as a rock, the church, and the keys.[20] The Gospel of

13. Luke 17:3–4; Matthew 18:21–22.
14. Tertullian, *On the Sense of Shame*, ch. 21.
15. Matthew 18:15–18.
16. 1 John 5:16–17.
17. Matthew 12:31–32; Luke 12:9–10.
18. Acts 15: 20, 25, and 29. See again Oscar D. Watkins, *A History of Penance*.
19. Matthew 16:18–19.
20. Matthew 18:18.

John uses different language about a statement of Christ's when he appeared to most of the disciples after his death and resurrection: if you forgive/remit (*aphienai*, literally, let go) the sins of any, let them be forgiven/remitted; if you retain them (*kratein*), let them be retained.[21]

There is a very important ambiguity in the term *aphienai*, already mentioned in chapter 2, and it remains difficult throughout to translate.[22] In case of doubt, I shall speak of forgiveness. If something is remitted, it is wiped from the slate, as if it had never occurred. When something is forgiven, on the contrary, it is a vital fact that the wrong was there, even though it has been forgiven. The question that was to arise was whether human procedures of absolution could do more than put an end to humanly prescribed punishments and wipe the wrongs from the *human* record, or whether human priests could claim on the basis of these texts to be doing more.

There is an ambiguity also in the idea of *binding*. It may be explained best by its paraphrase *kratein*, "to retain," which contrasts nicely with "letting go." The idea of binding will then be the negative one of *not* letting go, or *not* forgiving. Peter is not being invited to take the positive step of damning.[23] This is borne out by Church discussions, which are about whether or not the priest is to forgive; he is not called upon to damn.

Church Absolution from God, Not Man

In the Church the strongest motive for confessing and undergoing penance in order to gain absolution was fear of eternal punishment after death. Although the bishop or priest played an important part in absolution, the main role was reserved for God, and the exact character of the human part, though variously described, was minor. In the early centuries the priest was not given an agreed role promulgated everywhere, as in Luther's time, that of itself gave overwhelming influence to him. Origen in Alexandria (185–254) said that only a man who has received the Holy Spirit and become spiritual is able to remit (*aphienai*) whatever sins God remits. He does so as a minister (*hupêretein*) of God who alone has the power to remit, just as the prophets had spoken not their own words, but those of God's will.[24] Cyprian in

21. John 20:21–23.

22. This is very well explained by David Konstan, *Before Forgiveness*, Cambridge University Press 2010.

23. I thank John Wynne for making this point.

24. Origen, *On Prayer* 28.

Carthage (d. 258) allowed that God could amend human verdicts. We do
not prejudge (*praeiudicare*), said Cyprian. God can ratify or amend.[25]

Similarly, the Syrian *Didascalia apostolorum* (compiled between 252 and
270) declared, "But if there be a man who is innocent, and is condemned
by judges from respect of persons, it will not hurt him before God, but will
rather advantage him the more on account of the short time that he has
been unjustly judged by men."[26] According to Ambrose (340–397) in Milan, only God, in the person of the Holy Spirit, condones (*condonare*) sins.
Humans only exhibit their role as ministers (*ministerium*) for the remission
of sins.[27] In Rome, Jerome (346–420) allowed that it is only in a manner
(*quodammodo*) that the human priest judges people. God does not inquire
into the opinion of priests, but into the *life* of those he judges. Priests cannot condemn (*damnare*) the innocent or loose (*solvere*, "free") the guilty.
Rather, it is as the priests in the Book of Leviticus do not give people leprosy,
but *recognize* (*notitia*) lepers and the unclean and *distinguish* (*discernere*) the
clean and unclean. The manner in which (*quomodo*) they *make* the leper
unclean is the manner in which the bishop and priest, without binding (*al-
ligare, ligare*) or loosing the innocent or guilty, nonetheless, know who is to
be bound (*ligandus*) or loosed (*solvendus*), because they have heard through
their office the diversity of sins.[28]

None of these authors take it to be, in a literal sense, the human officia-
tor who remits sins and the same is true of Leo the Great, who was Pope
from 440 to 461. He held that God's indulgence at least during this life required the supplication of priests, but was provided by Christ and the Holy
Spirit. So priestly supplication is an opportunity, and if through negligent
delay it is missed because of the arrival of death, God reserves matters for
his own incomprehensible judgment. But God wills that we should fear
his power and fear what may happen to the negligent. So every Christian
should judge his *conscience*, and should avoid risking delay at a time when
by fuller satisfaction (*satisfactio*) of penalties he might come to deserve

25. Cyprian, *Letter* 55, to Antoninus, *Corpus Scriptorum ecclesiasticorun Latinorum* 3, pt. 1, pp. 636–37 (or, with different numbering, *Patrologia Latina* vol. 3, cols. 808–9); *Didascalia apostolorum*, ch. 11.

26. Translated from the surviving Syriac version of lost Greek by Margaret Dunlop Gibson, *Horae Semiticae*, no. 2, London 1903, excerpted by Oscar D. Watkins, *A History of Penance*, vol. 1, p. 255.

27. Ambrose, *On the Holy Spirit*, 3.18, *Patrologia Latina* vol. 16, cols. 807–10.

28. "Jerome *Commentary on Matthew*, bk. 3, on Matthew 16:19, *Patrologia Latina* vol. 26, col. 118.

God's indulgence (*indulgentia*).[29] Augustine of Hippo in Africa (354–430) says that he does not know whether the person will be condemned (*damnare*) who postpones penance until his deathbed, when it is too late to carry it out. If you want to avoid uncertainty, you should carry out penance while you are still healthy.[30]

Fear versus Shame

If all this attention to conscience was motivated by fear of eternal punishment, was the fear compatible with its being conscience? The issue had been raised not only, as we saw in chapter 1, in criticism of Epicurus' account of conscience, but also by Clement of Alexandria (150–215 CE), head of the Christian catechetical school there before Origen, in his *Miscellanies* (*Stromateis*). He says,[31] "There are two styles of penitent, the commoner is fear at one's deeds, the more special is the soul's shame (*dusôpia*) at itself arising from conscience (*suneidêsis*)." The implication seems to be that conscience is not based on fear. Later in this chapter, we shall encounter discussion of the relative value of contrition and *attrition*, where attrition is distress arising from the fear of eternal punishment. We would not ourselves think that distress wholly from fear could be a case of conscience. But fear could very well direct attention in such a way as to stir up conscience, and penitential practice seems to have counted on this.[32] The practice turns on the awareness of past wrongdoing which was part of the original conception of conscience.

First Concession: For Some Sins One Chance for Christians to Repent with Penance after Baptism

After Christ, with his disciples, and Paul, who like them became an apostle or emissary for Christianity, the first important text about Christian penitence is *The Shepherd of Hermas* written around 100 CE, or at least before 140. The shepherd who protects the prophet Hermas is called the Angel of Penitence. The most important issue is Hermas' question, whether there is ever a second chance, after serious sins have been remitted by the baptism which makes one a Christian, for the remission of *later* sins. The Angel of Penitence approves what Hermas has heard, that there is *not*, yet exceptions

29. Leo the Great, *Letter* 108, *Patrologia Latina* vol. 54, cols. 1011–14.

30. Augustine, *Sermon* 393, *Patrologia Latina* vol. 39, cols. 1713–15.

31. Clement of Alexandria, *Stromateis* 4.6.37.7

32. Fear was found also to redirect attention in the context of obtaining Donatist conversions in ch. 3.

are allowed both by the Angel of Penitence in his *commandments* and in the *visions* experienced by Hermas and the *parables* told to him. A persecution is expected, and a concession will be made for the post-baptismal sins of those who repent genuinely, not hypocritically (*en hupokrisei*), and do not waver (*dipsukhia*) in the coming persecution. The concession is that there can be penance and one single further remission of past sin up to a determined day, including remission of the sin of apostasy, blasphemous though it was, under the pressure of the last persecution, but not for any further sin after that, and certainly not for apostasy in the future persecution.[33] The advance from no remission after baptism to one remission after baptism seems to have become a widespread policy after *The Shepherd of Hermas*, despite the opposition of dissenters. The more liberal tradition of one more chance has an echo in the Greek Orthodox Church of today. Though regarding marriage in church as a sacrament with lifelong commitment, it allows remarriage in church once after divorce as a concession in a spirit of humanity, but replaces part of the ceremony with penitential prayers.[34]

Second Concession: One Chance for Christians to Repent with Penance for Sexual Sins

The second of three concessions about repentance seems to have been encouraged by the Bishop of Rome from 217/218 to 223, Callistus. We hear about him from his rigorist opponents, Hippolytus (160–236), the learned Greek writer, his rival in Rome for the post, and Tertullian (writing in Latin in Carthage, without using Callistus' name, but quite probably referring to him). Hippolytus tells us that Callistus cited Christ's command in Matthew 13 not prematurely to pick out the tares (weeds) for burning, for fear it might harm the wheat, taking the tares to be sinners in the church. Accordingly, Callistus accepted sins of sensual pleasure as something that could be forgiven (*aphiesthai*) by him. He also allowed clerks to marry and priests and bishops to remarry, while remaining clergy.[35] In *On Penitence*, the first of two works on the subject, Tertullian accepted what he later denied for

33. *Shepherd of Hermas* (*Visions*) 2.2.7–8 (or 6 in the continuous numbering of Whittaker); 2.3.4 (7), 3.5 (13); (*Commandments*) 4.3 (31); (*Parables*) 6.23 (62), 7.4 (66), 8.6.2 and 4 (72), 9.14.2 (91), 9.19.1 (96).

34. Kallistos Ware, Metropolitan of Diokleia, *The Orthodox Church*, Penguin 1963, revised 1993, pp. 294–96. I thank John Thorp for alerting me to the present Pope Francis's expressed interest in the position of his Greek Orthodox counterparts and to reform cited below on other issues in the Roman Catholic Church.

35. Hippolytus, *Refutation of all Heresies* 9.7

mortal sins, the view of Hermas that one second repentance could be allowed.[36] The proof of this second repentance calls for more than a revelation within conscience. It must be revealed in deed, and Tertullian goes on to describe penance as it was by then carried out in the church in *public*.[37]

In a later period, when he had joined the Montanist heresy, which forebade second marriages and remission in this life of capital sins, Tertullian wrote a more rigorist work, *On a Sense of Shame*. Chapter 1 of that work starts by deploring the fact that the bishop of bishops (Callistus?) has declared he remits adultery and fornication (sex outside marriage involving, or not involving, a married person) to those who have fulfilled their penance. But because some sin (*delictum*) is mortal (chapter 2), it is irremissible (*irremissibile*), and though penance should be undertaken, it cannot lead in that case to pardon (*venia*) from humans. Only God remits sins (chapter 3), and he can remit even mortal sins, so the penance is not in vain. This rigorist warning applies (chapter 5) to adultery, since it is one of three special sins along with idolatry and homicide. So how can the bishop of bishops condemn (*damnare*) the idolater and the homicide, but not the adulterer?—unless, indeed (chapter 9), the sinner subsequently becomes a martyr? When the Apostle Paul (chapter 13) delivered to Satan for the destruction of the flesh the man who committed incest with his stepmother,[38] Tertullian understands that the intended destruction was penance, and that it was not followed by restoration to grace. St. Paul in another letter reported restoring someone to grace (*kharisasthai*) after penance, but Tertullian denies it was the same man.[39] He ascribes to Paul's fellow apostle, Barnabas, the Letter to the Hebrews (chapter 20), and applies to the adulterer and fornicator its refusal to admit to repentance (*metanoia*) those who have fallen away (*parapiptein*) after baptism.[40] Only God (chapter 21) can condone and remit (*donare, dimittere*) mortal sins. Peter was not authorized to loose and bind the capital sins (*capitalia*) of believers.

According to Tertullian's description of public penance in *On Penitence*,[41] the penitent must wear sackcloth and ashes (a penance that the Gospel of Matthew 11:21 records for the cities of Tyre and Sidon); must conceal the body in drab clothing; must be cast down with grieving; must fast, groan, weep, and moan day and night; must fall prostrate to the priests; must kneel

36. Tertullian, *On Penitence*, ch. 7, *Patrologia Latina* vol. 1, cols. 1260–62.
37. Tertullian, *On Penitence*, ch. 9, *Patrologia Latina* vol. 1, cols. 1263–64.
38. First Letter to the Corinthians 5:3–5.
39. Second Letter to the Corinthians 2:5–11.
40. Letter to the Hebrews 6:4–6.
41. Tertullian, *On Penitence*, ch. 9, *Patrologia Latina* vol. 1, cols. 1263–64.

to those dear to God; must beg all his brothers to convey his prayer for mercy, that by means of temporal affliction, eternal penalties may be expunged.[42] In *On a Sense of Shame*, chapter 5, he speaks of sinners sitting in sackcloth, bristling in ashes, groaning as they breathe, and kneeling with prayers.

Third Concession: One Chance for Christians to Repent, with Penance, of Apostasy under Duress

There were to be other rigorist movements, but Callistus' recognition of penance for unchastity as able to lead to reconciliation was to remain the norm. The one-off concession in *The Shepherd of Hermas* for apostasy under a particular past persecution was the next concession to be developed. The persecution by the Roman Emperor Decius (249–251), through an edict of January 250, took the form of requiring sacrifice to pagan gods and the emperor, so that idolatry as well as apostasy under persecution became the subject of further reflection. Cyprian, Bishop of Carthage since 248, fled, rather than sacrifice. Some refused to sacrifice and became martyrs. Some sacrificed and became apostates, or "lapsed." Some lapsed "polluted their consciences" in a different way, not by sacrificing, but by buying certificates to say that they had. Of the lapsed in Carthage many appealed to those martyrs who were in prison to write them letters recommending absolution.[43] Cyprian was not willing to act on these letters, by permitting confession and the laying on of hands, except in the case of those apostates who appeared to be dying.[44] Others who did penance would be cared for by God, but must meanwhile await the decision of the whole Church.[45]

In 251, it was safe enough for Cyprian to hold a council in Carthage, attended by many bishops, to consider what to do. Cyprian sought its advice and read to it his treatise, *On the Lapsed* in which he described the day and night penance with sackcloth and ashes that would be required if God was ever to have mercy on apostates.[46] The council decided that, after individual examination, those who had merely bought certificates, but not carried out pagan sacrifice could apply to be restored after completion of penance. Those who had sacrificed might only be restored on the point of death, if they had been penitent from now until then. A second council called by

42. Tertullian, *On Penitence*, ch. 9, *Patrologia Latina* vol. 1, cols. 1263–64.
43. Cyprian, *Letter* 14, here and below in the numbering of Migne, *Patrologia Graeca* vol. 4.
44. Cyprian, *Letters* 12 and 13, Migne.
45. Cyprian, *Letters* 12 and 13, Migne.
46. Cyprian, *On the Lapsed* 35.

Cyprian in Carthage, granted peace (*pax*) to those lapsed who had been penitent since the day of their lapse, in order that they might join in yet another expected struggle.[47] Cyprian, like Callistus before him, used the parable of the tares. He took it to mean that rather than rooting out apostates, we should make sure that we become true wheat.[48] There was still dissent from the rigorist Novatian in Rome, an unsuccessful candidate for Pope, and it lasted for some centuries.

Alternatives to Last Chance: Origen; Successive Worlds for Purification; Pagan and Christian Versions of Purgatory after Death

The idea of a last chance, at least for Christians, was not the only one. Origen (ca. 185–253) was an early enough Christian to offer experimental theories, inspired by Greek thought, which avoided it. He envisaged a succession of worlds to provide painful correction and improvement for those, whether Christian or not, who have refused to obey the word of God.[49] The successive worlds would not repeat the same history, nor be endless,[50] or beginningless,[51] in the Stoic manner, but would allow for progress, and possibly only those who still needed correction would be reborn in these worlds,[52] as opposed to the final world in which our bodies would be photographic likenesses made of the indestructible gas *pneuma*.[53] To Jerome's disgust, the fallen angels themselves, even the devil, would eventually be saved.[54]

This more cheerful theory was rejected by Christianity, but the idea was embraced by some Christians, but not by the Greek Orthodox Church, of a third possibility for some after death, not heaven or hell, but a period of suffering in purgatory with the prospect of eventual release. Plato had already described the idea of some souls being judged after death to deserve punishment, temporary for most, in places of punishment beneath the earth until the time of their choosing their next incarnation, while other souls are

47. Cyprian, *Letter* 54, Migne.

48. Cyprian, *Letter* 51, Migne.

49. Origen, *On First Principles* 1.6.3, 2.3.1; cf. *Against Celsus*, bk. 6, ch. 26.

50. Origen, *On First Principles* 2.3.4–5

51. Origen, *On First Principles* 1.3.3, 2.1.4, 2.9.1–2, 4.4.8; *Homilies on Genesis* 14.3.

52. Origen, *On First Principles* 2.3.1

53. Origen, *On First Principles* 3.6.6, but for the more detailed, albeit hostile, report of the bishop Methodius, see my *Self: Ancient and Modern Insights about Individuality, Life, and Death*, University of Chicago Press and Oxford University Press 2006, pp. 72–77.

54. Left as a question in Rufinus' Latin translation of Origen 1.6.3, but reported by Jerome, *To Pammachius and Marcella, against Rufinus*, bk. 1, ch. 27.

judged to deserve reward until that time.[55] The Neoplatonist Ammonius' version of Platonic purgatory is reported by his Christian pupil, Philoponus in the early sixth century CE. Ammonius emphasizes the soul's *self*-purification and healing after death encouraged by pain inflicted in places of punishment under the earth. But pain requires a body made of *pneuma* that attends the soul, unless and until the series of purifications allows the soul to escape from being reincarnated in a body of flesh and to retain just its luminous body.[56]

The origins of the Christian idea of purgatory are controversial, but it seems to have many components, and it took time for them to be combined together. A recent study[57] has seen the Christian idea of purgatory above all in the English monk Bede (ca. 673–735) as a place visited immediately upon death by a few souls who are destined after the day of judgment to go to heaven, but who do not immediately join others in paradise, since they need first to be purged by fire of small remaining sins. The purging is no longer voluntarily undertaken, but is a form of punishment. But intercession by the living, including celebration of the mass, can provide help and speed the process and was later to be treated as the only source of help. Origen's alternative of eventual salvation for all is rejected, and the wicked are punished forever, starting even before the Day of Judgment. Elements of the idea of purgatory are found earlier in the Alexandrian Fathers Clement (d. before 215) and Origen (d. 253/254), and Pope Gregory the Great (540–604) supplied others. In between, Augustine (354–430) stimulated thought, but did not believe in a further opportunity of improving one's own position after death.

North Asian Provinces: Prolonged Public Penance in the Outer Parts of Church Building

In regard to penance on earth, the emphasis has been on Rome and Carthage, but in the churches of Asia Minor an entirely different system of penance had grown up, more lenient in that its aim was to bring all sinners eventually back into the Church, but harsher in the greater humiliation of the public penance and its astonishing duration. Gregory Thaumaturgus

55. Plato *Phaedrus* 249A; *Republic*, bk. 10, 614B–616A.

56. Philoponus, *Commentary on Aristotle's On the Soul from the Seminars of Ammonius with Some Observations of His Own* 17.26–18.33.

57. Isabel Moreira, *Heaven's Purge: Purgatory in Late Antiquity*, Oxford University Press 2010. John Newman's poem in Elgar's *Dream of Gerontius* provides an evocative modern conception of the journey to purgatory.

(miracle worker, ca. 210–270) was Bishop of Neo-Caesarea in Pontus, the province along the south of the Black Sea, from 233 until his death. Around 260, he describes a system of penance, with no acknowledged basis in earlier systems.[58] It did, however, build on stages in the training of converts, by distinguishing grades of penitent, and different stations within the church building where penitents were granted admission as they labored their way back by slow degrees to participation in the prayers of the Holy Communion. In the initial stage, as mourners, penitents had to wait outside the church altogether during the church services in penitential attire, beseeching the faithful for their prayers. In the next stage, as hearers, they were allowed into the vestibule or narthex, where they could hear, like the new converts, the scriptures and instructions. In the third stage, as fallers, they were admitted into the nave, or central part of the church, but on their knees with bowed head or prostrate, while the faithful stood, but they had to leave before the prayers of consecration. In a fourth stage, as bystanders, they could stand and remain during the prayers of Holy Communion, but could take no part in the sacrament itself with its consecrated bread or wine. In the final stage, this last was allowed, so that the penitent was restored to the faithful in full communion.

The duration of various stages is stated in the canons of the Council of Ancyra (314) in Galatia, the province immediately south of Gregory's. Typical for moderate sins is between one and three years in each stage. But some sins are singled out for up to twenty-five years, though no one is left unrestored to communion with the Church.[59] Basil, Bishop of Caesarea (329–379), also in the same province, wrote three letters in 374–375 that came to be called canonical. In them, he provides tariffs of up to thirty years and, like the Council of Ancyra, he distinguishes the stages of each penance. Again, everyone is restored, but an apostate is restored only at the approach of death.[60]

58. Gregory Thaumaturgus, *Canonical Epistle*, Canon 11

59. *Concilium Ancyranum*, ed. Mansi, 2.516–21: lying with beasts attracts fifteen to twenty-five years among the fallers and then five years among the bystanders, unintentional homicide, five or seven years among the fallers. A murderer will remain among the fallers, but be restored to communion at the approach of death.

60. Basil of Caesarea, *Epistolae* 188, 199, 217, in *Patrologia Graeca* vol. 32: Trigamists would receive five years, first as hearers, then as bystanders; fornicators a year each, or, in a later letter, two years each, as mourner, hearer, faller, and one year as bystander. An adulterer receives four years as mourner, five as hearer, four as faller, and two as bystander. For grosser unchastity, committed in ignorance and voluntarily confessed, thirty years penance will suffice; for unpremeditated homicide, eleven years, or in a later letter, ten years, two as mourner, three as hearer, four as faller, and one as bystander. A murderer may be reconciled before death, but only after four years as a mourner, five as a hearer, seven as a faller, and four as a bystander.

In 325, in between the Council of Ancyra and Basil, the Emperor Constantine held a conference at Nicaea, in the neighboring province of Bithynia, with 220 bishops, almost all Greek. This conference was definitive in establishing the Nicene Creed. But it also issued canons endorsing the graded system of penance and rejecting the objections of rigorists to the eventual reconcilability on earth of all Christian sinners.[61]

John Chrysostom's Concessions in Antioch

The graded system did not reach in Asia as far down south as Syria and it did not hold in the big eastern cities of Antioch in Syria, and later of Constantinople (founded by Constantine, May 11, 330). In Antioch after 381, John Chrysostom (347/349–407) ran one of the most attractive systems of penance. While still in his ascetic and monastic phase, he wrote in 372 to an apostate that God's mercy extends to the worst sins and to incomplete repentance (*metanoia*). For repentance is judged not by the length of time, but by the disposition of the soul.[62] After becoming a priest in Antioch in 386, at the age of thirty-nine, he called for confession not in the theater to others but to God, and described the system of public confession as intolerable publicity.[63] Five days of penance, or even one, might be enough, since the desire to reform is what matters.[64] He went on to suggest, as had Origen before him,[65] that there were many alternative modes of penitence that could be interchanged and combined in different ways, without any one being essential. In one version, you can move your conscience (*to suneidos*) as an accuser within, forgive others (*aphienai*), pray, give alms, and practice humility. Again, you could confess and feel contrition (*penthêsai*) as well as giving alms and practicing humility.[66] John Chrysostom was made Bishop of Constantinople and held the post from 398 to 404. According to Sisinnius, the rival Novatian Bishop in Constantinople, John said something even more unacceptable to him, that sinners could repent not just once, but a thousand times.[67] His opponents included such rigorists as these, and he was twice exiled from Constantinople and died in 407.

61. *Concilium Nicaenum*, ed. Mansi, 2.672–73.

62. John Chrysostom, *Letter* 6, *Patrologia Graeca* vol. 47, cols. 281–84.

63. John Chrysostom, Fifth *Homily against the Anomoeans, On the Incomprehensible Nature of God*, *Patrologia Graeca* vol. 47, col. 754, and *On Lazarus*, homily 4, *Patrologia Graeca* vol. 48, col. 1012.

64. John Chrysostom, *On Saint Philogonius* 4, *Patrologia Graeca* vol. 48, col. 754.

65. Origen, *On Leviticus*, homily 2, *Patrologia Graeca* vol. 12, col. 417.

66. John Chrysostom, *On the Devil as Tempter*, homily 2, *Patrologia Graeca* vol. 49, col. 263; *On Penitence*, homilies 2–3, *Patrologia Graeca* vol. 49, 285–89; 292–93.

67. Socrates, *Ecclesiastical History*, bk. 6, ch. 21.

Italy and Ambrose's Severity in the Imperial Seat of Milan

Meanwhile in the West, Milan had become the seat of the imperial court and capital of the Western Empire. Ambrose (340–397), who became Bishop of Milan in 374, faced a rival Novatian Church, and in his *On Penitence* argued against them that all sins could be remitted. He maintained, however, that penitents ought not to use marital relations (*usus copulae coniugalis*),[68] although unsurprisingly he found it hard to secure compliance. Ambrose secured tremendous prestige for the practice of public penance through the submission of Theodosius I, emperor from 379 to 395. Theodosius had in 387 accepted the silent remorse of Flavian, Bishop of Antioch, for the destruction by tax protestors of the emperor's statue in Antioch, as John Chrysostom reports.[69] But now in 390 Theodosius himself had sinned. Seven thousand inhabitants of Thessalonika had been massacred for sedition against their magistrates. Others had been sentenced to death or confiscation of property. According to Theodoret, twice in eight months Ambrose excluded the weeping emperor from the church building, although modern scholarship says that he stopped him by letter, not at the door.[70] Only after he had changed his edict to allow a thirty-day pause for examination before executions, was he permitted to enter the church. Theodoret says that he lay there prostrate, plucked out his hair, wept, and prayed for pardon, before he was admitted to the sacrament.[71]

Augustine Again versus the Purist Donatist Heresy

Augustine (354–430) as a young man had heard Ambrose's sermons in Milan. We have noticed how, as Bishop of Hippo in Africa from 395/396, he had to deal with the rigorist Donatist churches.[72] He says that his own town of Hippo was once all on the side of Donatus.[73] The Donatists were dis-

68. Ambrose, *On Penitence* 2.10 (96), *Patrologia Latina* vol. 16, col. 520.

69. John Chrysostom, *On the Statues, Patrologia Graeca* vol. 49, cols. 213–14.

70. Neil McLynn, *Ambrose of Milan,* University of California Press 1994.

71. Theodoret, *Ecclesiastical History* 5.17, *Die griechischen christlichen Schriftsteller,* vol. 44; *Patrologia Graeca* vol. 82, cols. 1231–38. Not at the door: Neil McLynn, *Ambrose of Milan,* 328.

72. W. H. C. Frend, *The Donatist Church,* Oxford University Press 1952, ch. 15, "St Augustine and the Donatists," pp. 238–39; Henry Chadwick, *The Early Church,* Pelican 1967, pp. 219–25. Particular aspects are discussed in Roland H. Bainton, "The parable of the tares," *Church History* 1, 1932, already cited in ch. 4, pp. 67–79, at 69–71; Roland H. Bainton, *Concerning Heretics Attributed to Sebastian Castellio,* Columbia University Press 1935, pp. 21–29.

73. Augustine, *Letter* 93, para. 5, cited in ch. 4 for Augustine's change of mind on the value of limited persecution, CSEL vol. 34, p. 462, line 1.

tinct from the Novatians, but like them, allowed no second reconciliation after baptism. They objected that the succession of bishops in the Catholic Church in Africa was invalid from 311 when Caecilian was consecrated as the Catholic Bishop of Carthage allegedly by apostates from the time of the Decian persecution. The Catholics were the tares, while the Donatists alone were the wheat. Augustine replied repeatedly. He insisted that Caecilianus was not proved guilty by his accusers.[74] He interpreted in an opposite sense Christ's command not to uproot the tares prematurely amidst the wheat. If the African Catholic Church were really the tares, then the Donatists were guilty of premature uprooting, by separating themselves, in the guise of wheat, from it. But in fact, the wheat, along with the tares, was meant to cover not just Donatist Africa, but the whole world, and the Donatists had cut themselves off from both.[75] Augustine also took a different view from the Donatists about what made priestly functions valid. In the related case of baptism, the Donatists were wrong to make baptism by heretics invalid. One might as well try to make baptism by *unrighteous* priests invalid. It is God who baptizes, and so validity does not depend on the character of the officiating priest.[76] Augustine finally had the Donatist case heard at a conference called at Carthage in 411, as a result of which the Emperor Honorius proscribed Donatism by edict, and imposed fines, exiled Donatist priests and confiscated Donatist property. Nonetheless, the Donatists survived for the best part of two further centuries, and were still active at the end of the sixth.

Celtic Private and Repeatable Penance Spreads from the Irish Church

Although in 597 St. Augustine (not of Hippo) was appointed the first Archbishop of Canterbury in England by Pope Gregory the Great, and converted many to Christianity in the kingdom of Kent, certain Christian practices of Celtic, not Roman, origin persisted in Western countries, prominent among them the system of penitence.[77] The monastery of Clonard in Ireland founded by St. Finian around 530 had contained not only monks, but lay people living in its grounds along with students reading Greek and Latin

74. Augustine, *Letter* 93, ch. 4 (ch. 5 already cited in ch. 4 above).

75. Augustine, *Letter* 76.2, CSEL vol. 34, pp. 326–27; *Against the Letters of Petilian*, bk. 2, ch. 79.174, CSEL vol. 52, p. 108.

76. Augustine, *On Baptism Against the Donatists*, e.g. bk. 7, ch. 14.27.7.

77. Again, I continue mainly to follow up to 950 CE the account of Oscar Watkins, *A History of Penance*, now in vol. 2.

and lay people undergoing penitence. It may be wondered if this wider community enhanced monastic understanding of family problems. St. Finian wrote a penitantial manual on the remedies of penance, which provided a tariff of penalties, demanding, but much lighter than those further East. The penalties, like the initial confession, were to be carried out in private and without the participation of any bishop. St. Columban (ca. 543–615) was trained at the daughter monastery of Bangor, and later took a mission to Britain and went on to found four monasteries in Gaul on the model of Clonard and Bangor, of which the most influencial was at Luxeuil. He too wrote a penitential for penance and reconciliation to be conducted, again in private, at his monasteries, not only for monks, but also for laity from outside. For adultery a married man was to make a payment to the wronged husband and abstain from his own wife for three years. This payment by by the adulterer to the wronged husband suggests attention to the wrong done to victims, not just to the sinner's relation to God or the church community.[78] A priest would decide on reconciliation without public ceremony, by simply allowing the penitent to take part in the regular sacrament of communion.

The only system of penance in Ireland and Wales was this one, and from Luxeuil it spread over Frankish lands through bishops and abbots who had trained there. In the seventh to eighth centuries, penitential manuals, indebted to that of Columban, were written on the continent. They were designed to help a priest in administering his system of private penitence for lay people and not only for monks.

In 668, Pope Vitalian in Rome appointed an Archbishop for Canterbury, who had been born and worked in a city of Asia, Tarsus in Cilicia, which is now southern Turkey. Theodore of Tarsus (602–690) brought to Canterbury Greek books which he had obtained on the way, and after arrival wrote a penitential manual to guide the local Celtic system of penance, which he adopted, but at the same time compared with Roman and Greek systems. Our own internationalism has not yet attained to this pitch. Theodore was only the second choice of the Pope, who made his preferred candidate accompany Theodore to England, partly in order to make sure that he did not introduce Greek practices contrary to Roman faith. Theodore declared in his penitential manual that he wanted the decrees of the Romans never to be altered by him.[79] But his penitential stated: "Reconciliation in public has

78. I thank Richard Kraut for the contrast.

79. Theodore, *Penitential*, bk. 1, ch. 5.2, Haddan and Stubbs, *Councils* 3.180.

not been appointed in this province, because there is no public penance," implying that the English system had always been private.[80] The penitential also stated that confession could be made to God alone, at least, so some manuscripts added, in case of necessity.[81] Theodore's penitential consisted of his answers to questions put to him about the remedy of penance, mostly by a priest, Eoda, who asked him questions drawn from a Celtic penitential manual, and recorded the answers.[82] Fasting is a common element of the penance and the tariff for killing is unexpectedly low.[83]

The privacy of penance made possible another major difference from the Greek and Roman systems, including those in Asia and Africa, that confession not only of monks, but of baptized *lay* people could be *recurrent*, and not once only, which had been the normal maximum concession elsewhere since the *Shepherd of Hermas*. It was later recorded that from the time of Theodore it had been the custom in the English Church, as if by force of law (*quasi legitime*), that not only clerks in monasteries, but also lay people with their wives and families should come to confession in the days before each Christmas, which suggests the possibility of repeated forgiveness.[84]

Private penance was accepted in the court of Charlemagne (King of the Franks from 768, crowned by the Pope as Roman emperor 800–814), and by 950 it has been described as unopposed north of the Alps. The northern penitential manuals were still strongly resisted in Rome. But at the same time, Alexander II, Pope from 1061–1073, gave a special license to two priests to conduct private penance, if their bishops agreed,[85] and allowed discretion to bishops in applying penance, based on the degree of contrition observed.[86]

80. Theodore, *Penitential*, bk. 1, ch.13, Haddan and Stubbs, *Councils* 3.187.

81. Theodore, *Penitential*, bk. 1, ch. 12.7, Haddan and Stubbs, *Councils* 3.187.

82. Theodore, *Penitential*, preface, Haddan and Stubbs, *Councils* 3.173

83. In the tariff, murder out of revenge for a slain relative receives only three or ten years' penance, reducible if relatives of the victim are paid. Murder of a layman by a layman, without surrender of arms, attracts seven years, three of them with fasting. Killing of a monk or clerk requires abandoning arms and entering a monastery, or seven years of penance. Killing a king or bishop falls under the king's jurisdiction. Lay drunkenness attracts fifteen days of penance, fornication one year, adultery four years, including two of continuous penance. Repeated theft calls for seven years of penance, reducible upon compensation or reconciliation.

84. *Dialogue of Egbert* (Bishop of York in 732–737), ed. Haddan and Stubbs *Councils*, 3.413.

85. Pope Alexander II, *Letter to Two Priests*, in Löwenfeld, *Epistolae pontificum Romanorum ineditae*, Leipzig 1885, p. 54.

86. Pope Alexander II, *Letter to Bishop Stephen of Auvergne*, in Löwenfeld, *Epistolae pontificum Romanorum ineditae*, Leipzig 1885, p. 55.

Value of *Contrition*: Eleventh- to Twelfth-Century France

Pope Alexander's stress around 1065 on contrition (*contrictio cordis, doloris affectus*) in a letter addressed to Auvergne is interesting. France, including Auvergne, being north of the Alps, was to become a center for the discussion of the relevance of *contrition* to absolution. Peter Abelard (1079–1142), one of the greatest philosophers of the Western Catholic Church, was teaching at Notre Dame in Paris around 1115. Seeking refuge elsewhere after his romantic and tragic love affair with Héloïse, he became the victim of successive charges of heresy, but toward the end of his life he wrote *Ethics* or *Know Thyself*, which was in circulation by 1139. In this, he took up the idea of *contrition*, defining penitence as a *contrition* of the heart, but one based not on fear of punishment, but on love of God.[87] True penitence, he said, was the first of three steps, in reconciling sinners to God, to be followed by confession and atonement.[88] But he argued that such contrition was worthy of forgiveness without delay. Even if the penitent did not have the opportunity for confession and atonement, he or she would not go to hell, although a compensating completion might be required temporarily in purgatory. Indeed, when Christ's disciple Peter denied his master, his very tears earned forgiveness, although we do not read of his confessing or atoning, as Ambrose had already noticed.[89] This treatment gives a higher place to *contrition* than to the procedures that the Church was able to conduct of confession and atonement. Luther was to emphasize contrition in another way, we shall see,[90] when he said, in explaining the fifth of his articles condemned by Papal Bull, that Christ absolved the woman taken in adultery without requiring any penalty—what Abelard calls atonement—and that this is possible where *contrition* is great.

Abelard from within the Church already complained of priests and bishops selling indulgences out of greed to shorten temporal penalties, while

87. The following references are from Peter Abelard, *Ethics* or *Know Thyself*, bk. 1, chs. 17–26, this one from under the headings "What is properly called penitence?"and "On fruitful penitence," in Paul Spade's numbering paragraphs 151–52, 164–65, in David Luscombe's edition pp. 76–79, 86–89.

88. Abelard, *Ethics* or *Know Thyself*, bk. 1, "On Reconciling Sins," p. 150 (Spade), pp. 76–77 (Luscombe).

89. Abelard, *Ethics* or *Know Thyself*, bk. 1, "On fruitful penitence," "That confession can sometimes be omitted," pp. 165–66, 186 (Spade), pp. 88–89, 100–101 (Luscombe). Ambrose, *On Repentance* bk. 2, ch. 10.

90. Ch. 6 below.

claiming to have inherited the power from Peter.[91] Such practices were not unique to Christianity, but were also known to Plato.[92]

Not long after 1139, Gratian in Italy included in his great compendium of canon law, the *Decretum*, under *On Penitence*,[93] the question whether anyone can satisfy God simply by contrition of the heart, without oral confession. But having given the arguments on both sides, he says (chap. 89) that the reader must decide for himself. Back in France around 1150 Peter Lombard (ca. 1100–1160) produced his magisterial *Sentences*, in four books, a comprehensive collection of theological questions and answers from previous Christian commentators. In *Sentences*, book 4, dist. 17, chapter 1, he raised the question whether sins can be forgiven by contrition alone, and, more decisive than Gratian on the subject, answered that confession is necessary if a priest is available, but otherwise it suffices to have the *intention* to confess, if one becomes available. This gave a further boost to *contrition*. Also in France, the idea of *attrition* was introduced in contrast to *contrition* by Alan of Lille (ca. 1128–1202).[94] It was sometimes thought of as a distress based on *fear* of eternal punishment, or great enough to lead to confession and satisfaction of penance, or as lacking only the grace needed for contrition. William of Auvergne (1180–1249) held that it was a first step in the removal of sin before there was confession. Some thought that through the priestly power of the keys transmitted through Peter to the Church it was possible for attrition to be converted into contrition either through the act of confession, or through the act of absolution, which had by now been switched to *precede* penance.

Thirteenth Century: Annual Confession Required, Move to Priest's "I Absolve You"

The emphasis on confession was restored in 1215 by the decision of the Fourth Lateran Council in Rome, when it made compulsory what had once been the practice of Theodore's Celtic Britain, that all Christian lay people must confess in church once a year. Annual confession had also been the

91. Abelard, *Ethics* or *Know Thyself*, bk. 1, "That confession can sometimes be omitted," pp. 201–3 (Spade), pp. 108–11 (Luscombe).

92. Plato, *Republic* 364 D–E.

93. Gratian, *Decretum causa* 33, question 3, dist. 1

94. Attrition is discussed by Thomas Tentler, *Sin and Confession on the Eve of the Reformation*, Princeton University Press 1977, 250–300.

custom at Christmas in Theodore's seventh-century England. This introduced an annual prospect of absolution, which contrasted with the practice of the earliest centuries, when the absolution at least of serious sins had been offered only once after baptism, but not again.

Thomas Aquinas (1225–1274) wrote in the wake of the 1215 decision, and regarded *confession* as essential, except that in the posthumously compiled *Supplement to the Summa theologiae,* he allowed that, if opportunity was missing, there might be no more than the *desire* to confess.[95] He also normally required *contrition,* unless the sinner had genuinely mistaken mere attrition for contrition, but, unlike Abelard, again in the posthumous *Supplement,* he saw contrition as having *fear* as its principal cause with hope as a joint cause.[96]

Thomas's biggest change was the increased power he gave to the priest in the act of *absolution.* Writing to the Master General of the Dominicans, he does not deny the view of some that thirty years earlier absolution had all been in the precatory form of a *prayer* that God would absolve ("May you absolve").[97] But Thomas thinks that the priest's absolution should be neither in the form of a prayer, nor in the form of a mere declaration that God has granted absolution, even though the rather vague absolutions of early centuries cited near the beginning of this chapter seemed all to have one of these forms or the other. Instead, Thomas wants the priest to say, "*I* absolve you," because the sacrament not only signifies, but *accomplishes* what it signifies. This is in spite of the fact that God alone absolves from sin, and the priests do so only as ministers (*per ministerium*), with their words working only as God's instruments (*instrumentaliter*).[98] The new wording added to the importance of priests, although it was no part of Thomas's purposes, if this later facilitated any of the abuses which Abelard had already deplored, and of which others were to complain. After, and in response to, the Protestant Reformation, the Council of Trent, which was held by the Catholic Church in 1545–1563, declared that "the form of the sacrament of penance, wherein its force principally consists, is placed in those words of the minister, I absolve thee, &c." The abbreviation "&c" omitted any following words, such as "in the name of the Father, the Son and the Holy Spirit," not necessarily because they did not add something important. But the priest's

95. Thomas Aquinas, *Summa theologiae,* suppl. question 6, article 1, *respondeo.*

96. Thomas Aquinas, *Summa theologiae,* suppl. question 1, article 1, *respondeo.*

97. Cited by Watkins, *A History of Penance,* 494–95, from *Opusculum* 22 in *D. Thomae Aquinatis doctoris angelici opuscula omnia,* Venice 1687, p. 343.

98. Thomas Aquinas, *Summa theologiae,* part 3, question 84, articles 3 and 5.

ability to absolve was based ultimately on the power given to Peter.[99] The modern Greek Orthodox Church retains the old precatory form, "May God absolve you," but in the eighteenth century the Russian Orthodox Church adopted the form "I absolve you."[100]

Each of the absolution formulas has its own problems. Thomas may have been wise to reject the formula, "may God absolve you," which does not give reassurance that he will. The formula, which he also rejected, "I declare God's absolution," was popular in antiquity and was to be favored by Luther. But, without further explanation, it is unclear how the priest would know God's decision. However, if Aquinas is right that the priest may say, "I absolve you," we need an explanation of why the priest is not forcing God's hand. Luther was to raise a different, but related, question: how can the sinner know that the priest's act will result in his or her absolution? Each question is based on a possible divergence between the priest's judgment and God's. In answering his version of the problem, the sinner's uncertainty, Luther, we shall see in the next chapter, offers a solution, and the Catholic Church at the Council of Trent sought to offer an alternative.

There was one more innovation relevant to the later situation of Luther. After 1215, there was a new wave of now very big handbooks or *summae* for the use of confessors, along with smaller manuals. The *summae* had to know about the new canon law established in Gratian's *Decretum* of about 1150. An important *summa* was written between 1240 and 1245 in four books by Raymond of Penaforte, and it has been regarded, along with the earlier work of Alain of Lille, also post-Gratian, as providing an early example of Christian casuistry.[101] Yet a further development in the fifteenth century was the printed take-home confession manuals for the use not of the priest, but of the confessing sinner.[102] There were now many questions to consider about one's sin. Some were adapted from questions ascribed to Cicero, but going back to Aristotle's discussion of voluntariness. An action may have been involuntary if one did not know Who, What is being done, Concerning what, Where, With what instrument, To what end, or In what manner.[103] There

99. Council of Trent, Session 14, Decree on Penance, ch. 3.

100. Kallistos Ware, *The Orthodox Church*, 288–90.

101. Albert R. Jonsen and Stephen Toulmin, *The Abuse of Casuistry*, University of California Press, 117–20, which reports other summae of this period.

102. The books of both sorts are described by Thomas Tentler, *Sin and Confession on the Eve of the Reformation*, Princeton University Press 1977, pp. 31–46. The *Odo Synodical Constitutions* of about 1197 are translated by John McNeill and Helena Gamer, *Medieval Handbooks of Penance*, Columbia University Press, 1938.

103. Aristotle *Nicomachean Ethics* 3.1, 1111a3–6; a version is ascribed to Cicero *De inventione* by Thomas Aquinas, *Summa theologiae* Ia IIae, question 7, answer 3.

were many rules if one was to learn how to make a *good* confession. Only mortal sins should be chosen, not venial. One's confession must not implicate another party.[104] One must remember all mortal sins *completely*. One must consider whether one has contrition, or only attrition. There may be alarming consequences if one presents a sin so heinous that the priest has to reserve it for decision by the bishop. These late developments were among those that led Luther to think that the Church was *terrorizing* conscience.

It may be said that Roman Catholic Christianity had institutionalized conscience. It had made a classified catalogue of the sins that should concern the conscience. But however much this may be true, it retained the *personal* element with which the concept began. As the take-home manuals showed, sinners were still supposed to share knowledge with *themselves* of what they had done wrong. As the need for contrition showed, they were supposed to feel personal guilt, however much they might also feel fear.

It should be said that the present climate of opinion in the Roman Catholic Church was transformed in 1965, albeit controversially, by the declaration *Dignitatis humanae* of the Second Vatican Council, which accorded religious freedom in belief and action to everyone.

Retrospect

The Church's systems of penitence prove to be full of the unexpected. Christ advised that quarrels should for preference be settled outside the Church. Within the Church, years of sackcloth had at first a benign aim: to restore sinners to the Church community. A greater severity was the burden of only one second chance after baptism. The eventual introduction of compulsory annual confession reflected the demise of any such burden. The idea of purgatory was late and not at first a source of threat or indulgences. More surprises will be found when we turn to Luther.

I have described the Christian system of penitence, partly because it was one of the most important incentives for taking conscience seriously, with its examination and watching of conscience, its confession of bad conscience, its contrition, its penance, its healing, and its absolution. But in the next chapter we shall see how some few aspects of the system as it developed became a subject for protest leading up to the Protestant Reformation. Thus understanding the system's later development is a necessary background for understanding the controversies it produced. Moreover, Luther was to react by providing very different views about conscience.

104. *Odo Synodical Constitutions*, as above.

SIX

Protesters and Protestants: "Terrorization" of Conscience and Two Senses of "Freedom" of Conscience, Fourteenth to Sixteenth Centuries

The reaction of protestors and Protestants not just to confessional practice, but to the whole system of penitence described in chapter 5, was relevant to conscience in a new way. We saw in chapter 3 some of the early demands for *freedom of religion* in the context of religious persecution of Christians and of heretics and other dissenters by Christians. Some of the new protests leading up to the Reformation were instead about something more specific, the Roman Catholic Church's alleged *terrorization of conscience* through the system of penitence. This was different from, but did not exclude, continuing demands by protestors for a more general freedom of religion. In fact, I shall say that Luther argued for both, although his more prominent case was against what he called the Pope's "terrorization" of conscience. In response to this "terrorization', he came to a radically different view about conscience, which filled his conscience with joy instead of despair.

A difficulty in describing protests is that the protestors will highlight worst cases, so that even to describe the protests may seem to be taking sides. But in fact, as the Protestants were themselves to find out, there are dangers in too much power accruing to any human authorities, whether to the priests of one denomination or another, or of one religion or another, or to magistrates, monarchs, or parliaments, or to the anti-religious rulers of an atheistic state like the Soviet Union.

Speaking of the Protestant Reformation, John Stuart Mill said: "The Reformation broke out at least twenty times before Luther, and was put down."[1]

1. J. S. Mill, *On Liberty*, ch. 2.

Following again the work of others,[2] I shall pick out from the two hundred years before Luther three Christian protesters whose criticisms included one aspect of the Catholic system of penitence, the priestly power of *absolution* of sins. This was based on the Church's claim to inherit the power of "The Keys," that is the power offered by Christ to Peter of loosing and binding sinners. Each of the three protesters both challenged the spiritual power of the Church authorities to absolve sins and sought to deny them secular power.[3] Neither the spiritual nor the secular challenge was in and of itself a general demand for freedom of conscience, and I have not labeled it as such. But the spiritual challenge was directed against one part of the control exercised over the consciences of the faithful: the absolution of sin.

Marsilius, Wyclif, Hus

Marsilius of Padua (1275/1280–ca. 1342), guided by the *Sentences* of Peter Lombard, insisted that in Matthew 16:18–19 it was Peter to whom Christ gave the keys of the kingdom of heaven and the power over whether or not to remit punishment after death for sins. The successor of Peter and of the other disciples was not the Pope as Bishop of Rome, but those who lived a life like the disciples', and the power of remitting or not was given to all priests, though with certain provisos which the Pope might not fulfill, especially concerning the priest's degree of sinfulness. In any case, the priest would not be deciding, but only as minister *showing* to the Church the decision of God, and the Pope himself might be in error. Excommunication from a church community could only be decided by the whole body of the faithful, or by a judge appointed by them (not necessarily a priest), or by their superior, or by a general council, and only on the basis of proof. Moreover, priests must be appointed by the multitude of believers, and only that multitude should control what they taught.[4] Marsilius also cited Hilary of Poitiers (ca. 315–367) writing to the Emperor Constantine that God wanted to be avowed willingly, not through force.[5]

2. For the two hundred years before Luther's birth, I have learned among others particularly from Gordon Leff, *Heresy in the Later Middle Ages: The Relation of Heterodoxy to Dissent, c. 1250–c.1450*, 2 vols, Manchester University Press 1967.

3. Marsilius of Padua, *Defender of the Peace* (1324), 2.4.3–4, 2.6; Wyclif, *On Civil Power* (1378); *On the Duties of the King* (ca. 1379): Jan Hus (Leff cites *Historia et monumenta Johannis Hus*, 176 r).

4. Marsilius of Padua, *Defender of the Peace* 2.6.3, 2.6.7–8, 2.6.12, 2.6.14, 2.7.1, 2.7.3, 2.28.17.

5. Ibid. 2.9.5, citing Hilary of Poitiers *Ep. ad Constant. Augustum*, 1.6, *Patrologia Latina* vol. 10, col. 561.

John Wyclif (1330–1384) in Oxford said that the power of the keys allowed the Pope only to *promulgate* to the Church God's decision about remission of sins, but the decision is effected only by God, and any priest or any Christian can declare it. Peter received the keys only as the most humble disciple and caretaker of the Church, and the power passes to priests who are fit. Priests, however, cannot know the state of mind of a sinner, and cannot compel God to confirm their fallible pronouncements.[6] The reduction of the power of the keys to *promulgation* had been canvassed since antiquity. It was quite as much a threat to views of priestly power then prevailing as was his better-known reinterpretation of the priest's role in turning bread into the body of Christ. Wyclif's and Marsilius's question of who inherits Peter's privilege draws attention to the more general question of inheritance. If it is taken that Peter was the rock on whom Christ said his church would be built,[7] it still remains a question whether Christ was offering the power of absolution to anyone other than Peter, or to the twelve disciples who had sacrificed everything for him.

Jan Hus (1371–1415) made the views of Wyclif more popular in Prague than they ever managed to become in England. He agreed with Wyclif in dismissing the Pope's claims to be the heir of Peter.[8] The power of the keys was used to terrify, but he denied that a priest can loose or bind, unless through God's doing so. Penitence includes contrition, confession, and satisfaction, but Christ on the basis of contrition alone let go the woman accused of adultery, telling her only to sin no more (John 8:11). Further, the remission of sin requires God's infinite power and mercy.[9] Hus and Wyclif both opposed the selling of indulgences, although they were not the first. We saw Peter Abelard some time before 1140, one of the Church's most brilliant members, although one much hounded, protesting, not under that name, against the sale by bishops of indulgences.[10] Wyclif may have escaped punishment partly through his friendship with the powerful John of Gaunt and partly by dying too soon, but Hus was charged with accepting Wyclif's views, and was burned alive entering the fire while singing the Creed.

6. John Wyclif, *On the Power of the Pope* (1379), chs. 1, 2, 5, 9; *On the Church* (c. 1378), ch. 15.

7. The alternative canvassed that Christ was the rock does not seem a plausible reading of Matthew 16:18–19.

8. Jan Hus, *On the Church* (1413), ch. 9.

9. Jan Hus, *On the Church*, ch. 10.

10. Ch. 5 above.

Luther

So far the protests selected have concentrated particularly on one aspect of the system of penitence, the claimed power of absolution. But Luther (1483–1546) was to take up all aspects, and to present not so much a modification of the Catholic Church's viewpoint as a radically different alternative. In 1545, a year before his death, he recalled his own change of mind back around 1515. He had originally been an Augustinian monk, suffering from an extremely disturbed conscience, and he was oppressed and angry to read about God's *righteousness* (*dikaiosunê*, "justice") in Paul's Letter to the Romans 1:17, which he took to be a determination to punish wrongdoing. His viewpoint changed entirely when he recognized that the verse in Paul adds: "He who through faith is righteous (*dikaios*) shall live." His despair was replaced by a sense of having entered the gates of Paradise, since now he understood God's righteousness as his merciful justifying of us, or making us righteous, however sinful, if only we have *faith* in the Gospel.[11]

By 1515–1516, no longer a monk, but a priest and permanent teacher at the University of Wittenberg, he lectured on Paul's Letter to the Romans, and, commented on chapter 14, where Paul is often taken to be saying what he says elsewhere,[12] that it is not enough for a Christian to have a clean conscience (*suneidêsis*) about what he or she eats, if that would encourage other Christians to eat the same things against their conviction (*pistis*, 14:23), since if those others merely think something unclean, it is unclean. Luther, however, takes *pistis* to mean faith. The passage then ascribes sin not to those who act without conviction, but to those who act without *faith* in the Gospel. Luther also introduced in this commentary an idea which he was to repeat in *On Penitence* (40) in 1518 and in the *Discussion of Confessing* (8) in 1520, which redirects attention from individual sins and compensating works to the whole person. He plausibly takes Romans 4:4–6 to mean that God does not accept a person on account of his works, but the works on ac-

11. Luther *Preface to the Latin Writings* (1545), in *Luthers Werke*, Weimar edition vol. 54. In my accounts of different works, I have used two sets of English translations, with the valuable introductions to them: *Luther's Works*, ed. J. Pelikan and Helmut T. Lehmann, 55 vols., and *Works of Martin Luther*, the Philadelphia edition, 8 vols., checking them for some points against the Weimar edition of the originals. For Luther's treatment of Psalm 130, "Out of the Depths," see Sarah Coakley, "On the Fearfulness of Forgiveness," in A. Andreopoulos et al., eds., *Meditations of the Heart*, Turhout 2011, 33–51.

12. First Letter to the Corinthians 8: 7–13.

count of the person. In *On the Freedom of a Christian* in 1520, he was to say that works derive their value from the person.[13]

The next year, 1516–1517, he delivered the first of two sets of lectures on Paul's Letter to the Galatians, emphasizing that mere conformity to law had been superseded. Revised versions were published in 1519 and 1523. The second set was delivered in 1531 and printed in revised versions of 1535 and 1538. Luther takes his theme from chapter 2, where Paul says that one is justified not by performing works prescribed by the law of Moses, but by *faith* in Christ. Attempts to rely on the law even put one under a curse. In commenting on Galatians 2.11–13, Luther invoked conscience as relevant, by speaking of the ignorant laws of the Pope as *introducing executioner's tortures (carnificia) for consciences.*[14] I shall return to his seminal treatment of Galatians in connection with the late lectures of 1531.

The early lectures already expressed Luther's new viewpoint that we cannot become righteous through performing the works of the law, but only by believing God's promise to forgive our sins. But in 1517 his new viewpoint proved relevant to something that changed the course of his career. Johann Tetzel arrived in Germany, sent to raise money for building St. Peter's basilica in Rome by selling papal indulgences, in return for which sins could be absolved without contrition or the satisfaction of penalties, even for those who were already dead and in purgatory. Luther saw this as abuse. The idea of purgatory, as described in chapter 5, had not started out as abusive. Bede gave little presents to those whom he asked to pray for his soul after death: they did not ask for any. The Irish monk Fursey (d. 649/650), experienced a vision in England in the early 530s that was written up in 657. In the account of his vision, he saw himself as accused of, and punished for, accepting a bequest for praying for the soul of an unabsolved sinner, when such bequests were supposed to be distributed to the poor, not used by the Church.[15] The aim in these earlier prayers for the departed was simply to save souls.

13. Commentary on Romans 4:4–6, *Luthers Werke*, Weimar edition vol. 56, p. 268, lines 4–6; *On Penitence* 40, *Luthers Werke*, Weimar edition vol. 1, pp. 319ff.; *Ratio Confitendi* 8, *Luthers Werke*, Weimar edition vol. 6, pp. 157–69; *On the Freedom of a Christian, Luthers Werke*, Weimar edition vol. 7, p. 63, lines 1–5. The redirection of attention to the whole person is emphasized by Michael G. Baylor, *Action and Person: Conscience in Late Scholasticism and the Young Luther*, Brill 1977.

14. *On Galatians* (1919), *Luthers Werke*, Weimar edition, vol. 2, p. 487, lines 16–17.

15. Both examples are taken from Isabel Moreira, *Heaven's Purge: Purgatory in Late Antiquity*, Oxford University Press 2010.

Tetzel's appeal for money, by contrast, for saving souls in purgatory, was completely opposed to Luther's beliefs. He wrote in Latin ninety-five theses against indulgences, in which he discussed contrition, repenting, remitting sins, satisfying penalties, and being absolved. He sent them, dated to October 31, 1517, with a cover letter to his Archbishop, Albrecht of Mainz. In this initial response, he conceded more of the opposing view than he would later. But he objected that the Pope can remit only his own penalties, not guilt (*culpa*), about which he can only *declare* God's remission. He allowed that God, who does remit guilt, first humbles the sinner and brings him into subjection to the priest. He protested against imposing posthumous penances in purgatory on the dying after absolution, pointing out that in earlier times penances had preceded absolution.[16] Luther had divorced the importance of conscience from its role in the penitential system.

The ninety-five theses were forwarded by the Archbishop to the Pope in December 1517 and friends arranged for them to be translated into German in January 1518. They had been tersely stated, and to ward off misinterpretations, Luther wrote *Resolutions* or explanations of them in 1518, and sent these with a covering letter to his mentor, Vicar of the Augustinian Order, John Staupitz, along with a letter to Pope Leo X, with a request that Staupitz forward both to the Pope. In the letter to Staupitz, the relevance to terrifying conscience is emphasized. Luther claimed that the innumerable and unbearable rules of the method of confessing are taught by *torturers* (*carnifices*). In contrast, Staupitz's earlier talks had moved him and the other students to *pity for many consciences* (*miserti conscientiarum multarum*).[17] Staupitz's declaration that true penitence begins with love of righteousness and of God had stuck in him like an arrow. As he started to look for confirmatory passages in the Bible, "Lo, there began a joyous game! The words frolicked with me everywhere! They laughed and gamboled around this saying. Before that there was scarcely a word in all the Scriptures more bitter to me than 'penitence.'" The enclosed letter to the Pope was still respectful. Luther claimed that he had reverenced the doctrine of the keys, though he also referred to the protection he enjoyed from the Elector of Saxony.

In the explanation or "resolution" of Thesis 7, he tried to find a role for the priest in exercising the keys of remission that would be compatible with his own very different view. God terrifies the sinner with recognition of his sin as a first step necessary for salvation, and relief can be gained only

16. Theses 5–13

17. *Letter to Staupitz Accompanying Resolutions, Luthers Werke,* Weimar edition, vol. 1, p. 525.

through the Church by confession. The priest then provides relief, but he does so only by *declaring* God's loosing. There is a sense in which the Pope or the priest remits guilt, but he does so in the way a counseling friend persuades a sick man to have faith in the doctor. What matters is the faith. Faith in the promise of Christ brings remission even if the priest acts from the worst motives. Conversely, contrition, confession, pardon, and the satisfaction of works of penance are useless unless the sinner believes in the promise made by Christ to Peter: "Whatever you loose (*luein*) on earth shall be loosed in heaven."

There was now a pause while the Pope sought through various emissaries to bring Luther to Rome and secure a retraction. Luther used the time partly for writing a series of clarifying works on penitence and confession, of which I shall mention three. In the Latin *Sermon on Penitence* of 1518, Luther addressed two of the three conventional parts of penitence—contrition and confession—omitting, as having been already discussed, the use of indulgences instead of fasts, prayers, and acts of charity, as methods of satisfying penances. Starting with *contrition*, he objected that thinking of one's individual sins and their damnability creates hypocrites motivated by fear, but still attracted by sin. That fear was distinguished by the Church as *attrition*, but it did not lead, as supposed, to *contrition*. Instead, for contrition, we need a different attitude. Love of justice such as we find in Christ and the saints should make us contrite that we are not like that. Love is prior to hate, and it is love of justice, not hate of sin, that we should discuss with our confessor. That way we can plan a new life, which is the best form of repentance. Fear does not produce contrition; you need to pray for it, as contrition comes from God's grace. The priest should not ask, and the sinner should not reply that he is contrite.

Luther next turned to *confession*. The customary method of confession requires confession of mortal sins only, not venial sins. But it is impossible to recognize all one's mortal sins, and often difficult to distinguish them from venial ones, which is why in the early Church only *manifest* mortal sins, ones that had become known, were confessed. For the rest, one should ask God to cleanse one from hidden sins, wanting to leave nothing unknown to his mercy. Once again, it is one's whole life, not individual sins, that one should confess to God as being damnable, while trusting in his mercy. You should rely not on your own contrition, which is neither sufficiently true, nor certain, but on Christ's promise to Peter about the keys. If you trust in that, you will be absolved with the priest's absolution, whatever the state of mind of yourself or of the priest. Even if contrition were genuine, it would not be sufficient without this trust. Much less can any good effect can be obtained, as supposed, from mere attrition combined with the absence of actual or proposed sin.

In October 1519 Luther published in German another sermon on penitence, *A Sermon on the Sacrament of Penance*, which contains his best explanation of how absolution works.[18] Luther addresses the Catholic Church's recognition of *uncertainty* about whether you have been absolved. He concedes that the priest does not know your degree of contrition or your faith. But this does not matter, he says, for the priest is simply obliged to give absolution when you confess and seek it, and your desire is sufficient reason for him to absolve you, which is not to forgive, but simply to *show, tell*, and *proclaim* that your sins are forgiven. The priest may be ignorant, bound in mortal sin, or jesting, because God's absolution depends not on the priest's character or ability, but on the sinner's *faith* in Christ's promise that everyone whom the priest looses will be loosed. This answers not only Luther's question about *uncertainty*, but also some of the questions raised in chapter 5. The priest is not second-guessing God. He does not need to know God's mind, but only to carry out his duty to loose the sinner who desires it. All he needs to know is that the sinner desires absolution. He must leave to God and to your faith the outcome of his utterance. Thus there is no danger of the priest forcing God's hand. Luther also circumvents another danger—that an ignorant priest might refuse to declare absolution. But Luther makes it the priest's duty to declare absolution, just so long as you want to be absolved.

There is more in this sermon. Having said that humans can remit works of satisfaction that they have imposed, whereas only God can remit guilt (*Schuld*), Luther added that God's remission creates a *joyful conscience* (*fröhlich Gewissen*).[19] This must be meant to contrast with the Church's procedure which only causes *fear*. Fear of God's judgment has a proper role to play, to make people seek comfort for their conscience, but Luther refers to the many manuals of penance as merely *frightening* people into making frequent confessions, without securing that benefit (16 and 19). Priests, bishop, or Pope are to be honored for the role they play, but that is only to bring you the *message* of God that you are loosed from sins (8). The Pope does no more than any priest, or, in the absence of a priest, any devout Christian who tells you that you are forgiven. With these others too, you simply need to believe

18. See for this esp. points 1, 12–15.

19. *A Sermon on the Sacrament of Penance*, second, third, and eleventh points, *Luthers Werke*, Weimar edition, vol. 2.

that you are forgiven, as you may when God has thus given a sign through another Christian (9 and 11).

The Catholic Council of Trent (1545–1563), addressed the doctrine on the sacrament of penance in November 1551, and provided an alternative account of why a priest's inadequacy would not interfere with absolution: "Even priests who are bound by mortal sin exercise as ministers of Christ the office of forgiving sins by virtue of the Holy Spirit conferred in ordination." It looks, in other words, as if, so far from second-guessing the Holy Spirit, or forcing a decision on the Holy Spirit, the priests are operating through the Holy Spirit. This would seem to answer the question of divergence between the priest's judgment and God's and with it Luther's version of that worry, how the sinner can be certain that the priest's act will absolve him. But the Council went on to add that the priest's act was equivalent to a judicial sentence and rejected Luther's idea that absolution could be obtained by faith alone without contrition and without serious inquiry by the priest. This makes it look as if, after all, the Holy Spirit will not guide the inattentive priest, or the one who is unqualified to act as a judge, so that his character and ability do matter, which would leave the question of the priest's possible divergence from God's verdict still to be resolved.[20]

There had been a past history of the subject of the inadequate priest. We saw Augustine in chapter 5 saying that a priest who was heretical or unrighteous could still conduct a valid baptism, because it was God who baptized. It was not only the Donatists, however, who thought that the priest needed to meet high standards. Earlier in this chapter, we noticed Marsilius and Wyclif requiring that for administering absolution the priest needed the qualities of Peter, even though Wyclif acknowledged at the same time that the priest could not know for sure the sinner's mind.

On March 25, 1520, Luther sent to press the strongest statement of his viewpoint so far, his *Discussion of Confession* written in Latin in thirteen sections, with a German translation made for him and published soon after the Latin one on May 8th. In this discussion he complained of the theologians who smite the whole world with "false terrors," with their distinction of mortal and venial sins. They leave no place in people's hearts for Christ, because of the confusion made by a "roaring sea of most wretched conscience" (*miserrimae conscientiae*).[21] One ought to give up in "despair" at the demand that once a year one should confess *all* one's mortal sins, which is

20. Council of Trent, Session 14, ch. 3, November 25, 1551, translated in Henry Denziger, *The Sources of Catholic Dogma*, no. 902, Herder, St. Louis 1957.

21. *A Discussion of Confession, Luthers Werke*, Weimar edition, vol. 6, p. 162, lines 20–21.

impossible. Once again appealing to the whole person, he recommends saying instead, "Behold, all that I am, my life, all that I do and say, is such that it is mortal and damnable." The theologians try to "drag consciences to utmost ruin" (*perditissime trahere conscientias*),[22] by bringing them not to recognize the truth of one's damnability. As for mortal sins, the Fathers, Augustine and Cyprian meant, according to Luther, that it is not these, but only criminal offences that are bound or loosed on earth (section 8). The theologians offer "a riot of distinctions." Is the sin due to fear or to inflaming love, has one sinned against the three theological virtues, the four cardinal sins, by the five senses, with the seven mortal sins, against the seven sacraments, the seven gifts of the Holy Spirit, or the eight beatitudes, with the nine sins of complicity (*peccata aliena*), against the twelve Articles of Faith with silent sins, or sins crying out to heaven? These concerns crowd out the pangs of conscience and determination to lead a better life. Instead, confession should be brief and chiefly about what troubles one (section 9). It would be best first to confess to God, and to tell God whether one is ready to change one's life. If not, it would be better to disobey the requirement to confess to a priest (section 3). As regards sins called venial, some may be mere temptations rather than sins, but in any case it merely "vexes" and "worries" people to think that they must avoid these, because in the flesh we cannot (section 5). With sins hidden in the heart, mere thoughts, or inclinations such as are inevitable, it may be impossible for us or for the priest to know about these sins. They are known only to God and are better confessed only to him (sections 6, 7, 9). There is no authority for the laws meant to "trouble consciences" (*conscientiae perturbandae*)[23] with sins of their own invention (section 10). It is not clear that the absolution of any sins should be delayed for referral to higher authorities, even for people who are excommunicated, although appeal to be loosed from the *penalty* of excommunication or other penalties can be so referred (section 12). Unrealistic and elaborate vows are "tyrannies" with which the "wretched consciences" (*miserae conscientiae*)[24] of penitent and confessing Christians are daily disturbed. They are rejected in favor of simply doing one's duty to household and neighbors (section 13). In 1520 Luther also burned the *Summa Angelica* of Angelus, which contained 975 main questions that a confessor could ask. He called it a *Summa Diabolica* of the Devil not an angel.

22. *A Discussion of Confession*, *Luthers Werke*, Weimar edition, vol. 6, p. 163, lines 6–7.
23. Ibid., p. 165, lines 24–26.
24. Ibid., p. 169, lines 6–11.

It was in 1520 only five years since Luther had started his lectures on Romans. But a new turn in his career was about to take place. He was interviewed more than once by Carl von Militz, a papal emissary, charged with bringing him to Rome. In October 1518 he was summoned instead to answer the Pope's legate Cajetan at the Diet held in Augsburg by the Holy Roman emperor, Charles V. But he there refused to retract anything, unless it could be shown that it conflicted with Scripture, not merely with the doctrines of the Church. In 1520, having waited three years, the Pope sent out on June 15th a bull (a sealed declaration) called *Exsurge, domine*, condemning forty-one numbered propositions found in Luther's works, and demanding that he retract them or be excommunicated. His works were also to be burned. Luther received the bull on October 10th, and this inspired him to a number of replies. The forty-one new numbers are not those of Luther's ninety-five articles, but of the Pope's selection of condemned propositions, taken from various writings of Luther already mentioned, including *The Sermon on Penitence* and the *Resolutions*.

The first condemned article attacked the idea that the Church's sacrament of penitence gave grace to everyone in the absence of unaddressed actual or proposed sin. The fifth denied a scriptural basis for the parts of penitence as the Pope conceived them: contrition, confession and satisfaction. The sixth complained that fear of eternal punishment makes contrition hypocritical. The seventh declared that changing to a new life is the best form of repentance. The eighth discouraged confessing any but known mortal sins. The ninth disparaged full and complete confession, in comparison with relying on God's mercy. The tenth made belief in forgiveness indispensible. The eleventh advocated belief in your absolution independently of your state of contrition. The twelfth declared that belief in absolution was probably sufficient to obtain it, even in the absence of contrition or serious intention on the part of the priest. Luther prepared four replies during 1520–1521. The most complete one, in 1521, was written in German, *The Ground and Reason for All the Articles of Dr Martin Luther Wrongly Condemned through the Roman Bull.*[25]

In this last, Luther explained the fifth article by saying that the three parts of penance do appear in Scripture, but the satisfaction of penances was not required by Christ when he absolved the woman taken in adultery, and that this is possible where contrition is great. The Pope, however, has the wrong reason for not requiring it, when he remits it on payment as an indulgence. Discussing the seventh condemned article from the *Sermon on Penitence*,

25. Luther, *Grund und Ursach, Luthers Werke*, Weimar edition, vol. 7, pp. 308–57.

Luther again emphasized the whole person, saying that the changed way of life in true repentance changes the *whole* man. The Pope, by contrast, prefers "gallows repentance," based on fear and hypocrisy, so that he can sell indulgences.

The year of the condemnation of forty-one articles, 1520, was not exhausted by the writings on penitence and confession together with replies to the condemnations on that and many other subjects. On the contrary, Luther wrote in that year a number of major works that are even better known. In two of them, he restricted the temporal power of priests. One of these from the beginning of the year was *A Sermon on the Ban*, the ban being excommunication, the very penalty with which Luther was about to be threatened. Although the Pope could exclude people from outward communion with the Church, he said, the Apostle Paul had used isolation only to improve people, and in any case the Pope could not interfere with the communion provided by the Holy Spirit. Nor might he impose restrictions on people's daily lives, nor use the sword.

By June, he saw little chance of reconciliation with the Catholic Church, and turned in the direction of national and international politics. He hoped for the support of the newly elected Roman emperor, Charles V, and of the German knights. Accordingly, he wrote *An Address to the Christian Nobility of the German Nation*, addressed also to the emperor and published by mid-August. In it he attacked the Pope's claims to authority and control over benefices and other financial perquisites in Germany at the expense of German Church rights. The Pope should not have authority over the Roman Empire, nor have bishops swear oaths to him, nor possess his own kingdoms in Italy. There should not be a separate canon law operated by the Church and territorial law should take precedence over that of the Holy Roman emperor. Priests were supposed to be appointed by consent and election of the community of the Church and the power of the keys was given to that whole community, and not ordained for determining doctrine or government,[26] but only for binding or loosing sins. In fact, the papal bull condemning forty-one propositions was issued at the very time in June when Luther was writing to the emperor and the German nobility, and was received in October.

In November, Luther was persuaded for a last time by the emissary Carl von Militz to attempt reconciliation, and he sent the Pope a new book, prefaced by a dedicatory letter, in which he expressed respect for him as an indi-

26. *An Address to the Christian Nobility of the German Nation, Luthers Werke*, Weimar edition, vol. 6, p. 412, lines 2–3.

vidual. But in the letter he called him a "lamb among wolves" and a "Daniel among the lions." The letter was backdated to September 6th, to avoid the appearance of intimidation by the bull. The new book, *On the Freedom of a Christian*, was sent as a sample of what Luther would like to write if he were left alone. It was not polemical, although it expressed his rival beliefs. He explained that although the moral law of Moses, the Ten Commandments, were to be followed, Christians were *freed* by faith in God's mercy and grace from depending for their salvation on their own efforts to follow. This kind of freedom was already available, unlike the freedom the Pope demanded from the terrorization of conscience. Through forgetting that all members of the Church are priests, a "terrible tyranny" and "intolerable bondage" had been set up to *human* works and laws. It is true that there is a role for preaching the terrors of the moral law given by God to Moses, in order to humble us into penitence. But we cannot stop there, for that would be to strike and not to heal. Grace and the remission of sin must also be preached, in order to teach faith, without which the system of penitence is taught in vain. Luther's stress on the need for grace would have flowed naturally from his Augustinian training. Augustine's insistence on original sin inherited from Adam, which makes it impossible for us to avoid new sin, led him to stress the need for God's grace at every step we take.

On December 10, 1520, Luther burned the papal bull, and on January 3, 1521, the threatened excommunication was carried out. On April 18, 1521, Luther appeared, as summoned, before the Holy Roman emperor at the Diet of Worms, after the Elector of Saxony had obtained from the emperor safe conduct to and from the meeting. He refused again to retract unless convinced by Scripture or reason, and his ground was relevant in a significant way to *conscience*. It was neither safe nor right, he said, to go against *conscience*.[27] These words were written by authors unknown on Luther's side, possibly in consultation with Luther, immediately before the most famous words attributed to him: "Here I stand. I can do no other. So help me God. Amen." The emperor declared Luther an outlaw, so that anyone could kill him, but he left the town surreptitiously, and, before he reached Wittenberg was escorted to the safety of Wartburg castle through the offices of the Elector of Saxony. There he started on his translation of the Bible, and poured out further writings, including in 1521 *On Confession: Whether the Pope Has the Power to Require It*.

So far only six years had passed since Luther started lecturing at Wittenberg. In 1521–1522, his career changed very much more in a political

27. *Luthers Werke*, Weimar edition, vol. 7, p. 838, line 8.

direction. First, he had to quieten certain rampages against churches in Germany, inspired, against his intentions, by his calls for radical reform. In 1523 he turned to the subject of the limits of civil power, addressing to his protector, the Elector of Saxony, a treatise in three parts, *On Secular Authority: How Far Should it be Obeyed?* After excluding secular power over religion, he restricted also the Church's power, using an argument from *ignorance.* The Church may not compel in matters where there is uncertainty whether God's word requires it. How one believes is a matter of each person's *conscience* (*Gewissen*).[28] Luther cited Augustine for the view that no one can compel belief and went on to give the argument, also Augustine's, that the sword is *ineffective* over faith and produces not conviction, but *hypocrisy.* But to this he added the further argument that force actually *strengthens* (*stercken*) heresy.[29] In 1525, he added yet another argument in preaching on Matthew 13, and Christ's command at 13:28–30 not prematurely to pick out the tares for burning for fear of uprooting the wheat as well. Luther accepted the interpretation of some of the early church fathers that allowed for reform—heretics might yet change their minds and become wheat.[30]

Later in 1525, he was embroiled in political matters again with the Peasants' War. At first he supported the peasants with a different kind of appeal to conscience, saying that that they must take up their cause "with good conscience" (*mit gutem Gewissen*),[31] and that force was not the answer. Instead, he recommended a commission of inquiry. But as the peasants became more aggressive, so did he, and in the first half of May, he wrote *Against the Robbing and Murdering Hordes of Peasants* and declared that princes, as ministers of God's wrath have a duty to punish with the sword, which they can do "with good conscience," because the peasants have a "bad conscience" (*böse Gewissen*).[32] In political and ecclesiastical matters, a startling intolerance has been ascribed to Luther's later days. Increasingly, he favored death

28. *On Secular Authority, Luthers Werke,* Weimar edition, vol. 11, p. 264.

29. Ibid., pp. 268–69.

30. Gospel for the fifth Sunday after Epiphany, 1525, Matthew 13, *Luthers Werke,* Weimar edition, vol. $17^{2,}$, p. 125. Roland H. Bainton, draws attention to this in "The parable of the tares as the proof text for religious liberty to the end of the seventeenth century," *Church History* 1, 1932, pp. 67–89 at p. 80. But in "The development and consistency of Luther's attitude to religious liberty," *Harvard Theological Review,* 22, 1929, 107–49, at 119, he pointed out that by 1530, in treating the 82nd Psalm, Luther thought that rejection of the Apostle's Creed should be treated as blasphemy, *Luthers Werke,* Weimar edition, vol. 31^1, p. 208.

31. *Admonition to Peace, Luthers Werke,* Weimar edition vol. 18, p. 300, lines 5–6.

32. *Against the Robbing and Murdering Hordes, Luthers Werke,* Weimar edition, vol. 18, 360.12—361.3.

at least for different *types* of people, whether or not for chosen individuals within his jurisdiction.[33]

From 1525, under a new Elector of Saxony, Luther was involved in *ecclesiastical* politics, organizing the Church in Saxon territory, and in 1530 he was party to the Augsburg Confession. This was a summary of what Lutherans believed, including on absolution and confession, delivered, in his enforced absence as an outlaw, at a new Imperial Diet in Augsburg. In the same year, he published a polemical work entitled *On the Keys,* which indulged to a large extent in ridicule. But besides repeating old ideas on the *affliction* and *disturbance* caused by the Pope's ordinances on the keys, it also contained some striking new ideas, one concerning again *uncertainty* over whether the priest's absolution would work. The Roman Church admitted that the key which loosed was capable of error, and they could not be *certain* whether the sinner whom they absolved had met the inner requirements they postulated for God's absolution. Apart from further taunts, Luther added, more interestingly, that it was a mistake to suppose that there were two absolutions. There is only one act, ours, of absolution, and when we perform it, God has already performed one and the same act. So there is no gap between two distinct acts for uncertainty to occupy, and for God to override the priest. It may have been easier for Luther to deny a gap between two acts, because he had so far reduced the role that the priest had to play.

There was an important return to old themes in Luther's lectures on Galatians in 1531 with revised editions in 1535 and 1538. Luther urged that in matters of troubled conscience one was to forget the law, and turn only to the promise of God's mercy as announced in the Gospel. In that sphere, the law merely terrorizes the conscience. But in matters of civil policy, one was to be concerned with the law and forget conscience. These were to be kept separate. Referring to this work in his *Grace Abounding to the Chief of Sinners* of 1666, John Bunyan (1628–1688) the author of *Pilgrim's Progress* was to say: "I must let fall before all men, I do prefer this book of Mr *Luther* upon the *Galathians,* (excepting the Holy Bible) before all the books that I have ever seen, as most fit for a wounded conscience." Luther's treatment of troubled conscience must have been as effective as anyone's up to the time of Freud, although his method and approach could hardly have been more different. This text, recalling his early lectures of 1516–1517, comes as a relief from his less tolerant mood.

33. Roland H. Bainton, "The development and consistency of Luther's attitude to religious liberty," *Harvard Theological Review* 22, 1929, 107–49, finds examples of intemperance early on as well. A minor example was quoted in note 30 above.

In Luther's treatment of conscience, we have seen more prominent and less prominent themes. More prominent was his objection to the Church's terrorization of conscience, and the contrast of a joyful conscience. But at Worms and in *On Secular Authority* two further themes were apparent. At Worms, he refused to retract because it was neither safe nor right to go against conscience. In other words, following conscience was *necessary*. In *On Secular Authority* he rejected *compulsion* of belief because how one believes is a matter of each person's *conscience*. In other words, conscience should be *free from compulsion*. This last insistence on freedom from compulsion of conscience was to be a dominant theme in the first half of the seventeenth century in Protestant England, the subject of chapter 8. By that time there was no Roman Catholic authority in England, but there had been in recent memory. Those who were insisting on freedom of conscience, though very keen that no Catholic authority should return, were demanding freedom to follow their own consciences.

Others have pointed out that Luther's idea of joyful conscience gave rise to the other idea of liberty of conscience, distinct from the demands for freedom to follow one's conscience: the idea of spiritual freedom *already* brought to the conscience by Christ's redemption of Christians.[34]

Calvin and Castellio

John Calvin (1509–1564) developed his form of Protestantism in Switzerland when Luther's was already established in Germany. His *Ordonnances* of 1537 for the organization of the Church in Geneva became law there in 1541, and set up a governing consistory elected by some members of the congregation. That model was adapted for the Scottish Presbyterian Church by John Knox, and by that route Calvin had more direct influence in England than Luther.

On the other hand, on the particular theme of conscience, Calvin had little to add, unless it was to emphasize that Luther's joyful conscience already enjoyed the other kind of freedom, a *Christian* freedom. In book 3 of his *Institutes of the Christian Religion*, written in Latin (1st ed. 1536; expanded in 1559, his first French translation in 1541), he reaffirmed Luther's view that "Christian consciences"—a term he used often—are *already* freed from the terror of the law, and are justified not by performing the works of the

34. Blair Worden, *God's Instruments: Political Conduct in the England of Oliver Cromwell*, Oxford University Press 2012, ch. 8, "Civil and religious liberty," at pp. 323–24.

law, but through faith in God's mercy.[35] This independence of the law gives to the consciences of the faithful a special Christian freedom (*conscientiis fidelium libertas*).[36] At the same time he agreed with Luther that scruples *oppress conscience* with doubt and despair, but our consciences are *freed* by Paul's Letter to the Romans 14:14, which shows that it is up to us what is unclean.[37]

In his discussion of the freedom of faithful consciences, Calvin offers a narrow definition of conscience based on only one of the functions recognized by St. Paul, as follows: "When they have a sense of the divine justice added as a witness which does not allow them to conceal their sins, but drags them forward as culprits to the bar of God, that sense is called conscience."[38] He immediately quotes St. Paul, Romans 2:15, which is concerned with the role of conscience as bearing witness on the Day of Judgment, as one's thoughts accuse or excuse one, while God judges. This expresses the idea that conscience reveals our possesion of the law and our recognition of conformity or noncomformity with it. Luther's account of conscience put a greater stress on *self*-awareness during life, and he also emphasized a different role for bad conscience. It was a necessary *preliminary* source of terror, preliminary to throwing ourselves on God's promise of mercy, which counts neither our sins nor our works, but our faith. However on justification being through faith, Calvin agreed.

On the subject of confession, Calvin was again broadly in agreement with Luther. In his *Institutes*, he held that one should confess to God. It is acceptable to confess to a human, if that gives solace, but one should not in that case confess all one's sins.[39]

Calvin's Christian freedom of conscience, as so far cited, is a freedom of Christians from the tyranny of religious law. But it does not, like Luther's *On Secular Authority*, limit the power of civil authorities concerning religious matters, or require freedom from compulsion of conscience. It does not express the defiance of Luther's famous insistence at Worms that it is neither safe nor right to go against conscience. Indeed, on these topics, Calvin appears to be disagreeing with Luther in book 4, chapter 20 of his *Institutes*, which constitutes a treatise *On Civil Government*. Here he allowed more power to secular rulers than had Luther. Magistrates had authority not only

35. *Institutes of the Christian Religion*, bk. 3, esp. chs. 2, 3, 11, 19.
36. *Institutes* 3.19.
37. *Institutes* 3.19.7–8.
38. *Institutes* 3.19.
39. *Institutes* 3.4.9, 3.4.12.

over the last six of the Ten Commandments, which prescribe rules for society, but also over the first four, which prescribe our attitude to God.[40] Far more clearly than Luther in his *On Secular Authority*, Calvin here pronounces the divine right of secular rulers. Paul's Letter to the Romans 13:5 says that one must be subject to rulers not only to avoid God's wrath, but also for *conscience's* sake. Calvin's 1559 version of the *Institutes* takes this to mean that the duty arises because it is God who gives power to rulers or to their office, so that to resist them is to resist God. God thus requires us to honor and obey rulers, however bad, because their right comes from him.[41] Two exceptions are allowed at the very end. There might be equivalents of the Athenian ephors or Roman tribunes of the plebs, whose role as magistrates was to curb injustice on the part of rulers. Again, one is not to obey rulers if that would mean disobeying God.[42]

As regards freedom from *compulsion* of conscience, Calvin was later accused of taking a very different view from Luther's *On Secular Authority*. He was to provoke a protest after Luther's death from Castellio, who was responding to a dismaying event in 1553. As a result of Calvin's denunciation, the Geneva Town Council burned Michael Servetus at the stake as a heretic for denying the doctrine of the Trinity, God's three persons, and for rejecting infant baptism. Calvin would have preferred the more merciful death of the sword, but defended the decision in his *Declaratio orthodoxae fidei* of the next year. But Sebastian Castellio (1515–1563), Calvin's one-time friend, himself a fugitive from the sight of the Catholic inquisition burning people in Savoy in France, remonstrated under the pseudonym of Bellius in his *On Heretics: Whether They Should Be Persecuted*, published in Latin in 1554, with a French translation following.[43] A later work, *Against the Book of Calvin*, appeared only posthumously. In *On Heretics*, Castellio collected quotations bearing on the conscience of heretics, using among others some of the ancient sources mentioned above in chapter 3. In his short dedication of the Latin version to the Duke of Würtemberg, he argues that whereas knowledge of right conduct is engraved in our hearts, to use the terms of St. Paul's Letter to the Romans 2:15, this is not the case with matters of doctrine. On

40. *Institutes* 4.20.9.

41. *Institutes* 4.20.22–25.

42. *Institutes* 4.20.31–32.

43. I have made use of Roland H. Bainton, *Concerning Heretics Attributed to Sebastian Castellio*, Columbia University Press 1935, reprinted by Octagon Books, New York 1979, with discussion and illustrative passages in translation, including Castellio's dedication of his work to Duke Christoph of Würtemberg; also of Rainer Forst, *Toleranz im Konflikt*, Suhrkamp, Frankfurt 2003, pp. 167–72

this he uses the appeal to *ignorance*. The death penalty is used by the mighty concerning topics on which opinions are almost as numerous as men and which have been disputed for centuries without anyone arriving at knowledge. Those called heretics, he says, are people who are *acting according to conscience* and who *dare not violate their conscience*,[44] although they may be in error. We call heretics those with whom we disagree on matters of doctrine, and almost every sect regards every other sect as heretic, so that as you travel, you would need for safety to change your faith as often as you changed your currency. Castellio died during his own trial for heresy in 1563.

Different Meanings of Freedom of Conscience

This chapter has found two great founders of the Protestant Reformation, Luther and Calvin, in agreement on replacing the Church's "terrorization" of consciences by substituting faith in God's mercy. They agreed also on the freedom given to Christian consciences by that mercy. But we have noticed that "freedom of conscience" could mean very different things. Christian freedom of conscience continued to be invoked in reference to Christ's redemption of sinners. But objections to compulsion of conscience, like that in Luther's *On Secular Authority*, treated freedom of conscience as something to be demanded, rather than as something *already* given to Christians, and it foreshadowed demands for freedom of conscience in the seventeenth century, even if Luther later showed a more authoritarian side. Calvin's Presbyterian heirs in the English Parliament, by contrast, were to be accused of refusing freedom of conscience to others.

Retrospect

Luther's treatment of penitence was again full of the unexpected. The penance he most objected to was the lightest, indulgence payments, not the ancient rigors of sackcloth. His worthlessness of the whole person was part of a joyful conception that would free his conscience from despair. In the next two chapters I shall look first at the dilemmas of conscience created partly by a splintering of religious authority encouraged by the Protestant Reformation, and at the casuists' concern with the morality of particular decisions from which Luther had sought to escape. In chapter 8, I shall consider seventeenth-century demands for freedom of conscience.

44. For the references to conscience, see Roland H. Bainton, *Concerning Heretics Attributed to Sebastian Castellio*, pp. 124–25.

SEVEN

Advice on Particular Moral Dilemmas: Casuistry, Mid-Sixteenth to Mid-Seventeenth Centuries

Moral Dilemmas: Need for Advice Intensified by Multiple Claims of Allegiance after the Reformation

The Protestant Reformation had unforeseen consequences. What was not foreseen was that the break would lead to new moral dilemmas and a revived interest in acts of conscience. For it divided the Western Church not only into Catholics and Protestants, but also into many Protestant denominations and sects, and this led to severe problems of conflicting demands for allegiance that preyed upon consciences. Resolving these cases of conflict of conscience was a problem of conscience concerning future conduct that for Protestants to an extent replaced the backward-looking confession of *past* sin, after confession for them had ceased to be compulsory. For Catholics, the new problems were *added* to the problems of the confessional.[1] We encountered in chapter 4 medieval treatments of one type of moral dilemma, moral double bind, but that discussion was conducted on the whole at a general level. What was new was the provision of specialist advice on actual and particular or highly specific cases of moral dilemmas with close attention to circumstances. This study of cases of conscience was called casuistry.

In England, although many Protestants, including the three Oxford martyrs Cranmer, Latimer, and Ridley, were burned at the stake under the brief reign in England of Catholic Queen Mary Tudor (1553–1558), it has been

1. There are two works that I take here as my main guide: Albert R. Jonsen and Stephen Toulmin, *The Abuse of Casuistry*, University of California Press 1988, with corrective observations drawn from Keith Thomas, "Cases of conscience in seventeenth century England," in John Morrill, Paul Slack, and Daniel Woolf, eds., *Public Duty and Private Conscience in Seventeenth Century England*, Oxford University Press 1993.

estimated that 183 Catholics were executed under her Protestant successor, Queen Elizabeth (1558–1603). Catholics had to hide their allegiance from 1559 when her *Oath of Supremacy* required office holders to swear allegiance to her, not the Pope, as head of the Church, on pain of a charge of treason, and her *Act of Uniformity* outlawed celebration of the Roman Catholic Mass, and imposed fines for not attending Anglican service every Sunday. The Jesuit Edmund Campion returned to England in 1580 from training as a Catholic missionary in France, and managed to print his case for Catholicism in hiding at Stonor, but was caught and executed in 1581. In 1585, Jesuits were banished, and it was declared treason for priests ordained abroad to return to England. Under the next monarch, James I (1603–1625), Robert Catesby consulted a Jesuit casuist on morality before leading the unsuccessful Gunpowder Plot in 1605 to blow up the Protestant Parliament. The following year, James I made all Catholics in the realm swear an *Oath of Allegiance*, without any equivocation or secret reservation according to which they would not kill him, if the Pope declared him deposed. The explicit prohibition of evasions, to be repeated in subsequent oaths, is a sign of the slippery practices which were later, rather unfairly, to be treated as the mark of all casuistry.

King Henry IV of France, protector of the Protestant Huguenots, was assassinated in 1610. So the Spanish Jesuit Suarez chose a sensitive time in 1613 to publish against James his *Defence of the Catholic Faith Against the Errors of the English Sect.* He rejected the right of James to rule over the consciences of Catholics, and he allowed the killing of a ruler, although only after a legitimate sentence had been declared on the grounds that the ruler was not serving the common good. Charles I, successor of James from 1625–1649, repeatedly asked his Anglican bishops to solve questions of conscience before he made decisions. In 1640 he had Parliament impose on clergymen, schoolmasters, and many others the *Et Cetera Oath* to uphold against Rome the Anglican Church and its governance by bishops. They were to swear according to the plain and common sense and understanding of the words provided, without any equivocation, mental evasion, or secret reservation whatsoever. In 1641 he required everyone over eighteen to swear a *Protestation* of loyalty to himself and the Anglican Church against Popery.

Most of the oaths so far mentioned created problems of conscience for Catholics, but Protestants were also to be affected. Elizabeth's *Act of Uniformity* requiring Anglican worship affected Protestants too. In the two Civil Wars of 1642–1646 and 1648 between King Charles I and Parliament, each side in turn sought the alliance of the Presbyterian sect—first Parliament through the *Solemn League and Covenant* of 1643, which offered reform of English religion in return for the help of a Scottish Presbyterian army; then Charles I in the *Engagement* of 1648 with Presbyterians who had supported the earlier covenant. In between in 1646, the victorious Parliament abolished the Anglican Church's institution of bishops. But in 1648 Parliament was itself forcibly purged of Presbyterians who sympathized with King Charles by the largely Puritan New Model Army which it had appointed to defeat him. With the execution of the defeated King Charles in 1649, Parliament introduced an *Engagement Oath* requiring fidelity to the new king-free Commonwealth and lasting until 1654. With the restoration of the monarchy in 1660, the *Engagement Oath* was declared illegal, and those who had flourished under the Commonwealth were in great danger.

Protestants and Catholics alike needed moral guidance in this dangerous period, and it was provided partly by *casuistry*. This was particularly developed by the Jesuit movement between the mid-sixteenth and mid-seventeenth centuries. But casuists arose also among English Protestants, in Cambridge with two priests from the Puritan wing of the Anglican Church, William Perkins in publications of 1596 and posthumously between 1603 and 1608, and his pupil William Ames publishing in 1639. There was also the nonconformist Richard Baxter, whose main casuistic work was published in 1673. Among the Royalist Anglicans there was Robert Sanderson in Oxford and Jeremy Taylor, both of whom benefited from the restoration of the monarchy in 1660. Thomas Hobbes, it has been argued, was very conscious of casuistry in his *Leviathan* of 1651, but sought to replace it, as something far too lax, with his own principles.

Ancient Stoic Beginnings

The beginnings of casuistry were recorded by Cicero in Latin in the first century BCE in his *On Duties*. He there described the Stoics of the second century BCE and their interest in particular moral decisions or specific types of moral decision. Although these were not expressed in terms of conscience, the ones discussed tended to involve moral considerations. Admittedly, Cicero did not discuss examples of moral double bind, since his interest extended to asking which course was morally better, but not to asking which was less bad.

Cicero cites the lost Greek text *On Duties* by Panaetius, who was head of the Stoic school in Athens from 129–09 BCE. Panaetius set out to discuss decisions on what was morally right (*honestum*), what advantageous, and apparent clashes between the two. Cicero thought he should have added discussion of how to identify which was morally *better* of *two* courses and which *more* advantageous, and since Panaetius never reached his discussion of a clash between the moral and the advantageous, Cicero supplied a discussion in his own book 3.[2] He was convinced that there could not be a real clash. Although killing a person is normally wrong, killing a tyrant is not a case of following advantage instead of morality; it is moral as well as advantageous, because circumstances matter. Cicero records discussions from the two Stoic heads preceding Panaetius, Diogenes of Babylon (d. ca. 152 BCE) and his pupil Antipater of Tarsus (head from 152–29 BCE), as well as of Panaetius' own pupil Hecato. These discussions take very specific cases of moral dilemma, although the *grounds* for decision are not here equally specific. In selling a house, should you reveal to the purchaser that there is rotten fabric? In a shipwreck, if there is only one plank afloat for two men overboard, which should have the plank? Panaetius himself was doing what could be identified as casuistry, for example, in his treatment of *personae*.[3] In making decisions in life, one should consider not only what Kant would stress two thousand years later, one's role as a rational being, but also, without forgetting rationality, much more specific roles, the rank or gender to which you were born, the work you had chosen in life, your abilities, your age, for example. Rationality alone does not give enough guidance. One is a rational male or female, son or daughter, Greek or Roman. There is a very good discussion of how to choose a career. Should you follow your father's? Not if you do not have those abilities.[4]

For some people the right decision is unique. When Julius Caesar, in violation of the Roman republic, seized power by conquest and advanced on Utica in what is now Tunisia, the younger Cato, the Stoic, committed suicide rather than parley with Caesar. This Roman illustration of Panaetius' principles is supplied by Cicero. It was right for Cato to commit suicide, but not for anyone else *in the same circumstances*. Kant, we know from student lecture notes, had heard of this case, although his student at least had not understood properly the Stoic rationale.[5] It does not strictly contradict what Kant was to say, that rationality requires us to consider that what is right for

2. Cicero, *On Duties* 1.9–10; 3.7–20.

3. Reported with his own Roman examples by Cicero, *On Duties*, bk. 1, esp. 107–25.

4. Cicero, *On Duties* 1.120–1.

5. Kant, *Lectures on Ethics*, trans. Louis Infield, London 1930, p. 149; and by Peter Heath Cambridge 1997, discussed by Richard Sorabji, *Self: Ancient and Modern Insights about Individuality, Life, and Death*, Oxford University Press and University of Chicago Press 2006, 165–66.

one is right for all in the same circumstances. Kant put even more stress on impartiality than Adam Smith before him. No doubt Panaetius could have agreed with Kant, that if there *had* been anyone else exactly like Cato (treating his character as one of the circumstances), it would have been morally right for him *too* to commit suicide. But the morally relevant point was that there *was* no one else like Cato; he had stood all his life for a uniquely uncompromising austerity and fidelity to the Roman republic. One would have to know many anecdotes about him to understand this; it could not be summed up in a few adjectives.[6] When Roman emperors replaced the Roman republic, Stoics still consulted their *personae*. Senators had been robbed of their political power, but notable Stoics still accepted, at the risk of their lives, Epictetus tells us, the senatorial role of expressing their disagreement with the emperor,[7] and under the Emperor Nero, Stoicism was made a capital charge for Thrasea Paetus, a biographer of Cato.[8]

What is considered here is particular circumstances, or very specific types of circumstance. I have discussed elsewhere the interest in the particular or specific in Stoic ethics and have found it in most ancient schools of philosophy, even if less so in Platonism.[9] Admittedly, the Stoics spoke also of a moral *law* of nature within each person, but it was seen in chapter 1 that this law did not take the form of a set of general or universal moral rules like the Bible's Ten Commandments. The example of such a law or formula given five times by Cicero in book 3 of his *On Duties*, and later by Seneca, is that the bonds of human fellowship must be fostered, not violated. This was general enough to cover the duties of human relationships (and the Stoics did not entertain duties *to* their impersonal God, important though he was for morality).[10] At the same time, it left the interest, and in some cases all the hard work of decision, focused on the particular.

6. Cicero, *On Duties* 1. 112. Cf. Peter Winch, "The universalisability of moral judgement," *Monist*, 49, 1965, 196–214.

7. Epictetus, *Discourses* 1.2, esp. 8–29.

8. Miriam Griffin, "Political thought in the age of Nero," *Neronia VI, Rome à l'époque néronienne*, Collection Latomus 268, 2002, pp. 325–37.

9. In Stoic ethics: Richard Sorabji, *Gandhi and the Stoics: Modern Experiments on Ancient Values*, Oxford University Press and University of Chicago Press 2012, ch. 6 "Persona and *svadharma*: is duty universalizable or unique to the individual?"; Ch. 7, "Hesitations about general rules in morality." In other schools: my "Philosophy and life in Greek and Roman philosophy: three aspects," lecture at the Royal Institute of Philosophy, London, 2012, to be published in its *Proceedings*, 2014.

10. God's rationality was to be imitated. The *eupatheiai*, or good emotions, include joy at God's good governance of the universe, but only a sage could get this right: it was supererogatory, not an ordinary duty.

Gratian's Canon Law and Handbooks for Hearing Confession

The subsequent history of casuistry has been traced by Albert Jonsen and Stephen Toulmin.[11] They cite Aristotle and Thomas Aquinas for interest in the particular, but casuistry they find in Cicero, in the Jewish Talmudic tradition, and Christian casuistry in primitive form in Pope Gregory I "the Great" (540–604), who provides the three dilemmas of moral double bind mentioned in chapter 4, and who gives the advice to choose the lesser evil. They regard the early penitential manuals discussed in chapter 5 as prototypes. But a more important step toward mature Christian casuistry they find in the development of the Church's canon law under Gregory VII, Pope from 1073.[12] In 1070, the *Digest* of Justinian had been rediscovered, a compilation of legal rulings from several centuries made under the Byzantine Emperor Justinian (ca. 482–565 CE). This now served as a model for a compilation of rulings in the Church, which needed to be clarified and reconciled with each other. Earlier Christian thinkers such as Augustine might be much cited. He had introduced into Christianity, partly drawing on Cicero, the idea of just war. But his views on when it was just to go to war had not been crystallized by him into criteria. That was left to the canon lawyers and continued by Thomas Aquinas.[13] The culminating work in canon law was the *Decretum* of Gratian of about 1140. It was taught by case study in the University of Bologna. Canon Law was reflected in the new range of *summae* to guide priests hearing confession, including the *Summa* of Raymond Penaforte from 1240 to 1245 and the earlier *Liber poenitentalis* of Alain of Lille, both mentioned in the discussion of penitence in chapter 5.

Thomas Aquinas's Use of Aristotle's Interest in Particular Cases

After 1215, when the Fourth Lateran Council made confession once a year compulsory, interest in conscience and its companion *synderesis* was intensified. In 1257–1258, Thomas Aquinas said that the general principles grasped by *synderesis* were the general principles of natural law.[14] Thus, as he

11. Albert R. Jonsen and Stephen Toulmin, *The Abuse of Casuistry*.

12. Useful here is Harold J. Berman, *Law and Revolution: The Formation of the Western Legal Tradition*, Harvard University Press 1983, ch. 5.

13. Richard Sorabji, "Just war from ancient origins to the Conquistador debate and its modern relevance," in Richard Sorabji and David Rodin, eds., *The Ethics of War: Shared Problems in Different Traditions*, Ashgate, Aldershot 2006, ch. 1.

14. Thomas Aquinas, *On Truth*, question 16, answer 1.

says elsewhere, these principles are the same for all—for example, that borrowed goods should be returned. Nonetheless, the conclusion to be drawn from them is not the same for all, if the return of a borrowed weapon would be used wrongfully. Circumstances matter.[15] Aristotle's *Nicomachean Ethics* had been rediscovered around 1245, and Thomas was in the forefront in commenting on it. He cites Aristotle's enumeration of the particular circumstances that would make an action involuntary and free from blame: in Aristotle's original, nonculpable ignorance of who, what, concerning what, where, with what instrument, for what purpose and in what manner. Thomas believes that Cicero's *De inventione* had a similar list of questions for the orator to consider.[16] He holds that circumstances though not part of the essence of an act can decide whether it is good or bad, as taking something becomes bad if it is another's and worse if taken from a holy place.[17] The recovery of Aristotle's text also made available his treatment of equity, *epieikeia*, or the discretion exercised by the wise judge to allow for the particularities of the case that a general law could not foresee. Aristotle compared the ruler used by builders in Lesbos, which, being made of lead, could bend round corners.[18]

Jesuit Order 1540 and Protestant Casuist Works

The heyday of casuistry was a response to the Reformation and the Counter-Reformation inaugurated by the Catholic Church at the Council of Trent from 1545 to 1563. The Jesuit order, founded by Ignatius of Loyola in 1540, had headquarters in Rome and had consultants at the council. Its members were trained and supplied training in cases of conscience and by 1600 it had colleges worldwide in Europe, South America, and India. The Jesuits were the leading, though not the sole, practitioners of casuistry.

A number of English Protestant writers on casuistry offered definitions of conscience in their texts, and some of them, while retaining the basic idea that conscience involves self-judgment, gave conscience a certain

15. Thomas Aquinas, *Summa theologiae* Ia IIae, question 94, article 4. The point had been anticipated in Plato, *Republic* 1.331C., but Thomas would not yet have had direct access to that.

16. Aristotle, *Nicomachean Ethics* 3.1, 1111a3–6; Cicero, *De inventione* 1.26. Thomas Aquinas, *Summa theologiae* Ia IIae, question 7, article 3.

17. Thomas Aquinas, *Summa theologiae* Ia IIae, question 18, article 10.

18. Aristotle, *Nicomachean Ethics*, bk. 5, chs. 8–10, Lesbian ruler at 1137b30. Equity is discussed in my *Necessity, Cause and Blame*, Duckworth, London 1980; and Chicago University Press 2006; Bloomsbury, London 2010, chs. 16–18.

reference to God. William Ames (1576–1633), in his *Conscience with the Power and Cases Thereof,* of about 1630, translated into English in 1637, thought that we and conscience *regard* its judgments as being God's.[19] He started his book by saying, "The conscience of man is a man's judgment of himself, according to the judgment of God in him" (1.1.1). He continued: "Conscience stands in the place of God himself" (1.3.2 and 6); and "he that doth against it doth against God's will, . . . because what the conscience doth declare, it declareth as God's will" (1.4.6). This idea is a development of St. Paul rather than what he explicitly says, and it contrasts, we shall see in chapters 9 and 10, with later resecularization. But the role of God in Ames is still subjective. Conscience *considers* that it is speaking for God. But Ames does not say that God endorses everything that conscience says. He does say in *The Substance of the Christian Religion* (Doct. 1, Reas. 1), speaking not of conscience but of the law of God written in the heart on which conscience draws, that it is as it were the voice of God. But since, according to Paul, the law is written in our hearts *by God,* it actually is the word of God, and Ames's qualification "as it were" must be allowing that the law is not present strictly as a *voice.* Other English casuists applied the term "voice of God" to such a variety of phenomena that it would not have been recognized as a synonym for conscience.[20]

19. I thank Jerome Schneewind for drawing my attention to his quotations from Ames in *The Invention of Autonomy,* Cambridge University Press, Cambridge 1998, p. 93.

20. Jeremy Taylor (1613–1667) in *Ductor Dubitantium or the Rule of Conscience,* 1660, treated the voice of God not as the conscience that accuses or excuses us, but as passing sentence *after* our conscience has spoken and consigning us, if need be, to hell. Richard Baxter (1615–1691) spoke repeatedly about the voice of God, but typically not as a synonym for conscience. He normally referred to warnings about eternal punishment or salvation, whether delivered as God's word in the Bible, or by any other messenger in the Bible, such as the curses heard by King David in relation to his acquiring Uriah's wife Bathsheba by getting her husband killed (*The Life of Faith; The Saints' Everlasting Rest; A Call to the Unconverted to Turn and Live*). Conscience is mentioned when Baxter says, "And then it is your work to . . . hearken more to the voice of God and conscience than of the slanderer" (*A Treatise of Self-denial*). But in the light of his other usage, it seems likely that conscience is here a *second* voice to be heeded, not identical with God's voice. The term "voice of God" had been used even more loosely by Ames's teacher in Cambridge, William Perkins, in *A Discourse of Conscience,* 1596, where he included the sacraments as the *visible* voice along with preaching as the *audible* voice of God. In the noncasuist milieu of the eighteenth century, Joseph Butler was to use the term "voice of God" almost equally loosely, identifying it not with conscience but with our *nature,* a nature in which God had deliberately given conscience the highest authority: "Our nature, i.e. the voice of God in us, carries us to the exercise of charity and benevolence" (Joseph Butler, Sermon 6, sec.7, in *Fifteen Sermons Preached at the Rolls Chapel*).

Successes and Failures

In 1656, Blaise Pascal's attack on casuistry in his *Provincial Letters* gave the very word a bad name. The attack was partly based on the probabilism, first introduced by a Dominican, Bartolomeo Medina, not a Jesuit, in 1577, which allowed one to make moral decisions whose correctness had a lower degree of probability. But other devices had been recognized long before Pascal—for example, in the oaths required in England in 1606 and 1640, which forbade relying on unspoken qualifications, or deliberate equivocations. In England, in addition, some of the moral dilemmas were abated by the new King William who came from Holland in 1688, when his *Act of Toleration* of 1689 allowed freedom to nonconformists at least in matters of worship, provided they had taken yet another oath of allegiance, though not to all sects, nor to Catholics.

Despite the decline of casuistry, the main moral that Jonsen and Toulmin draw in their book, *The Abuse of Casuistry*, is that, though it led to such abuses, its focus on the particular and specific was a positive merit. I have tried to illustrate this merit with such examples as that of the Stoic Panaetius' appeal to individual, as well as universally shared, *personae* in making decisions in life.

EIGHT

Freedom of Conscience and the Individual: Seventeenth-Century England and Holland

It was the frequent resort to experts in casuistry that especially prompted Keith Thomas's description of the seventeenth century as the age of conscience. But it could also be called the age of conscience for a further reason: the appeals to *freedom* of conscience. It was not a freedom of conscience like that of Luther's period, in which one major group was demanding freedom from another, Protestant from Catholic. The seventeenth century was concerned with the freedom of minorities or of particular congregations or of individual consciences. Casuistry could be concerned with both past and future, with past wrongdoing and with avoiding future wrongdoing. But freedom of conscience is primarily concerned with the forward-looking roles of conscience, the awareness of what it would be wrong or not wrong to do or not do in the future.

Part 1 up to 1660

Four English Baptists Call for Freedom of Individual Conscience, 1612–1620

The Baptists believed in *adult* baptism, some of them renouncing their own infant baptism. The first of four English Baptists to call for freedom of individual conscience[1] was John Smyth, who was at Christ's College, Cambridge, as a student until 1590 and as a teacher until 1598 at the same time as two other notable writers on conscience, mentioned for their casuist

1. See H. Leon McBeth, *English Baptist Literature on Religious Liberty to 1689*, Arno Press, New York, 1980, and Edward Bean Underhill, ed., *Tracts on Liberty of Conscience and Persecution, 1614–1661*, London 1846.

writings in chapter 7,[2] and like John Milton at a later date. Smyth was not then a Baptist, but became one gradually. He took refuge in Holland with the group of which he was pastor, and that developed into what is considered the first English Baptist church. In 1612, having come closer to the Mennonites, he signed a Mennonite confession in which article 84 addresses individual freedom of conscience: "The magistrate is not by virtue of his office to meddle with religion, or matters of conscience, to force or compel men to this or that form of religion or doctrine: but to leave Christian religion free, to every man's conscience, and to handle only civil transgressions (Rom[ans] xii), injuries and wrongs of man against man, in murder, adultery, theft, etc." The Baptists did not, like some other groups, oppose magisterial power, nor the use of the sword, in nonspiritual matters. But Smyth went as far as denying church membership to magistrates.

Thomas Helwys, a disciple of Smyth, assisted his flight to Holland and later took a group there himself and accepted adult baptism. But in 1611 or 1612, he returned to England and set up the first Baptist Church there. In 1612, he dedicated to King James I *A Short Declaration of the Mistery of Iniquity*, and sent it to him. In the book he said of members of the Romish religion, "If they be true and faithfull subjects of the king, . . . wee do freely profess that our Lord the King hath no more power over their consciences than over ours, and that is none at all. . . . Let them be heretikes, Turcks, Jewes, or whatsoever it apperteynes not to the earthly power to punish them in the least measure [in spiritual matters]." He anticipates the argument that Locke was to make his principal consideration, addressing the king as follows: "Oh, let the King judge, is it not most equall, that men should chuse their religion themselves seeing that they onely must stand themselves before the judgment seat of God to answere for themselves, when it shal be no excuse for them to say, wee were commanded or compelled to be of this religion by the King, or by them that had authority from him."[3] Helwys was sent to Newgate prison, where he had died by 1616.

2. Of two members of the Puritan wing of the Anglican Church, William Perkins (1552–1602) was a fellow of Christ's from 1584 to 1594. Moving to become lecturer of St. Andrews Church, Cambridge, he published in 1596 *A Discourse of Conscience*, and a posthumous publication was *The Cases of Conscience*, between 1603 and 1608. William Ames, was Perkins's pupil at Christ's from 1594, and after getting his MA in 1601, became for a while a fellow of Christ's. But after controversies he eventually moved to Holland and in 1639 published *Conscience with the Power and Cases Thereof*.

3. Thomas Helwys, *A Short Declaration of the Mistery of Iniquity*, facsimile, Kingsgate Press, London 1935, p. 46.

Leonard Busher published *Religion's Peace: A Plea for Liberty of Conscience* in 1614. Addressing the king, he says, "No prince or people can possibly attain that one true religion of the gospel which is acceptable to God by Jesus Christ, merely by birth." Although he sought to confine arguments to the New Testament, rejecting appeal to church fathers, he uses the arguments familiar from Augustine that persecution for beliefs is ineffective and produces only hypocrites, and that people should be converted, not killed. Busher was in exile in Holland in the 1640s.

John Murton may have been baptized by Smyth, went to Holland, and became Helwys's chief helper. He returned with him to England and, after Helwys's imprisonment, became in effect his successor. He published, probably in 1615 *Objections Answered by Way of Dialogue, Wherein Is Proved . . . That No Man Ought to Be Persecuted for His Religion* (London), and in 1620 *A Most Humble Supplication of Many of the King's Majesty's Loyal Subjects, Ready to Testify All Civil Obedience by the Oath of Allegiance, or Otherwise, and That of Conscience* (London). He used the familiar argument that persecution does not change belief, but only produces hypocritical pretense, and he discussed the New Testament parable of picking the tares too soon and of compelling the hedge dwellers to come in to the feast. He was in prison in 1615 and smuggled out his 1620 treatise, written in milk, to our next figure, Roger Williams, who was inspired by it to write his *Bloudy Tenant*.

Roger Williams, Baptist Convert

Roger Williams (1603–1684) was another early English supporter of freedom of conscience, who studied at Pembroke Hall, Cambridge, and was ordained an Anglican in 1629. Horrified the next year by witnessing the persecution of a Puritan, he left England for the Massachussetts Bay Colony in America. After criticizing the seizure of land from American Indians, and the proposed State imposition of an oath of loyalty, he avoided arrest by fleeing in the winter of 1635–1636 to the settlement he later called Providence. In 1639 he was rebaptized as a Baptist. At first, he lived for periods with American Indians, but later visited England twice to gain a charter for the group of settlements that became the state of Rhode Island, and he wrote into the charter freedom of conscience and protection for American Indians. The first visit in 1643 resulted in a charter from Charles I (b. 1600), king of England from 1625 until his execution in 1649. After the Restoration of the monarchy in 1660, Williams returned and renegotiated the charter with Charles II (1630–1685). The freedom of conscience secured has been illuminatingly analyzed by Martha Nussbaum.[4] He called for freedom of conscience in belief and in acts of worship, with only the provisos that it was not used for licentiousness or profanity and not for injuring others or disturbing the peace. Very unusual for a Protestant in this period was his extending freedom of conscience to Roman Catholics. We shall seldom find that again.

In 1644 he replied to John Cotton of Massachussetts and his support for religious persecution with *The Bloudy Tenent of Persecution* and in 1652 to Cotton's riposte with *The Bloody Tenent Yet More Bloody*. Some of the arguments on both sides were concisely presented in 1651 in Williams's letter of admonition to Governor John Endicott of the Massachussetts Bay Colony, from whose jurisdiction he had earlier escaped.[5] In the space of four pages within this ten-page letter,[6] Williams argues that it is by oppressing Turkish, Popish, or Protestant consciences, superstitions as they may be, that the persecutor turns them into heretics, blasphemers, regicides, and (in 1605) would-be blowers up of Parliament. He would put the point by saying in *Yet More Bloody* that the persecution itself *hardens* consciences,[7] just as Luther had said that it *strengthens* heretics. To the governor he used the argument which in another version, we saw, for a time attracted St. Augustine, that torture—and, Williams added, argument—is not easily *effective* in removing even a deluded conscience. This, he claimed, was especially true of English consciences, as a former Pope is said to have acknowledged. He had earlier in chapter 40 of *The Bloudy Tenent* coupled the argument from *ineffectiveness* with that from *hypocrisy*, saying that *only* God could release opponents of the truth, open their eyes and produce faith and repentance, whereas the sword of steel could create only *hypocrisy*. To the governor he added that conscience is found in all mankind more or less, in Jews, Turks, Papists, Protestants, pagans, etc. In *Yet More Bloody*, he had said that conscience was the man,[8] a view much revived of late in the idea that conscience helps to constitute personal identity.[9] In England itself, he told the governor, the consciences of

4. Martha Nussbaum, *Liberty of Conscience*, Basic Books 2008, ch. 2. I benefited from her allowing me a preview of her book.

5. Roger Williams, *The Correspondence of Roger Williams*, ed. Glenn La Fantasie, Brown University Press, Providence RI, vol. 1, pp. 337–47.

6. Ibid., pp. 338–41.

7. The *Complete Writings of Roger Williams*, New York 1963, vol. 4, p. 474.

8. *Complete Writings*, 4, 440.

9. See Michael Sandel, *Democracy's Discontent*, Harvard University Press 1996, p. 67; Amy Gutmann, *Identity in Democracy*, Princeton University Press 2003, p. 171; Kwame Anthony Appiah, *The Ethics of Identity*, Princeton University Press 2005, p. 99; William Galston, *The Practice of Liberal Pluralism*, Cambridge University Press 2005, p. 67; cf. Jocelyn Maclure and Charles Taylor, *Secularism and Freedom of Conscience*, Harvard University Press 2011, pp. 76, 89, 91, 108.

the most holy men, especially in the days of the Catholic Queen Mary, had been mistaken, an argument from our *ignorance*, and *The Bloudy Tenent* had given other examples of fluctuations in human opinion.

Although King Charles I gave Williams the charter establishing Rhode Island and endowing it with freedom of conscience, Charles's own interest in conscience was rather in squaring his decisions with conscience with the aid of casuistical advice. Roger Williams knew our next figure, John Milton, and wrote to a friend that he taught him Dutch, while learning many more languages from him.[10]

The English Revolution

In England, the discussion of freedom of conscience in the seventeenth century was bound up with revolutionary events from the time of the two Civil Wars (1642–1646 and 1648), and the abolition of bishops (1646) and of the monarchy (1649) until their restoration (1660) and the invitation to William of Orange from liberal Holland to replace the Stewart kings (1688). Because ideas were so much intertwined with what was happening in the nation, I present a summarized timetable of events.

Timetable for Revolution in Seventeenth-Century England

1642–1646: First English Civil War.

1643: Parliament's Solemn League and Covenant with Scottish Presbyterians in which they send an army in return for the reform of English religion.

1643: Milton, *The Doctrine and Discipline of Divorce*, first edition.

1644: Milton, *Areopagitica* for freedom of publication in protest at Parliament's licensing order of 1643.

1645: Parliament created New Model Army, which defeated King Charles I.

October 1646: Anglican bishops abolished.

March 1647: Parliament, dominated by Presbyterians, tries to dissolve Model Army.

October–November 1647: Putney debates: Levellers argue with Oliver Cromwell and Ireton for three days, including on suffrage for all free men and for women.

10. Williams's letter is quoted by Barbara K. Lewalski, *The Life of John Milton, A Critical Biography*, Blackwell, Oxford 2000, p. 285.

October 24, 1648: Treaty of Westphalia, England, not represented: local sovereign's choice of his realm's public religion extended beyond Catholicism and Lutheranism to Calvinism. Private Christian worship need not be any of these.

1648: Second Civil War. Charles I offers to Parliament to establish Presbyterianism, but defeated. Army purges Parliament of Presbyterians seeking accommodation with him.

December 16, 1648, and January 8–11, 1649: Whitehall debates, Levellers vs. Cromwell/Ireton focus on freedom of conscience.

January 30, 1649: Charles I beheaded.

February 1649: Milton publishes *The Tenure of Kings and Magistrates* in support of regicide.

March and May 1649: "Rump" Parliament abolishes monarchy and declares Commonwealth of 1649–1653.

1649: Milton appointed foreign secretary to Commonwealth by Parliament.

May 1649: Levellers' mutiny defeated.

1650: Diggers suppressed.

1649–51 Hobbes in exile with royalists in Paris, writes *Leviathan*, and returns to Commonwealth in England where it is published.

1653–1658: Oliver Cromwell's Protectorate succeeds Commonwealth after his conquests in Ireland and Scotland.

1654: Milton's *Defensio secunda* published for free discussion of truth.

1658: Cromwell dies, succeeded by son in 1658–1659.

1659–1660: Commonwealth resumed.

April 1660: Charles's Declaration of Breda from exile offers amnesty and liberty to "tender consciences," but both subject to Parliament agreeing.

May 1660: Restoration of Charles II. October: Regicides executed.

August 1662: *Act of Uniformity* restores Anglican bishops. In 1660–1662 non-Episcopalian priests ejected.

December 1662: Charles II's first Declaration of Indulgence.

1667: Locke enters service of Ashley, opponent of absolute monarchy, who later in 1672 became first Earl of Shaftesbury, and Locke writes for him his less known *Essay on Toleration*.

1672 and 1673: Charles II's Second Declaration of Indulgence, withdrawn on Parliament's insistence.

1673: Milton's *Of True Religion* published for tolerant discussion.

1673: Test Act on transubstantiation removes Catholics from Parliament for 150 years.

1675: Shaftesbury falls; Locke retreats to France.

1678: Shaftesbury returns to power and Locke rejoins his service.

1679: Hobbes dies.

1681: Shaftesbury is imprisoned. William Penn, Quaker, founds Pennsylvania with religious toleration, but not for Catholics.

1683: Locke retires to Holland.

1685–1688: James II reigns.

1687, 1688: James's First and Second Declarations of Indulgence.

1688: James flees to France. William of Orange from Holland invited to take Crown in peaceful "Glorious Revolution." Locke returns.

1689: Locke's first and second *Letter Concerning Toleration. Act of Toleration* excludes Catholics.

John Milton

John Milton (1608–1674) set out to be a poet, but he claimed in 1642, on the outbreak of the First Civil War, that considerations of conscience required him to turn to prose on political events.[11] The epic poems for which he is most famous, *Paradise Lost* and *Paradise Regained*, were postponed until after the restoration of the monarchy in 1660. The political writing of the intervening revolutionary period is full of references to conscience. Often the subject is freedom or oppression of conscience, although his advances in the field of freedom do not extend to Catholics or women. Milton studied from 1625, like so many others, in Christ's College, Cambridge, to become an Anglican priest, but the Anglicans had bishops and he switched for a time to the Presbyterians, whose priests were elected by congregations in a system derived from Calvin. By 1646, however, he finished his poem, "On the new forcers of conscience under the Long Parliament," by saying: "New *Presbyter* is but old Priest writ large," and thereafter he urged the independence of Church from State, as giving more room to individual conscience.

Two of Milton's first prose works were on subjects unusual at the time. In 1643, during the first Civil War, he published *The Doctrine and Discipline of Divorce*, with a second edition the following year. The matter of divorce in marriage should be left to the *conscience* of the master of the family, with the law only ensuring that the terms of divorce be just and equal. Christ had left the matter to conscience, and it was the popes who sought revenue and authority by taking over judgment for themselves.

11. Blair Worden, *God's Instruments: Political Conduct in the England of Oliver Cromwell*, Oxford University Press 2012, 356.

In 1644, still in the middle of the Civil War, he published *Areopagitica: A Speech for the Liberty of Unlicensed Printing*. He argued that at first, church councils and bishops only declared what books were not commendable, "leaving it to each one's *conscience* to read or to lay by." But eventually the popes and the Inquisition of the Roman Catholic Church extended laws of censorship further and further and increased the punishment for violations. He maintained it was more Christian that many be tolerated, rather than all compelled. But he also added the argument, not for the last time, that "the knowledge and survey of vice is in this world so necessary to the constituting of human virtue, and the scanning of error to the confirmation of truth"—a subject to which he returned. His idea about virtue was that true virtue has seen and rejected the supposed benefits of vice. In seeking toleration, he made an exception of the Roman Catholic Church: "I mean not tolerated Popery, and open superstition, which, as it extirpates all religions and civil supremacies, so itself should be extirpate, provided first that all charitable and compassionate means be used to win and regain the weak and the misled."

Within *two weeks* of the execution of Charles I in 1649, he defended the regicides and attacked monarchy in *The Tenure of Kings and Magistrates*. In his calls for liberty of conscience, he was talking about freedom of religion, and it was priests that he more often described as *oppressors of conscience*, although he included at least one monarch, Mary Tudor, and certainly had in mind Charles I as well. Later that year, in *Eikonoklastês* on the image of the late king, he complained that the king had tried to make his *private conscience* into "a *universal conscience*, the whole kingdom's conscience," wording suggestive of what Hobbes was to recommend for his sovereign two years later. Also in 1649, Milton was appointed by Parliament as foreign secretary to the Commonwealth, which made use of his command of Latin and foreign languages, although from 1653 his increasing blindness was to limit his role. In February 1650, in *The Ready and Easy Way to Establish a Free Commonwealth and the Excellence Thereof, Compared with the Inconveniences and Dangers of Readmitting Kingship in This Nation*, he argued that only a free commonwealth, not a monarchy, could provide liberty of *conscience*.

In 1652 he wrote a sonnet to Oliver Cromwell with some admonitions and in 1654, after Cromwell had become Lord Protector of England, he defended him in his *Pro populo anglicano defensio secunda*. Cromwell and the king's opponents, he said, took up arms only in order to defend the laws and the rights of *conscience*. He further urged Cromwell to "permit the free discussion of truth without any hazard to the author, or any subjection to the caprice of an individual," and anticipated the rationale better known from J. S. Mill in the nineteenth century, by adding, "which is the best way to make truth flourish and knowledge abound." This repeats, or is at least in the same spirit as, the argument of the *Areopagitica*, that the scanning of error is necessary to the *confirmation* of truth. Immediately next, he urged Cromwell not to dread hearing any truth or falsehood, but to listen least to those who think they cannot be free until they have fettered the minds of others.

In 1659, after the death of Oliver Cromwell, in *A Treatise of Civil Power in Ecclesiastical Causes*, he urged the new Supreme Council established by Cromwell's son to remember that any law against *conscience* might at a later date be turned against their own conscience. He also used an argument from *ignorance*. It was the main foundation of Protestant religion, he said, that there was no external authority but Holy Scripture, and no internal authority but the Holy Spirit interpreting that scripture only to ourselves, about whose presence we cannot be certain. So "no man . . . can judge definitively the sense of scripture to another man's conscience, which is well known to be a maxim of the Protestant religion." Christ accused the Pharisees of forcing the conscience that was not to be forced.[12] The law could do this under Moses, but may no longer under the Gospel. Against Catholics he used the invalid argument that because Catholic conscience was enthralled to a human, the Pope, it was not enthralled to God and so almost became no conscience.

He had by this time become disillusioned with rule by one man, whether it was Cromwell or a king. With extraordinary daring, early in 1660, he went on writing against monarchy or rule by one man to within a few weeks of the return of Charles II as king. In an enlarged edition of *The Ready and Easy Way to Establish a Free Commonwealth* in 1660, he said that monarchy was anti-Christian. Upon the Restoration of the monarchy in 1660 a number of those who had supported the execution of Charles I were hanged, drawn, and quartered, and Milton, already blind, went into hiding for sixteen weeks. In the event, he suffered only brief imprisonment and a fine, and the House of Commons called for two of his books to be burned. This was the period when he wrote *Paradise Lost* and his other epics. He returned to political prose only in 1673, the year before his death, with *Of True Religion*, in which he argued that one of the safeguards against Popery was to

12. Matthew 23:23.

tolerate other opinions, hear them patiently, and examine them. Moreover, to repeat for a third time the argument about the best *route to truth,* he urged that reading controversies sharpens judgment and confirms truth already recognized. Again the usual exception is made. If the Roman Catholics complain that we violate their *consciences,* we are not in this matter warranted to regard conscience that is grounded on authority instead of Scripture.

In these texts, Milton had gone beyond Roger Williams, who connected freedom of conscience with *religious* belief and practice. Rather unusually, Milton had connected it also with more secular matters, freedom in the husband's decision on divorce, and freedom to publish and read.

The Levellers

The Levellers were one of the most interesting groups in the history of British democracy. Drawn from the New Model Army which defeated Charles I, they engaged in several days of open debate with Oliver Cromwell, a commander of that army, and its commissary-general, his son-in-law, Henry Ireton. The debates were held first at Putney between October 28th and November 1st, 1647, and then in Whitehall on December 14th, 1648, and January 8th–11th and 13th, 1649. At Putney in 1647, the Levellers, led by Thomas Rainborough, called for democratic reforms. Some of the reforms demanded then or later were not to be instituted for three centuries, if then: suffrage for all freeborn, including women, and parliaments whose power would be constrained by lasting for only two years. It was at that time not Parliament, dominated by Presbyterians, but the army, which guaranteed a wider share of liberty. Parliament in 1647 tried to dismiss the New Model Army they had appointed without back pay, and alarmed at its continuing power, sought an accommodation with Charles I. The debates closest to our subject were those of 1648–1649 at Whitehall on a different subject—freedom of *conscience* in religion. The Levellers argued for freedom for everyone in religious belief and practice in opposition to those Presbyterians in Parliament who were seeking a compulsory national Presbyterian Church controlled by the State. Cromwell and Ireton, like John Milton, took a middle position, and were known as Independents. They wanted religious toleration within limits.

The debates are remarkable, among other things, for the speakers' appeals to their consciences. How did Cromwell and Ireton reply? Did they insist on their army rank? On the contrary, Cromwell, as much as Rainborough, claimed to be speaking according to his conscience, and affirmed that he too must be allowed liberty of conscience, while Ireton also claimed the right of conscience.[13] The debates read as if Cromwell was at first taking the Levellers' proposals very seriously. But in the event he reneged to a large extent, which led in 1649, within two years of the first debates, to the Levellers' mutiny and military defeat by Cromwell.

In the Whitehall debates, thorny questions were raised by the Independent side. For the Levellers, Captain Clarke used the old "ineffective" argument: one *cannot* change one's opinions, so should be left free in religion. For the other side, Philip Nye sought to discredit appeal to freedom of conscience by referring to a bigamist sent for execution to Newgate prison, who had pleaded for bigamy as something encouraged by his conscience.[14] Ireton canvassed an issue which had earlier been raised by Luther and Calvin: how far and in what sense the New Testament replaced the Old, either in ceremonial and judicial laws or in moral laws. As regards the moral laws, Luther had insisted on the importance of teaching the Ten Commandments, but no longer as law which terrifies the conscience. Calvin had considered that magistrates must enforce the Ten Commandments, but on the ground that St. Paul's Law engraved in our minds is a "testimony" of the natural law.[15] In the debates, Ireton conceded that some of the laws which magistrates had to enforce in the Old Testament ceased to be valid with the coming of Christ. But, in conformity with Calvin, he argued that magistrates should enforce even the first four of the Ten Commandments, the ones then under discussion, which concerned God and religion, because there is "testimony" for them which men can judge through what is written in their hearts and he appealed to the light of nature. For the Levellers, John Goodwin replied in part that Ireton's case depended not directly on the light of nature, but on inferences from it.[16]

In the earlier Putney debates, Ireton had raised an alarm: "All the main thing that I speak for is that I would have an eye to property." If Rainborough says that there is an equal right of nature to vote, then will there not be an equal right of nature to take the property of others, and even remove all property? Rainborough replied that the Ten Commandments include a law of God, "thou shalt not steal," which would prevent removing property, yet

13. The contemporary record of the debates, with analysis and other relevant documents and literature is supplied by A. S. P. Woodhouse, *Puritanism and Liberty: Being the Army Debates (1647–9) from the Clarke Manuscripts*, Dent and Sons, London, last available of three eds., 1938/1986. For Cromwell's appeals to his conscience, see pp. 8, 76, 78, 85, 97; for Ireton's p. 77.

14. A. S. P. Woodhouse, *Puritanism and Liberty*, 146.

15. Luther *Commentary on Galatians* (1535) 2.21; Calvin, *Institutes of Christian Religion* (1536), bk. 4, ch. 20.

16. A. S. P. Woodhouse, *Puritanism and Liberty*, 154–59.

at the same time the law of God does not deal with particulars, and so has nothing that either side can cite about the right to a *particular* property.[17]

Immediately after the Putney debates in December 1648, John Lilburne, perhaps the best known of the Levellers, took a new course: an *Agreement of the People* which he proposed to Cromwell should be drawn up. His own published version of the agreement announced the dissolution of the current Parliament by April 1649, and its replacement by "representatives of the people."[18] But one clause, number 7, particularly concerned freedom of conscience. His original intention was, with army support, to gain the backing of regiments and of people in the country, and then to impose the agreement on the current Parliament. After learning that Ireton and the army had, contrary to his intention, submitted their own rewritten version to Parliament, he published his own second draft on December 16, 1648, as "Second Agreement of the People." He claimed that his draft conformed to what had been agreed, except—on one point—by Ireton. Clause 7 on freedom of conscience had three parts, the second concerning freedom from military conscription. Firstly, the people's representatives (who were to succeed the present Parliament) must allow worship in accordance with conscience, though at their discretion they could offer the nation public direction in religion, provided it was noncompulsive and not in support of Popery or Anglicanism ("Prelacy"). Secondly, they could not press-gang people into war, if war, or even that *particular* war, was against their consciences. Thirdly, there should be an amnesty for all except those whom the present Parliament chose to punish for supporting the king. This second part expands the idea of freedom of conscience to conscientious objection to war.[19]

Besides debates and proposed agreements, a further medium of Leveller influence was the publication of innumerable pamphlets from printing presses that could never be stopped, and of books.[20] Two important ones had been produced before the two years of particular political prominence.

17. Ibid., 61–62

18. Provision was made for new representatives of the people to be elected, from newly mapped constituencies, with rules extending the vote to the poor and restricting eligibility to stand for election, duration of office, and scope of permitted legislation. It restricted the use of lawyers and introduced local arbitration tribunals. This last would have pleased Gandhi, who saw the law as a form of violence and advocated arbitration tribunals.

19. A. S. P. Woodhouse, *Puritanism and Liberty*, 361–62. A refinement of the first part of clause 7 was given in Lilburne's *Final Agreement of the people*, recorded in note 26. See also Lilburne's *History of the Second Agreement*, pp. 342–55.

20. Both the books I mention are discussed by H. N. Brailsford, *The Levellers and the English Revolution*, Cresset Press, London 1961, at pp. 55–56 and 66–67.

In 1645, Richard Overton published *The Arraignment of Mr Persecution*, whose style is thought to have influenced John Bunyan's *Pilgrim's Progress*. He makes very good use of an argument from *ignorance*: we ourselves learn only by degrees, and what we once believed we may later look back on as heresy, so we should not persecute others for their ignorance. The next year, 1646, William Walwyn, whom Lilburne had unsuccessfully nominated to draw up *The Agreement of the People*, contributed one of his series of pamphlets, *A Whisper in the eare of Mr Edward Thomas, Minister*. This was a reply to a defender of the proposal to form a compulsory national Presbyterian Church. Walwyn used the argument that persecution over beliefs is *ineffective*, because threatened victims will proffer *hypocritical* assent. In his *The Compassionate Samaritaine* of 1644, he had used the argument from *ignorance*: "The uncertainty of knowledge in this life: no man, nor no sort of men can presume of an unerring spirit. . . . Since there remains a possibility of error, notwithstanding never so great presumptions of the contrary, one sort of men are not to compel another, since this hazard is run thereby, that he who is in an error, may be the constrainer of him who is in the truth." I pick out these themes because they keep recurring in the history of the subject. A different version of the argument from *ignorance* is found in Milton and other versions later in Locke and Bayle. Walwyn's argument on *ineffectiveness* and *hypocrisy* we have found mentioned by St. Augustine as a view he had abandoned, and again by Luther, and below we shall see that Hobbes, Locke, and Bayle made different uses of the "ineffective" and "hypocrisy" arguments.

Disillusioned by Cromwell's backtracking on their discussions, the Levellers mutinied and were defeated by Cromwell and Fairfax. Of them 340 were imprisoned in 1649 in the church at Burford in Oxfordshire, and three of them shot outside. The movement had lasted little more than five years.

Thomas Hobbes and Oliver Cromwell

Thomas Hobbes (1588–1679) was almost opposite to the Levellers in his treatment of conscience. He was also aligned not with the Stoics, who saw humans as naturally sociable, but with the Epicureans, who saw humans as naturally competitive, and as entering into social relations only by a contract, in order to avoid the dangers of uncontrolled competition. The need for a sovereign should not depend on the idea of a divine right of kings. A sovereign is needed in order to provide the security sought in the social contract. He offered his most famous defense of sovereignty in the *Leviathan*, which was written in the two years 1649–1651, starting immediately after the execution of Charles I. It might be supposed that it was a defense of the monarchy. For Hobbes had taught the son of Charles I, later to become Charles II. He was in exile with the Royalists in France and gave a copy of *Leviathan* to the future Charles II. But a recent book has stressed that Charles did not like the work and the Royalists thought Hobbes a traitor. Hobbes returned from France to England and published *Leviathan* in English in London, when Cromwell was in the ascendant. In fact, the work served at least as much as a defense of Cromwell's later position from 1653 as Lord Protector as it did of Stewart kingship. When the monarchy was restored in 1660, Hobbes, it is said, had to destroy some of his papers and protest that he was indeed a Royalist.[21]

Hobbes drew remarkable conclusions about private conscience. Using a false etymology, he argued that the word gained respect because originally it was applied to a co-witnessed fact. But then it passed through two stages which he takes to be inferior. Most unusually, he correctly identifies what I have taken to be the original meaning, but as a meaning which came second. People applied the term to knowledge of their own personal secrets. Finally, in the most decadent stage of all, they used it of their own private *opinions*, however absurd.[22] This private conscience is to be obeyed only where there is no civil law: that is, in the state of nature before any social contract. Once there is a contract, private conscience can be followed only where the sovereign has not laid down a law, or by the sovereign himself. In a commonwealth the law is the *public* conscience by which people have undertaken to be guided, and it is a mistake to consider it a sin to disobey private conscience there. The view of Peter Abelard, Thomas Aquinas, and much of the Latin Middle Ages is thus rejected. On the contrary, following such private opinions disintegrates the commonwealth.[23] Just as God gave positive commands to Abraham to pass as civil sovereign to his family, so members of a commonwealth are to obey the laws of their sovereign about the outward acts and practice of religion. As for inner beliefs, they are neither voluntary nor knowable to human governors. So there need be no fear that sovereignty can remove private *belief*.[24]

21. Jeffrey Collins, *The Allegiance of Thomas Hobbes*, Oxford University Press 2005.

22. *Leviathan*, ch. 7, ed. Richard Tuck, p. 48. The three stages are clearly distinguished by Mark Hanin, "Thomas Hobbes' theory of conscience," *History of Political Thought*, vol. 33, 2012, pp. 55–85. Cf. *The Elements of Law Natural and Politic*, pt. 2, ch. 25.12: "The conscience being nothing else but a man's settled judgment and opinion."

23. *Leviathan*, ch. 29, ed. Tuck, p. 223.

24. *Leviathan*, ch. 40, ed.Tuck, p. 323.

This is an opposite use of the "hypocrisy" argument to that we have so far encountered. It was there considered a danger that untrammeled sovereignty would lead to persecution for religious belief, as it so often had. Hobbes is maintaining that no such danger need exist. Even if a sovereign were to command us to say with our tongue that we do not believe in Jesus Christ, we can do so, for "profession with the tongue is but an external thing": a sentiment already deployed by Euripides in a play repeatedly cited in chapter 1.[25] What the sovereign cannot do is prevent us by command from actually *believing*.[26] The sovereign is thus apparently satisfied with what the traditional argument considered *hypocrisy*.

Why is Hobbes interested in stressing that the sovereign is not interfering with *belief*? It is surely connected with his having just identified private conscience in this decadent age with mere *opinion*. But it was seen from chapter 1 onward that conscience from the beginning had involved belief not merely about the truth of theological ideas, but about what it had been, or would be, *wrong* for one to do (e.g., to gainsay one's beliefs). Conscience thus had always concerned *action* as well as belief, and it had always applied to one's *own* action. Conscience can therefore be oppressed not only by punishing belief, but also by punishing *action*. Hobbes admits that in the state of nature *actions* can be contrary to conscience, when he speaks of what a man *does* in the state of nature often being against his conscience.[27] Why then does he allege that conscience has now become a mere opinion? If he wants to convince the sovereign's subjects that their conscience is not being violated, he will need to convince them not merely that the sovereign cannot interfere with theological belief, but also that he will not interfere with beliefs of conscience such as that it would be wrong for them to deny their theological beliefs, the fault once known as apostasy.

But it may be thought that he is not trying to convince them that their conscience is left free, but merely pointing out that his sovereign will not, like many rulers, persecute them in addition with a view to changing their beliefs *as well as* their actions. That would certainly be a mercy. He spares them persecution for belief, because he accepts the argument that Augustine abandoned, that it would not be *effective*: "As for the inward *thought* and *beleef* (sic) of men, which humane government can take no notice of, (for God onely knoweth the heart), they are not voluntary, nor the effect of the laws,

25. Euripides, *Hippolytus* 380–87: Told in confidence of his stepmother's guilty love for him, Hippolytus says of his promise not to speak, "My tongue swore, but my mind is unsworn," lines 656–60.

26. *Leviathan*, ch. 42, ed. Tuck, p. 343.

27. *Leviathan*, ch. 29, ed. Tuck p. 223. I thank Dennis Klimchuk for the point.

but of the unrevealed will, and of the power of God; and consequently fall not under obligation."[28] If Hobbes had come to share Augustine's second thoughts, that a little bit of persecution can redirect belief, he would have lost the stated motive for this concession. But he has extra arguments which he offers to the sovereign and to pastors. He warns the sovereign that it is against natural law to try to force a man to accuse himself of opinions, when his actions are compliant.[29] He also opposes pastors excommunicating people over every small controversy of faith, as creating a needless burden of conscience,[30] although he adds no sanction to deter zealous pastors. If he intends to concede that his sovereign is violating conscience in the matter of actions, how does he intend to persuade subjects to accept the violation? He will still have the argument that the sovereign alone supplies the security that the subjects need, which in turn rests on his preferring the Epicurean view that what is natural for humans is mutual hostility over the Stoic view that what is natural is amicability. His further view that the security of a commonwealth requires rule by one man was, of course, the opposite of the conclusion to which Milton came. It would be difficult to persuade subjects that such violation of conscience was a necessary price for security, which is why he may have been trying to convince them that their consciences were not being violated. But, on the account of conscience so far encountered, that claim would also be unpersuasive to them.

It is remarkable that Oliver Cromwell offered this very misrepresentation of what people mean by conscience, in his refusal to allow celebration of mass in Catholic Ireland in 1649, the same year as his suppression of the Levellers. This suggests that he may have so interpreted Hobbes's picture of the sovereign's rights and applied it, at least in this case, to himself. Rejecting the attempt by the governor of New Ross to include freedom of conscience in the terms of surrender, he wrote, "I meddle not with any man's conscience." His letter reads as follows:

> For the Governor in Ross: These:
> Before Ross, 19th October 1649.
> SIR, . . .
>
> For that which you mention concerning liberty of conscience, I meddle not with any man's conscience. But if by liberty of conscience you mean

28. *Leviathan*, ch. 40. For Augustine's view in 408 CE, see ch. 3 above.
29. *Leviathan*, ch. 46, ed. Tuck, p. 471.
30. *Leviathan*, ch. 42, ed. Tuck, p. 351.

> liberty to exercise the Mass, I judge it best to use plain dealing, and to let you know, where the Parliament of England have power, that will not be allowed of.

The mistake of Cromwell has been repeated in modern times, but in connection with freedom of *religious* belief, rather than of conscience. The US Supreme Court in *Reynolds v. United States* in 1878 confirmed the conviction of a Mormon for exercising his religious belief in polygamy, arguing that the First Amendment of the Constitution protected his belief, but not his practice.[31]

The Quakers and Diggers

The Quakers appeared on the scene only in the 1650s after most of the events so far described had happened, and at first they appeared in a form far less socially acceptable than they subsequently attained.[32] They relied on an inner light to guide them, and James Nayler (1618–1660) was as prominent a leader as George Fox (1624–1691). Nayler rode into Bristol in 1656 in the manner of Christ on a donkey with women strewing the path before him. He was convicted of blasphemy by Parliament, pilloried, flogged, branded, pierced through the tongue, and imprisoned for two years. Various other Quakers went naked except for a loin cloth, or said that the Bible was not the word of God. Even George Fox interrupted services, and denounced Protestant ministers who took tithes or a salary as hireling priests and churches as steeplehouses. Their recruiting led to fights, and also brought into the movement Ranters after they were suppressed in 1650–1651 for denying many of the doctrines of Christianity. Lilburne, the former Leveller, also joined the Quakers in 1655. John Locke, we shall see, criticized the Quakers on civil grounds, because their refusal to take off their hats encouraged disrespect for magistrates. So too might their addressing everyone in the familiar second person singular as "thou." The refusal to take oaths was tolerated by Locke in his late work in the case of Quakers, though not in the

31. *Reynolds v United States* 98 U.S. 145, 164 (1878), a case cited by Michael Sandel, *Democracy's Discontent*, 58.

32. I draw particularly on Christopher Hill's famous book, *The World Turned Upside Down: Radical Ideas during the English Revolution*, Maurice Temple Smith 1972 and Penguin 1975, not only for the Levellers, but also on ch. 10 for the Quakers and on ch. 7 of his *A Turbulent Seditious and Factious People: John Bunyan and his Church*, Oxford University Press 1988, published under the title *A Tinker and a Poor Man: John Bunyan and his Church, 1628–1688*, Knopf 1989.

case of atheists,[33] presumably because Quakers had the different ground that even their ordinary promises were true. Even Roger Williams criticized the Quakers for their heckling and wrote *George Fox Digged Out of His Burrowes* in 1676. The Baptist John Bunyan (1628–1688) was less accommodating to them. In *Grace Abounding* (1666),[34] he accused them of eight heretical views hardly compatible with Christianity. As a result of their early reputation, more than a century later in 1793 Immanuel Kant understood that they might be atheists.[35] It is not surprising that Quaker Acts were introduced in 1662, two years after the restoration of the monarchy, requiring the taking of lawful oaths and forbidding Quakers to assemble outside their houses in groups of more than five. It has been estimated that fifteen thousand were put in prison and 450 died there. Under the very severe persecution, their consciences were still guided by the inner light.

Nonetheless, the Quakers reacted under George Fox by getting rid of Ranters and other undesirables from their ranks. Already in 1661 the first statement of pacifism had been issued, in order to ward off charges of sedition. As pacifism grew within the movement, it succeeded in making Quakerism more acceptable, because less of a threat to the authorities. There was less emphasis on the individual's inner light and conscience, and more concern with agreed principles. An asset was the membership from 1666 of William Penn (1644–1718), the founder of Pennsylvania. His charters for the State from 1681 to 1701 benefited Catholics as well as Quakers by extending freedom of worship to all who believed in one God. Penn criticized Ranter disunity, and argued for more central authority for Quakers. In 1681 he wrote in his *A Brief Examination and State of Liberty Spiritual* that they could not afford to wait for a motion of the spirit for everything. On the other hand, the Quakers did keep the idea that within each congregation an agreed sense of the meeting within Quaker principles should be discovered and followed. They might be thought to have found a middle way between the random following of different individual consciences and the reimposition of priestly power over congregations.

There had been an earlier pacifist movement, the Diggers, under Gerrard Winstanley (1609–1676), but it was connected with a belief in sharing land to grow produce among the poor. The Diggers were in both respects unlike

33. First *Letter Concerning Toleration*, translated by William Popple, ed. Tully, p. 51, in David Wootton, *John Locke: Political Writings*, Hackett 2003, 426.

34. Sec. 124.

35. Vigilantius' notes on Kant's lectures of 1793 on *Metaphysics of Morals*, translated by Peter Heath in Peter Heath and J. B. Schneewind, eds., *Lectures on Ethics*, Cambridge University Press 1997, p. 327.

the Levellers, who were army men and believed in private property, albeit more equitably distributed. The Diggers camped on the land together, and got their name because they dug unused private or common land to grow and share the produce. It was this, not the pacifism, which led to their suppression by Fairfax, commander in chief of the New Model Army. Their digging was very short-lived, lasting from 1649 to 1650, but Winstanley's writing and ideas had a longer life.[36] Winstanley said that everyone had a teacher within, the Father or Creator, and he himself had a trance in which he heard a voice saying, "Eat together. Work together." Some of his ideas came to be shared later by the Quakers. He banned not only the use of arms, but also the taking of oaths, and he would not take his hat off to Fairfax. His refusal to employ a defense lawyer, as well as his refusal to take up arms would have pleased Gandhi, had he known about him, and he has been more widely compared with Gandhi especially for his belief that God and the truth could be found in anyone, and his value-laden conception of nature.[37]

Part 2 from 1660

John Locke

John Locke (1632–1704) was one of the most influential defenders of freedom of conscience, but he did not start out that way, and even in one of his last and best known works he also raised some daunting questions. A certain intolerance is shown in Locke's two early *Tracts*, written in English in 1660 and in Latin in 1661, but neither of them published. They were written in the immediate wake of the interregnum and of its many demands for freedom of conscience, which Locke considers often inappropriate. The title of the two tracts picks out a very particular subject: *Question: whether the civil magistrate may lawfully impose and determine the use of indifferent things in reference to religious worship*. Locke regarded the outward form of Christian worship as being of itself a matter of *indifference*, since *it was not laid down by divine law*. The principal magistrate of all the people was entitled, according to the *Tracts*, to require or prohibit any indifferent action for the purpose of public order or safety. The monarchy had just been restored with Charles II in 1660, and people were waiting to see whether Parliament would impose

36. George H. Sabine, ed., *The Works of Gerrard Winstanley with an Appendix of Documents*, Russell and Russell 1941.

37. Akeel Bilgrami, "Gandhi the philosopher," *Economic and Political Weekly* 38, 2003, 4159–65; repr. in *Secularism, Identity and Enhancement*, Harvard University Press 2014.

a single compulsory form of worship. Philip Abrams as translator of the Latin Tract suggests that the two *Tracts* remained unpublished because Parliament did in 1661 make the Anglican form of worship mandatory for priests.

In the first tract, despite using the conciliatory language of Charles I and saying that all agree conscience is to be "tenderly" dealt with and not to be *imposed on*,[38] he immediately goes on to argue that some actions are *indifferent* and adds[39] that it is wrong to think it an *imposition* for the magistrate to determine *indifferent* outward action, contrary to a man's persuasion. He acknowledges that conscience is an opinion that concerns *action*, when he says: "conscience being nothing but an opinion of the truth of any practical proposition, which may concern any *actions* as well moral as religious, civil as ecclesiastical" (my italics). He repeats the reference to action in the second tract, we shall see, by calling the law of conscience a judgment about things to be *done* in life.[40] He also recognizes that the sovereign's restrictions on action *bind* consciences, because they impose a duty. But none of this, in his view, means that these restrictions *impose on* conscience.

As a further example of restrictions that do not impose, he holds that Quakers should be required to show respect to a magistrate by taking their hats off, contrary to their belief in equal respect for all. This, he says, does not impose on their conscience—and here he gives a narrow definition not of conscience, but of *imposing* on conscience. *Imposing*, he says, is the pressing of laws upon belief or practice as if they were divine laws, necessary to the individual's salvation and obliging the conscience *directly of themselves*, rather than in some indirect or other way (e.g., because the magistrate has commanded them). The magistrate could presumably also require further actions of Quakers, since they are indifferent by Locke's criterion of not being prohibited by divine law. For example, the magistrate could presumably violate the Quaker belief, which Locke later respected, that oaths should not be sworn because all Quaker statements should be equally true, and that meetings should start in silence with no officiating priest appointed, so that on equal terms anyone moved by the inner light could offer a comment to the general sense of the meeting. Interference with provision for attending to the inner light would be a particular form of interference with the guidance of conscience. Locke also refers back to the political ground

38. First Tract, ed. Philip Abrams, under the title of John Locke's *Two Tracts on Government*, Cambridge University Press 1967, p. 138.

39. First Tract, ed. Philip Abrams, *Two Tracts on Government*, 138–39.

40. Second Tract, *Two Tracts on Government*, Abrams's translation from Latin, 225.

for the magistrate's need to bind conscience, with a dig at rival claims for freedom of conscience. The magistrate should restore peace and prevent society being torn to pieces by quarrels over these issues by "everyone that could pretend to conscience and draw a sword."[41]

The second tract adds that liberty of conscience is preserved, because the magistrate does not require the assent of the *judgment* that his law has any necessity independent of his commanding it. The magistrate does thus bind the conscience to *act*, but not to *judge* that it binds by divine law,[42] and conscience is *directly* bound only by divine law. Other laws bind only indirectly, by being *grounded* on divine law. For example, we are bound to obey magistrates in matters of indifference by a text of St. Paul, Romans 13:1–5, which says that we must obey government, because it is instituted by God, and it acts as the servant of God in opposing resistance with wrath and the sword. We must obey not only because of the wrath, but also because of *conscience*, because it is God's institution. Thus conscience is presented as being on the side of obedience, not disobedience, in matters which are in themselves indifferent, and so not prohibited by divine law. The present passage recalls also the political rationale for the magistrate's powers, when it says that a vow or private error of conscience cannot nullify the edicts of the magistrate, or the order of society would collapse.[43] It is further explained that a law is obligatory if the magistrate calls for indifferent religious ceremonies in the mere *belief* that it leads to public welfare and order.[44] The reiterated attacks on those who during the interregnum stirred up strife under the slogan of conscience[45] do not repudiate conscience itself. On the contrary, conscience is enhanced as being in effect an inner legislator using the light of nature implanted in our hearts by God: "The law of conscience we call that fundamental judgment of the practical intellect concerning any possible truth of a moral proposition about things to be *done* in life. God implanted the light of nature in our hearts and willed that there should be an inner legislator (in effect) constantly present in us whose edicts it should not be lawful for us to transgress even a nail's breadth."[46]

Locke's next work on the subject, *An Essay Concerning Toleration* (1667), also remained unpublished and, unlike his *Letters* on the subject, received

41. First Tract, ed. Philip Abrams, *Two Tracts on Government*, 162.
42. Second Tract, *Two Tracts on Government*, Abrams's translation from Latin, 239.
43. Ibid., Abrams's translation from Latin, 225–27.
44. Ibid., Abrams's translation from Latin, 237–38.
45. Ibid., Abrams's translation from Latin, 211–12; 237–38.
46. Ibid., Abrams's translation from Latin, 225.

no critical edition until 2006.[47] But for the first time it reveals his interest in toleration, within limits. It may at the time have been seen only by his employer. In that year, after much intolerance from Anglican bishops and Parliament in matters of religion, Locke entered the service of the future First Earl of Shaftesbury, who wanted a somewhat greater measure of tolerance, and later opposed the succession of James II for fear that his rule would be still more absolutist and Roman Catholic. The *Essay* already contains many of the ideas that appeared in Locke's series of *Letters* about toleration that were to be published beginning twenty-three years later in 1689. Locke's *Essay Concerning Toleration* included an argument anticipated by Thomas Helwys, the Baptist: the magistrate is not concerned with my *eternal salvation* for the whole of infinite time, which depends on my voluntary choice and is of more concern to me than is anything in his power. This could be used both to support the old "ineffectiveness" argument by reference to the individual's having insufficient motive to obey the magistrate, and to question the magistrate's having sufficient right to command the individual. My way to salvation through worship has to be a voluntary choice of my mind, not any exterior performance such as the magistrate can enforce. No consideration could be sufficient to force a man from that which he was fully persuaded was the way to infinite happiness, and those whose views were unchanged during the recent tumults can see this for themselves. Further, he argues, religious worship is the homage to God that I judge acceptable to him, and therefore has in its own nature no reference to the community and cannot disturb it.[48]

With the "ineffective" argument Locke combined the "hypocrite" argument. Compulsion from the magistrate, being ineffective in changing belief, can only produce hypocrites pretending belief—and, for that matter, enemies of the magistrate. The magistrate's concern is only the security of his people and preserving the peace, not the souls of men. On the other hand, if the magistrate does insist on people renouncing their opinions and assenting to the contrary, they should do what their consciences require and accept the penalties, thereby securing their happiness in the future world, and preserving the peace in this.[49]

47. J. R. and Philip Milton, eds., *John Locke: An Essay Concerning Toleration*, Oxford University Press 2006.

48. Ibid., 273–74; see for yourselves: p. 294.

49. Ibid., 278–81.

There are limits to toleration. Locke mentions the Quakers again, not, I think, as outstandingly heinous, but as clearly falling under the magistrate's jurisdiction. Compulsion, he repeats, may be acceptable for making them take off their hats, since the disrespect to the magistrate of their refusal could endanger government.[50] Moreover, Papists are not to be tolerated, because, once in power, they will deny toleration to others, and they can violate their obligations to their own prince because of blind allegiance to an infallible Pope who controls them by claiming to hold the keys of their consciences, which can determine their entry to heaven.[51]

Locke's *Two Treatises on Government* (as distinct from the two *Tracts*) were published in 1690, but it has been argued that publication was delayed, and that they were mostly written in 1679–1681, during the debate on excluding the future James II as heir to the throne. In his *Second Treatise on Government* Locke introduces, like Hobbes, a theory of social contract. The original state of nature had been one of war with power restricted only by conscience. In order to escape from this state, people made a contract to surrender their liberty.[52] But if they are once persuaded in conscience that laws, liberties, lives, and perhaps religion are in danger, they cannot be prevented from resisting such illegal force.[53]

In 1689, Locke's most famous contribution, his first *Letter Concerning Toleration*, was published in Latin and translated by William Popple into English. It is thought that the final draft was written in Holland where he had fled because of his opposition to the Catholic King James II. There in Rotterdam he met Pierre Bayle in 1686, a refugee from Louis XIV of France and from his persecution of the Huguenots, the French Calvinist Protestants earlier protected by Charles IV. Locke received Bayle's work on the subject of toleration published that year, *Philosophical Commentary on These Words of Jesus Christ "Compel Them to Come In,"* and had sent Bayle his own not-yet-published first *Letter* in Latin.

Much in the first *Letter Concerning Toleration* had been said by Locke before. At the beginning he offers three arguments for toleration. The first is that the civil ruler cannot rationally be given a mandate from people to choose their faith and worship for them, because of the point from the earlier unpublished *Essay Concerning Toleration* that it is not in his power to

50. Ibid., 286–87.
51. Ibid., 291.
52. Locke, *Second Treatise on Government*, secs. 19–21, 96–105.
53. Ibid., sec. 209.

secure for them the eternal salvation which depends on that choice of faith and worship. Second comes the ineffectiveness argument, that the ruler cannot induce by force the conviction that true (and, he adds, "saving") religion requires. Third, even if the ruler could change people's beliefs, he could not know which religion would give them salvation. This third is an additional argument based on our *ignorance* of who is right:

> If one of these churches hath this power of treating the other ill, I ask which of them it is to whom that power belongs, and by what right? It will be answered, undoubtedly, that it is the orthodox church which has the right of authority over the erroneous or heretical. This is, in great and specious words, to say just nothing at all. For every church is orthodox to itself; to others, erroneous or heretical. . . . The decision of that question belongs only to the Supreme judge of all men, to whom also alone belongs the punishment of the erroneous.[54]

Because the magistrate himself does not know the answer, if each one insists on his own church, only those few souls will be saved who happen to be born in the area whose magistrate has got it right.[55]

Locke calls the *principal consideration* the point found in Thomas Helwys, that I will not secure my own *salvation* if I conform against my conscience.[56] Such hypocrisy would even be an obstacle to salvation.[57] Indeed, salvation is mentioned in all three of his opening arguments, and its expanded role is a new feature of Locke's case. Locke further tries to define separate spheres for the magistrate and the religious search for eternal salvation.[58] He also

54. John Locke, *A Letter Concerning Toleration*, trans. William Popple, ed. J. Tully, Hackett 1983, p. 32; *Epistola de tolerantia, A Letter on Toleration*, ed. R. Klibansky, trans. J. W. Gough, Oxford University Press 1968, 80–83. I have learned about the relation of Locke, Proast, and Bayle particularly from Rainer Forst, "Pierre Bayle's reflexive theory of toleration," in Melissa S. Williams and Jeremy Waldron, eds., *Toleration and Its Limits*, New York University Press (*Nomos* 48) 2008, pp. 78–113. Jeremy Waldron's own "Locke: Toleration and the rationality of persecution" in Susan Mendus, ed., *Justifying Toleration: Conceptual and Historical Perspectives*, Cambridge University Press 1988, is a classic, reprinted also in her and John Horton eds, *John Locke: A Letter Concerning Toleration in Focus*, Routledge 1988, pp. 98–124.

55. Locke, *Letter Concerning Toleration*, ed. J. Tully, 28; *Epistola de tolerantia*, ed. R. Klibansky and trans. J. W. Gough, 70–71.

56. Locke, *Letter Concerning Toleration*, trans. William Popple and ed. J. Tully, Hackett, Indianapolis 1983, 38; or *Epistola de tolerantia*, ed. R. Klibansky and trans. J. W. Gough, 98–99.

57. Locke, *Letter Concerning Toleration*, ed. J. Tully, 27; *Epistola de tolerantia*, ed. R. Klibansky and trans. J. W. Gough, 68–69.

58. *Letter Concerning Toleration*, pp. 26–28, 42, 46–47, 48–49; *Epistola de tolerantia*, ed. R. Klibansky and trans. J. W. Gough, 64–71, 110–11, 122–23, 126–29.

reveals further limits to his toleration. He attacks subservience to an external authority—the Mufti of Constantinople may here stand for the Pope—as incompatible with obeying a Christian magistrate, and atheists are not to be tolerated at all.[59]

Within the same year, 1689, Locke had to write *A Second Letter Concerning Toleration* in reply to an Anglican priest, Jonas Proast. He would not have had to rewrite, if he had studied Augustine's letter of 408 CE. For Proast used the objection which Augustine had already recognized in the early fifth century, that compulsion may after all change one's beliefs indirectly by redirecting one's attention. This could happen both through the banning of books and through punishment. Hence compulsion can produce sincere change of belief instead of hypocrisy. This affects what Locke called his principal consideration, because it means that compulsion might give someone the sincere belief needed for his salvation. Locke tries to blunt the force of the objection, by shifting the weight of his case to his argument from *ignorance*. By this time he owned a copy of Bayle's treatise, which had put more weight on the argument from ignorance from the start. Men in the wrong way are to be punished, but the question is who are in the wrong way. Each of two differing parties has no more reason than the other to say, unless it can convince the other, in which case punishment becomes irrelevant. Fair debate should not presuppose the point at issue, that your church is right, which can no more be granted to you than it can to a Papist, Lutheran, Presbyterian, Anabaptist, or even Jew or "Mohametan."[60] Locke sought to blunt Proast's point, secondly, by saying that this good effect from political compulsion would not be general, whereas the persecution required to secure some cases of conversion would have to be very general.[61]

I have described some of Locke's arguments and Proast's objection to him as having been available in antiquity. Indeed his case reveals how much can be gained from the history of philosophy. But Jeremy Waldron has "excavated" some impressive and less well-known sentiments from Locke and from other Enlightenment writers—Bayle, Voltaire, and Diderot—objecting to hate speech and insisting on civility in disagreement. In antiquity this is

59. *Letter Concerning Toleration*, 50–51; *Epistola de tolerantia*, ed. R. Klibansky and trans. J. W. Gough, 134–35.

60. Locke, *Second Letter Concerning Toleration*, 1690, and *Third Letter for Toleration*, 1692, quoting the Second, in *The Works of John Locke*, 9th ed., printed for T. Longman et al., London 1794, vol. 5, e.g. pp. 89, 126, 418–19.

61. Locke, *Second Letter Concerning Toleration*, 1690, in *The Works of John Locke*, 9th ed., printed for T. Longman et al., London 1794, vol. 5, pp. 125–26.

sometimes found in the treatment of sinners, but more rarely in the treatment of heretics.

In his equally late publication, *An Essay Concerning Human Understanding* (1689), Locke is concerned with knowledge and he includes our knowledge of moral principles. He wishes to show that we have no innate ideas. Moral principles are not the same as conscience, which he does not mention here. But conscience draws on them, and so if they are unreliable, this puts a question over the reliability of conscience. In the *Essay*, he speaks as follows of moral principles: "Doctrines that have been derived from no better original than the superstition of a nurse, or the authority of an old woman, may, by length of time and consent of neighbors, grow up to the dignity of principles in religion or morality."[62] In earlier drafts B and C of 1671 and 1685 he speaks similarly, if less trenchantly. Draft C cites as a common source of moral rules not writing in the heart, but education, company, and customs.[63] This is a direct rejection of St. Paul's law written in our hearts. But Locke seems not to have recognized that, as explained in chapter 1, Paul's law is not innate and he thought our *knowledge* of it fallible, and that moreover two of the greatest church fathers, Origen and Augustine, warned that we do not read the law in our hearts at first and may fail to read it at all.

Locke attempted his own solution to the question how to gain knowledge of moral principles.[64] In 4.3.18, he considers that in principle "from self-evident propositions, by necessary consequences, as incontestable as those in mathematics, the measures of right and wrong might be made out, to anyone that will apply himself with the same indifferency and attention to the one as he does to the other of these sciences." As foundations of our duty and rules of action to place morality among the sciences capable of demonstration, he suggests two ideas that, in his view, are sufficiently clear for the purpose: the ideas of God and of ourselves as rational creatures. He does not mention traditional perplexities about these ideas: whether we might not form an idea not only of God, but also of an island or of anything else, making sure that the idea implied existence, without there *actually* being anything corresponding to our idea. Again, is there a sense in which all humans can be assigned rationality but no animals can be? The first of

62. John Locke, *Essay Concerning Human Understanding*, bk. 1, ch. 3, aec. 22, at least in the much approved 4th ed. of 1699 with imprint of 1700, the last printed in his lifetime.

63. Draft B. I thank John R. Milton for checking the drafts for me.

64. I am indebted to the comments of Elliot Rossiter, Ben Hill, and Lorne Falkenstein at the University of Western Ontario.

his two examples of demonstrable principles is equally startling: "'Where there is no property, there is no injustice' is a proposition as certain as any in Euclid." A second is "no government allows absolute liberty." But even if this were accepted, the problems would start when we asked what liberties should or should not be allowed. Locke himself grants that the project has not been *started*. His whole approach to improving the reliability of principles is entirely different from that which I shall advocate in chapter 12. The result of this is that although Locke has issued a trenchant warning that many consciences have no reliable basis at all, he has not supplied any convincing basis for his confidence about how this might be rectified.

Of course, even if consciences are unreliable, this does not damage the case for freedom of conscience. Indeed, one of Locke's best arguments for freedom of conscience is that none of us can know who is right. It had equally been an important feature of Roger Williams's position that he thought freedom of conscience should be defended, even when he thought the conscience in question was unreliable. Britain in 1916 exempted conscientious objectors from military service, regardless of whether their objection was erroneous. It was also the view of the US Supreme Court that it should not consider the moral value of a religious belief (and eventually of certain other conscientious beliefs), in deciding whether that belief earned exemption from such laws as military conscription, under the First Amendment to the US Constitution. The issue of defending the freedom of *erroneous* consciences had been treated more fully by Locke's contemporary, Pierre Bayle, and it raises difficult issues about the limits of freedom of conscience.

Pierre Bayle

Pierre Bayle (1647–1706) was a Protestant Hugenuot who fled to Holland from the persecution of Protestants by the Catholic Louis XIV of France, and wrote major works on freedom of conscience. The most famous was his *Philosophical Commentary on These Words of Jesus Christ "Compel Them to Come In"* of which the first two parts were published in 1686, the third in 1687, and a supplement in 1688. The reference was to Christ's parable in Luke 14:23 about summoning the poor to a feast after others had declined. It had been reapplied by Augustine to justify the coercion of religious dissenters. Bayle's brother had already died in prison, a victim of the "Convertists." Bayle used the argument that Locke had already employed many years earlier in his unpublished *Essay Concerning Toleration*, that religious adoration is incompatible with *hypocrisy*, and, again like Luther, Roger Williams, William Walwyn, and Locke, he spoke at first as if persecution was *ineffective* at producing anything, or anything more than hypocrisy.[65] But his *Philosophical Commentary* considered an admirable number of objections and, like Augustine but unlike Walwyn and Locke, he recognized that compulsion need not always produce hypocrisy, when he turned round and drew attention to "the only possible thing to be held against me." The objection that he foresaw was that although instruction was indeed the only *legitimate* means of securing conversion, nonetheless in order to put this means into practice, by removing *resistance* to instruction, violence might be needed as an *indirect* course for removing obstacles.[66]

For the present he had available a reply based on the idea of our *ignorance*. Different arguments from *ignorance* had already been used by Roger Williams, Milton and the Levellers Richard Overton, and William Walwyn. But Bayle put his in much the same terms as Locke was to use in his *Second Letter Concerning Toleration*. All persuasions believe that they are the true Church, and so they must not beg this question in their disputes.[67] Although everyone has the natural inner light of universal reason, we have to judge everything by our own private light. There is no infallibility here.[68] Bayle is less restrictive than Locke. Tolerance for one is tolerance for others, including Jews and Turks.[69] There are limits: atheists are tolerated, but not the *advocacy* of atheism. Papists should not be allowed to force the consciences of *others*. But that does not mean that we should try, as many countries do, to force them to change their religion. We need laws only to stop them meddling, and we should never ourselves force their conscience, enforcing or rewarding change of religion, nor should we prevent the private practice of their religion, and their teaching of it to their children. We should not abuse their persons, impair their prosperity, confiscate their property, or restrict their access to the law, but should merely prevent them disturbing the state.[70] Here he already anticipates his fallback position that freedom of conscience must be restricted for those whose conscience erroneously calls for persecution.

Not only is this more liberal than Locke, but he differed from Locke in other ways, producing an argument that has been called the "Reciprocity Ar-

65. *Pierre Bayle's Philosophical Commentary*, pt. 1, ch. 2, *Oeuvres diverses*, the Hague 1727–31, vol. 2, p. 171b, translated from French by Amie Godman Tannenbaum, Peter Lang 1987, pp. 35–36.

66. Bayle, *Philosophical Commentary*, pt. 1, ch. 2, Tannenbaum, p. 37.

67. *Preface*, pp. 13–14.

68. Pt. 1, ch. 1, Tannenbaum pp. 31, 33; pt. 2, ch. 10, sec. 4, Tannenbaum, p. 181.

69. Pt. 1, ch. 7, Tannenbaum p. 145.

70. Pierre Bayle, *Philosophical Commentary*, pt. 1, chs. 5 and 7, trans. Tannenbaum pp. 129, 147.

gument."[71] If "compel them to come in" was meant to create an obligation of conscience, since conscience always creates an obligation, partly because it is *interpreted* as (he does not say it *is*) the voice of God, there will be an obligation on every Christian heretic to compel the true church by persecution to come in to his heresy. Moreover, God will be partly responsible for the resulting strife between sects, because he will have foreseen the result of the compulsion supposedly advocated. The obligation on the heretic to persecute is not morally good, but it is always morally better to follow conscience than not. So Bayle recognizes a *moral double bind*, with a solution that is obligatory, but in this case outrageous. The Reciprocity argument is very relevant to the usual seventeenth-century view in England that Catholics cannot be tolerated, because if they returned to power, they would not be tolerant. To offer a simpler version, if the intolerance of them is based on the idea that the intolerant cannot be tolerated, Catholics would be right not to tolerate their intolerant opponents.

Because the subject matter of Bayle's work on "compel them to come in" is heretical doctrines, he uses the term "conscience" *both* for conscience as we have been thinking of it *and* for disputed theological doctrines about God which are matters of conscience in that people feel conscience-bound to live by them and to impose them on others, so that they too have implications for action. Bayle is not talking, like Hobbes, about theological doctrines *divorced* from practical implications. His extension of the term "conscience" is understandable, but for clarity I will distinguish the extended cases, though he does not, by calling them *matter-of-conscience doctrines*. Matter-of-conscience doctrines may include not only doctrines about God, but also moral principles like that in *Philosophical Commentary*, part 2, chapter 9, the erroneous principle that murder is a virtuous action.[72] He calls this an error of conscience, although I would rather have called it an error in the general principles which conscience applies to the particular case.

Bayle's initial thesis is that even an *erroneous* matter-of-conscience doctrine imposes an overriding obligation. He foresaw in his part 2 the objection that this principle could be turned against his toleration of erroneous conscience. For the erroneous consciences he was tolerating might indeed require people to suppress beliefs held as a matter of conscience by others. This paradox is the one he later described as "the most perplexing

71. John Kilcullen, *Sincerity and Truth: Essays on Arnauld, Bayle and Toleration*, Oxford University Press 1988. I take my account from Michael Hickson, "*Reductio ad malum*: Bayle's early skepticism about Theodicy," *Modern Schoolman* 88, 2012, pp. 201–21, esp. 213–19.

72. Pierre Bayle, *Philosophical Commentary*, pt. 2, ch. 9, Tannenbaum, pp. 165–66, cited to me by Hickson.

objection that can be put to me."[73] If it is God's will that even erroneous matter-of-conscience doctrines should impose an overriding obligation, then it is his will that sincere conscientious persecutors should persecute. But that creates the paradox that in the name of following conscience God requires heretics to compel others to transgress their own conscience. Bayle did not think that his own initial replies escaped the paradox, but he did not think either that paradox could be avoided by the use he rejected of "compel them to come in" to endorse persecution. He thought paradox inevitable for both sides and drew a different conclusion. I here follow recent work of high interest by Michael Hickson that takes us back to the philosopher, statesman, and orator Themistius of the fourth century discussed above in chapter 3.[74]

Bayle was still writing his *Entretiens de Maxime et de Thémiste* when he died in 1706. Hickson first establishes that the reference is to our Themistius. Reviewing in *Nouvelles de la République de lettres* an edition of Themistius, Bayle had said in the 1680s that Themistius persuaded the Emperor Valens to moderate his persecution of supporters of the (eventually victorious) Nicaean view that Christ was begotten of God, and was not merely his creation. One argument put to Valens, Bayle claims, was that each person captures only some part of the truth,[75] and God is pleased to humble humans to himself by making himself difficult to know.[76] In his most famous work, the *Dictionnaire historique et critique*, Bayle's article "Jovian," remark C, discusses the purpose of Themistius' praise of Jovian's anticipated toleration in his Oration 5, where one of the arguments, cited in chapter 3 above, was that God allows diversity of belief, and another that there is no one road to God, because that makes us more zealous in seeking him and makes us feel awe and astonishment at him. Bayle may have been going beyond Themistius, in his remarks on Oration 6 to Valens on the virtue of humanity (*philanthrôpia*), because that says no more on diversity than that while all lean on God, some do so more clearly, some more dimly.[77]

73. Pierre Bayle, *Philosophical Commentary*, pt. 2, in *Oeuvres diverses*, vol. 2, p. 430b, translated Tannenbaum pp. 166–67; *Supplement to Philosophical Commentary*, in *Oeuvres diverses*, vol. 2, 539b–540a.

74. Michael Hickson, "The message of Bayle's last title: providence and toleration in the *Entretiens de Maxime et de Thémiste*," *Journal of the History of Ideas* 71, 2009, 547–67.

75. A view, incidentally, accepted by Mahatma Gandhi.

76. Pierre Bayle, *Oeuvres diverses*, vol. 1, 178b–179a.

77. Themistius Oration 6, ed. Schenkel, 77c, translated in Peter Heather and David Moncur, *Politics, Philosophy and Empire in the Fourth Century: Select Orations of Themistius*, Liverpool University Press 2001, ch. 3, p. 188.

Bayle may also not have known the identity of Maximus, if, as Hickson suggests, he thought of the much earlier Maximus of Tyre, rather than the obscure Maximus the Platonist miracle- worker of Ephesus. Themistius wrote in defense of Aristotle against Maximus, who was on the side of Boethus (of Sidon). The Emperor Julian judged their opposed writings and gave his vote to Maximus.[78] Julian probably supported Maximus because he adored the Neoplatonist Iamblichus, himself reputed to be a miracle worker. A text which looks like the one described has been edited by Marwan Rashed in 2013 and translated by him into French from the manuscript surviving in Tashkent in Arabic translation of Themistius, *In Response to Maximus and Boethus*. It is about how to justify the second and third figures of Aristotle's syllogisms. Themistius, an excellent philosopher, appears to demolish Maximus, but Julian had studied under Themistius and probably disliked his pro-Aristotelian stance, since it was against the lofty spiritualism of Iamblichus. The distance between them is suggested by the rebuff he wrote to Themistius' encomium, in his *Letter to Themistius*.[79]

Hickson clarifies the moral that Bayle wishes to draw from the diversity of theological opinion, and presumably from the above-cited inevitability of insoluble paradox for rival views. He refers to Bayle's *Dictionnaire* 4, "Clarification on the Manichaeans" (638). People should tolerate each other's rival theological opinions on the Justice of God, because it is as true in the field of astronomy as in that of religious controversy that the one true opinion may seem the least probable. There were three theories of the planetary system, those in chronological order of Ptolemy, Tycho Brahe, and Copernicus, the first two of which assumed that the planets circled a stationary earth. It was known by Ptolemy's time in the second century CE that the planets appear closer to the earth and larger, or more distant and smaller, during the course of the year, and this had been accounted for by postulating epicycles (rotating orbits on rotating orbits) or eccentrics (orbits with a different center from the earth's center). But Copernicus' later idea that the earth moves round the sun was discredited for requiring a much larger increase or decrease in apparent planetary size than could be observed. It took the telescope to show that the greater increase and

78. Ammonius on Aristotle's *Prior Analytics* 31.17–22.

79. For details, see Peter Heather and David Moncur, *Politics, Philosophy and Empire*, 139–40; Simon Swain, *Themistius, Julian and Greek Political Theory under Rome*, Cambridge University Press 2013, 89–91, 132–179. Julian's letter denies that Aristotle would have wanted in an emperor the active life Themistius recommended, rather than a contemplative life.

diminution he required was actually observable, and so what had seemed to make Copernicus' theory implausible finished up by confirming it. In theological disputes, no equivalent of the telescope will become available, to enable us to find the one true account, and presumably to solve apparent paradox. Hence we should tolerate each other's rival doctrines, however unlikely they may seem. Error will then be confined to our doctrines about theology, but our conscience need not add the error of thinking that doctrinal error must be suppressed. The final motivation for toleration may then have been the prevention of irresoluble strife, rather than any right to freedom of conscience for its own sake. Conscientious belief in suppression of doctrine would not be given freedom. Toleration is a wider notion than freedom of conscience, which is only one of its motives, and here the motive was keeping the peace. But the appeal to toleration of theological doctrine for this motive was enough to uphold Bayle's original objection to the misuse of the words "compel them to come in."

Bayle was accused by Jurieu, in his *Droits des deux souverains* in 1687, of encouraging an attitude of *indifference* toward the correctness of one's own theological doctrine, since according to Bayle, conscience required one to live by one's doctrines, even if erroneous, and God would accept that you had thereby done your duty. But Bayle replied in the preface to his *Supplement to the Philosophical Commentary* that this was an unjustified criticism. He had already in part 2 of the *Philosophical Commentary* repeatedly urged that you must examine your theological doctrines, and were in conscience bound to try to get them right. It was only if you had made this examination that God would be content with you. He wrote for example, "This demonstrates necessarily that God proposes the truth to us in such a way that he leaves it to us to examine what he proposes, and to investigate whether it is indeed the truth. From which it follows that he demands no more of us than to examine and to investigate with diligence; and that he is content with us whenever we assent to those objects that appear to us true, and love them as gifts from heaven, after we have examined them to the best of our ability."[80] This view would have implications for your conscience, that you should not live by a theological doctrine without having examined it, and that you should not hastily criticize the theological doctrine of others until you had checked your own. Bayle thus contributes not only to the question of how

80. *Philosophical Commentary* pt. 2, ch. 10, sec. 3, in *Oeuvres Diverses*, vol. 2, p. 436b, translated also in Tannenbaum, pp. 178–79. I am indebted to Michael Hickson for drawing my attention to the controversy and to this quotation, and the next.

to make your *doctrines* more reliable, but also, within limits, to the question of how to make your *application* of them more reliable.

Early in the *Philosophical Commentary* he discusses moral principles (the ones on which conscience draws), as opposed to the speculative truths which I have been calling doctrines, and he recommends a method for rising above personal interest and local custom in assessing them. Passion and the force of custom are obstacles to recognizing the natural light (meaning conscience):

> To avoid these two obstacles, I should want a man, if he wishes to know the natural light distinctly in relation to morals, to rise above his personal interest and the custom of his country and ask the following in general. Is such and such a thing just? And if it was a matter of introducing it into a country where it was not in use, and where he would be free to take it up or not, would one see upon a cold examination that it was sufficiently just to deserve adoption? I think this act of abstraction would dissipate a number of clouds which sometimes intrude between our mind and that primitive and universal light that emanates from God to show to all men the general principles of equity. It would thus be the touchstone for all precepts and for all individual laws without exception, even for those which God reveals to us directly by extraordinary means, either by speaking himself into our ears, or by sending us prophets inspired by him.[81]

It looks as if, in Bayle's view, God proposes to us through prophets or direct messages only enough to give some imperfect part of the truth for us to examine further, which is all that Themistius supposed we have and is also all we have in astronomy. This increases our fallibility far beyond mistakes in applying, or failures in reading, a complete law written in our hearts.

Spinoza

Spinoza (1632–1677) was excommunicated at the age of twenty-three from the Jewish community in Amsterdam in 1656, having opposed a rabbi on the fundamentals of Jewish religion the previous year. On a recent account,[82]

81. *Philosophical Commentary* pt. 1, ch. 1, in *Oeuvres diverses*, vol. 2, 368b–369a, translated also in Tannenbaum, p. 30.

82. Jonathan Israel, *Radical Enlightenment: Philosophy and the Making of Modernity, 1650–1750*, Oxford University Press 2001, pp. 159–74.

he had been studying philosophy in private, and especially Descartes, for at least five years since 1650. By 1661 he had worked out a system, fully stated in his *Ethics* of 1677, in which his God, though central, was closer to the Stoic God than to anything in the revealed religions. These he rejected, and he was regarded as an atheist. The same source has argued that his later work of 1670 and 1677 places more emphasis on the *individual's* freedom of conscience than do the later-published works of Locke.[83] Locke urges freedom of conscience for the congregations and individual members of many, but not all, persuasions about religion. Spinoza recommends a dominant state religion, but freedom for dissenting individuals to speak and teach (*dicere, docere,* occasionally *loqui*) their beliefs, and for individuals to set up as many divergent churches as they choose, with only one restriction. Churches diverging from the state religion should have only small congregations and be set well apart from each other. This favors not Locke's selected forms of religion, but any persuasion, so long as it does not disrupt the national religion.[84]

Earlier in 1670, Spinoza's preface to his *Tractatus theologico-politicus* had presented the work as concerned with freedom of conscience. He claimed to be enjoying the privilege of living in a State, Holland again, "where each may worship God as his conscience dictates," and he offered to demonstrate that "without such freedom, piety cannot flourish, nor the public peace be secure." In chapter 20, he applied the "ineffectiveness" argument not only to belief, but also to speaking. In a commonwealth there can never be a happy outcome to the attempt to have men, despite their contrary opinions (*sentire*), to speak (*loqui*) only as prescribed by the supreme powers'. Repeating the insistence on speaking and teaching (*dicere, docere*) twice more, he added only the qualification that the person speaking or teaching his opinion, should defend it through rational conviction alone, and should also submit his opinion to the judgment of the sovereign power, "which alone is competent to enact and repeal laws." The State's role in religion is confined to concern with charity and just dealing, and that is why it may be concerned with (unjust) actions, but should not seek to interfere with what people *say*.[85]

83. Ibid., see esp. pp. 265–70.

84. Spinoza, *Tractatus politicus,* ch. 8, 1677, translated in A. G. Wernham, Spinoza, *The Political Works,* Oxford University Press 1958, 411.

85. Spinoza, *Tractatus theologico-politicus,* ch. 20, translated from the edition of Gebhardt, by Samuel Shirley, Brill 1989, pp. 292–93 and 299.

Arguments of the Seventeenth Century Repeated from Antiquity and in the Eighteenth and Nineteenth Centuries

Let us take stock of the arguments for freedom of conscience that we have encountered in the seventeenth century, and see which ones were being repeated from earlier times. The century repeatedly used in different forms arguments from the *ineffectiveness* of persecution that we found in Tertullian in the third century CE, and warnings about ineffectiveness and creating *hypocrites* that we found in Themistius and Libanius in the fourth century and found to be recognized, but rejected, by Augustine in the fifth. Arguments from *ineffectiveness,* with or without *hypocrisy,* also appeared in Luther, Williams, the Leveller debates, Hobbes, Locke, and Bayle. Williams's warning about *hardening* consciences echoed Luther's about *strengthening* heretics. We saw arguments from there being *no one right road* to God and his preferring diversity in different versions in Themistius, Symmachus, and Bayle, and arguments from ignorance of the one road in Castellio, and then in Williams, Milton, Overton, Walwyn, Locke, and Bayle. Uses of the first argument will recur in Gandhi, and of the second in Kant. We found that Milton already expressed the idea more fully developed by Mill of free expression as *confirming truth.* In Mill's arguments for toleration, the discussion is no longer couched in terms of *conscience* and its freedom. The terminology of conscience is still alive in Kant, but does not constitute his main argument for tolerance.[86]

Differences among Freedoms of Conscience, Freedom of Religion, and Toleration

We have already seen in chapter 6 that freedom of conscience had different meanings in the Reformation, as something already granted to Christians by God's mercy, or something still to be fought for against terrorization. We can now see better some further distinctions. Despite their overlap, freedom of conscience and freedom of religion are distinct considerations. We can also see how these two freedoms are only two of many different grounds for advocating *toleration,* which is a far wider concept, as emerged from considering Pierre Bayle and as a recent comprehensive history of *toleration*

86. Rainer Forst, *Toleranz im Konflikt,* Suhrkamp, Frankfurt 2003, pp. 418–37, locates this in the idea of a religion of reason common to all faiths despite their mistaken insistence on inessentials.

makes clear.[87] For example, Augustine's motives for toleration included not only freedom of conscience, but also love of one's neighbor, awaiting God's judgment, and the hope that toleration would unite the Church.[88] Another common motive for toleration, keeping the peace, is also different from an interest in conscience. This throws light on the relation between the freedom of conscience discussed in the seventeenth century and the freedom of religion discussed between 200 and 400 CE. Many of the arguments, we have just seen, are remarkably similar, with a few transpositions, according to whether compulsion is said to create bogus religious worship (in the early centuries along with Locke's *Essay Concerning Toleration* and Bayle), or bogus belief concealing the conscientious belief (in the later centuries). But in the seventeenth century Milton also considered freedom of conscience in matters of divorce and publication and the Levellers in military conscription, and, as a case recorded by Philip Nye, polygamy. Conscientious objection to conscription was not presented by the Levellers as a matter of religious belief, and we shall see that by the time of the First World War it was allowed in England on grounds of socialist belief. Conversely, freedom of religion can be allowed, simply to make it easier to govern. This would have been true when Queen Victoria sought to avoid repetition of the Indian uprising of 1857, by declaring that Britain would not in future interfere in Indian religions. This was not due to an interest in conscience, and she would not have made concessions for conscientious objection to colonial rule, or for conscientious objections by Indians to practices within their own religions with which she did not wish to interfere.

Some things might be better classified under freedom of religion, some under freedom of conscience. One or the other of these is addressed by the argument that force is *ineffective* in changing conscientious belief, or in producing genuine worship, and by the argument that we cannot *know* that imposition of our own conscientious or religious beliefs would reduce error. A certain interest in conscientious or religious belief *as such* is shown by support given to religious or conscientious beliefs out of respect for the fact that they are held, despite strong rejection of their content. This might have been the position of Roger Williams about some American Indian beliefs, and was the initial position of Bayle. It may have been that of British magistrates exempting socialist conscientious objectors in the First World

87. Ibid., 70–78.
88. Ibid., 70–78.

War, despite themselves thinking the war effort of the greatest importance. In other cases that have been treated under freedom of conscience, there was an ulterior objective at stake, as in Helwys's and Locke's appeal to the greater importance of one's eternal salvation, or Milton's appeal to freedom of conscience as the best route to finding truth. By Milton this was applied to religion, but by John Stuart Mill it was applied also to the sciences, and the religious application was not the only one that interested him.[89] He also did not put the point particularly in terms of freedom of conscience, perhaps because his conception of conscience was an atypical one that gave it a merely instrumental value as a painful feeling. I shall finish by turning to Kant and Mill again because of the continuity in them of themes *other* than conscience.

Eighteenth to Nineteenth Centuries: Immanuel Kant and John Stuart Mill

If we look ahead to later discussions of toleration after the seventeenth century, we find that Immanuel Kant (1724–1804) still invoked the idea of *ignorance*, but included a further element: the degree of *probability* on the basis of which one could act in conscience, which had been a favorite subject of Catholic casuists in the sixteenth century.[90] Kant in the context of persecution seems to require *certainty*, like Walwyn and others before him. In the notes taken by Vigilantius on Kant's lectures of 1793 on the Metaphysics of Morals, Kant argued that nobody should be punished for religious dissidence, since this is due to erroneous judgment of the understanding, not to a defect of conscience or lack of conscientiousness. What is conscienceless is to take a thing as right or wrong on the basis of mere probability. It shows a want of conscience to use an uncertain interpretation of the words "compel them to come in," in order to threaten to burn someone at the stake for not believing Roman Catholic doctrine.[91] It would be a lack of conscience, he argues in *Religion within the Boundaries of Mere Reason* of 1793, if an inquisitor condemned someone to death for unbelief, since he could never be certain

89. Scientific belief can of course indirectly affect religious belief, as it did in Mill's time and earlier.

90. See Robert Aleksander Maryks, *Saint Cicero and the Jesuits*, Ashgate 2008.

91. Vigilantius' *Notes on Kant's Lectures on the Metaphysics of Morals*, vol. 27, 614–15, in the German Academy edition of Kant's Works, 1900–, translated by Peter Heath in Peter Heath and J. B. Schneewind, eds., *Lectures on Ethics*, Cambridge University Press 1997, 358–59.

that he was not possibly doing wrong. It also violates a holy freedom to tempt consciences by offering or denying civil advantages for accepting or not accepting ecclesiastical doctrines which are merely probable.[92]

In chapter 2 of his *On Liberty* of 1869, John Stuart Mill (1806–1873), speaking of freedom of speech rather than freedom of conscience, provided the fullest development of Milton's idea of diversity of opinion as *confirming truth*. If the opinion of others is correct, one has an opportunity of learning. If it is mistaken, the truth will stand out more clearly. *Ignorance* is again important, because the search for truth presupposes that we do not know which view is true. If it had been made a heresy to question the scientific views of Newton, we would be *less* sure of their truth. Mill thinks it the source of everything to be respected in man that he can correct his mistakes by discussion and experience. He rejects the view that some opinions are useful, whether or not true. He also qualifies the "ineffective" argument that true belief cannot be suppressed by persecution. This is where he says that the Reformation broke out at least twenty times before Luther, and was put down. Even so, suppression is less effective at killing heresy than free discussion. Going beyond Milton, he says that free discussion is needed for an intellectually active people. Without it, even true opinions are superstition. Cicero pointed out that to know one's own case one needs to study one's adversary's. Without discussion, a belief is not living, and regulates conduct only up to a point, and one does not even know the full meaning of what one believes. Current rival opinions may each have only part of the truth, and one may need a third view as a supplement. Christian belief may need supplementing by non-Christian. Although he finds Protestantism more tolerant than the Roman Catholic Church, his case would require Protestants to engage with Catholic views as likely to contain a portion of the truth.

This case for freedom of discussion was not intended to protect defamation of religious or racial groups or their members. In the same chapter, it has been pointed out,[93] Mill says that we can avoid those whom we disapprove, but may not parade our avoidance, and only spontaneous reactions of horror are permitted. I imagine that Mill would have allowed civil expression of the belief that some races have lower intelligence as measured by

92. Immanuel Kant, *Religion within the Boundaries of Mere Reason*, part 3, division 2, Academy vol. 6, 133–134 and part 4, second part, §4, Academy vol. 6. 186, translated by Allen W. Wood and George di Giovanni, Cambridge University Press, 1998, 136–137 and 179.

93. Jeremy Waldron, *The Harm in Hate Speech*, Harvard University Press 2012, pp. 225–26, 229.

intelligence testing, and would have welcomed the result that it discredited the claim of intelligence testing to be culturally neutral.

Comparison of the great variety of views on the limits to freedom of conscience might have the Millian effect of assisting decisions on appropriate policies. The subject will be resumed later in chapter 11.

NINE

Four Rehabilitations of Conscience and Connection with Sentiment: Eighteenth Century

Conscience Based on Custom or Superstition? Four Rehabilitations: Butler, Smith, Rousseau, Kant

We have seen that Thomas Hobbes (1588–1679) in the seventeenth century dismissed conscience as mere opinion. John Locke provided a worrying reason for agreeing with this charge, when he treated the principles on which conscience draws as often no more than the superstition of a nurse. Before either of them, the French philosopher Montaigne (1533–1592), steeped in the newly available skepticism of antiquity, had said, "The laws of conscience, which we say are born from nature, are born from custom; everyone having an inward veneration for the opinions and manners approved and received around him, cannot, without very great reluctance, depart from them, nor apply himself to them without applause."[1]

As against the attacks on conscience or moral principles as mere opinion, due to custom or superstition, the eighteenth century saw the beginnings of a rehabilitation of conscience. Three eighteenth-century thinkers who sought to rehabilitate conscience in their different ways were Bishop Joseph Butler, Adam Smith, and Jean-Jacques Rousseau, all of whom appealed to the ancient Stoics. The first two argued that the value of conscience is not necessarily impaired by its admittedly drawing on the opinions of other humans. Kant offers not so much a rehabilitation as an exemption, by presenting conscience as not the sort of thing to which reliability is relevant.

1. Michel de Montaigne, *Essays*, bk. 1, ch. 22, "Of Custom."

Limitations on the Role of Deity

At the same time, the rehabilitations did not depend entirely on the role of God. Even though Butler and Smith gave God important roles, they were somewhat indirect roles, and some arguments for the value of conscience could have gone through even if reference to God had been omitted. In 1711, the Third Earl of Shaftesbury, Anthony Ashley Cooper (1671–1713, not Locke's employer the first Earl), published a revised edition of a manuscript of his that had been circulating in 1691, and had been published by Toland in 1699, without Shaftesbury's name: *An Inquiry Concerning Virtue and Merit*. In it he argued that we have a natural sense of right and wrong. This sense is *not* due to knowledge of God, but is in us before we acquire any knowledge of God, or of his rewards and punishments. Francis Hutcheson (1694–1746) agreed. He spoke in his *An Inquiry Concerning Moral Good and Evil* of 1725 of our having a moral sense, which directly senses moral good and evil, and responds to it independently of any self-interest, including self-interest in God's reward or punishment, and independently of any desire to follow his will.[2] These are early steps in the secularization of the idea of conscience, although Hutcheson allowed that religious reading and belief can *confirm* our moral sense. By the end of the century, we shall see, Kant was able to describe conscience independently of our knowledge of God's *objective* existence.

Replacement of Reason by Sentiment: Henry More, Shaftesbury, Hutcheson, Hume, and Nineteenth-Century Feeling

Already the Cambridge Platonist Henry More (1614–1687) had introduced a boniform faculty, which was an inward *sense* or *passion* that gives us delectation when what is good proves grateful to it. In 1711, the Third Earl of Shaftesbury argued in his *An Inquiry Concerning Virtue and Merit* that our sense of right and wrong is a *sense*. Shaftesbury thinks it *horridly offensive and odious* to a rational creature to have the "Reflection in his Mind of any unjust Action or Behaviour, which he knows to be naturally odious or non-deserving," and this *state of mind* is what he thinks is properly called conscience.[3] Francis Hutcheson spoke in his *An Inquiry Concerning Moral Good*

2. Francis Hutcheson, *An Inquiry Concerning Moral Good and Evil*, sec. 2.7; sec. 4.5 (pp. 90–91, 125, sections 101, 142, in L. A. Selby-Bigge, *British Moralists*, Oxford University Press 1897).

3. Shaftesbury, *An Inquiry Concerning Virtue and Merit*, bk. 1, pt. 3, sec. 3; bk. 2, pt. 2, sec. 1, pp. 23–24 and 46–47, secs. 24 and 49 in L. A. Selby-Bigge, *British Moralists*.

and Evil of 1725 of moral *sentiment*, and of the moral *sense*, which is *pleased or displeased* by good or evil.[4] In the eighteenth century, David Hume (1711–1776) also spoke of a moral *sense* and connected conscience with *passion* instead of *reason*: "reason is wholly inactive and can never be the source of so active a principle as conscience, or a sense of morals."[5]

Some nineteenth-century English writers called conscience a *feeling*: John Stuart Mill and perhaps Cardinal Newman. Mill, who defines "the *essence* of conscience" as "a feeling in our own mind; a pain more or less intense, attendant on violation of duty" seems to be thinking of it as a *sensation*.[6] A sensation can indeed motivate, but if conscience is only a sensation, it will presumably be *produced by* value judgments about wrong, which are now no longer incorporated within conscience itself. Conscience will then be reduced to a status like that of the *bites* referred to in chapter 2, which were discussed from antiquity through the middle ages. The bites of conscience were originally a mere *effect* of bad conscience, with bad conscience itself being a belief about one's wrongdoing. If conscience is turned into a sensation, it will be equated with what was once a mere effect. Even if conscience is a *sentiment* of approval or disapproval, such a sentiment will presumably be an *effect* of value judgments about wrong or not wrong which caused the sentiments, although if one can identify the grounds of one's approval or disapproval, the relation of sentiments to judgments may become closer.

Joseph Butler: The Authority of Conscience as Its Function

I turn now to the rehabilitations of conscience by Joseph Butler and Adam Smith. Butler (1692–1752) still treated conscience as a form of reason, but assigned it a unique authority based on its psychological function, an authority far above any of the passions. He presented his case in 1726 in the second and third of *Fifteen Sermons Preached in the Rolls Chapel*, and in his preface to the sermons. In these two sermons, he took as his text one of the major focuses of our chapter 1, St. Paul, Romans 2:14: "For even when the Gentiles, which have not the law, do by nature the things contained in the law, these having not the law, are a law unto themselves." In Sermon 2 (1) Butler looked at the interrelations of our various psychological movements. In the preface (14) he had compared looking at the parts of a watch to

4. Francis Hutcheson, *An Inquiry Concerning Moral Good and Evil*, sec. 2.7; sec. 4.5, p. 90–91, 125, secs. 101, 142, in L.A.Selby-Bigge, *British Moralists*.

5. Hume, *A Treatise of Human Nature*, bk. 3, pt. 1, sec. 1.

6. Mill, *Utilitarianism*, 1863, ch. 3. Newman, *A Grammar of Assent*, 1870, ch. 5, § 1 : conscience and a moral sense of pleasure and pain are aspects of the same feeling.

discover the end which in combination they served. Besides appetites, passions, and affections, humans have a principle of reflection or conscience, which adjusts and corrects the other inward movements and affections. He starts Sermon 2 (1) by following Plato when the latter defines the *ergon* or function of a type of thing as what it alone does or what it does best, and, like Plato, he gives the example of an eye and its sight.[7] I have elsewhere argued that with a *natural* organ like an eye its function is an effect that confers a good on the species that owns it.[8] Neither Plato's definition nor mine introduces the idea of an *intended* purpose. That would be legitimate, I believe, only with the function of an *artifact* like a watch. Butler brings in intention only at the next stage. If the nature of a creature is adapted to such and such purposes only, or to those purposes more than to any other, there is reason to believe that the author of that nature, God, *intended* it for those purposes. This means (Sermon 2 [12–14]) that conscience has a certain *authority*, and *supremacy*, a term already used in the preface (14), which is not to say that it has the most power (Sermon 2 [13–14]), because it may be overruled by passions. It would have been open to Butler to derive its authority from the role it naturally plays, and that would have been a secular argument. I do not know to what extent he intends to derive its authority from that of God. But he seems to invoke both considerations in the Third Sermon when he says that it has authority from being our natural guide, the guide assigned us by the author of our nature. The authority means not that it will be obeyed, but that it ought to be obeyed.

So far Butler has been glossing Paul's reference to the Gentiles being able by *nature* to do the things contained in the law. But he also addresses Paul's idea of the Gentiles being a law unto themselves. In Sermon 3 (3), he glosses being a law unto oneself as having the rule of right within, if only one will honestly attend to it. This law within is the law that St. Paul describes in his next verse as being written in our hearts. In saying that we need honestly to attend to it, Butler is accepting the fallibility of conscience or of our awareness of it, as Paul himself does in his First Letter to the Corinthians, 4.4 and 8.7–13. The authority of conscience in Butler does not imply our infallibility, contrary to what has sometimes been thought,[9] any more than it implies its power. For Butler discusses in Sermons 7 and 10 how self-deception can get in the way of our attending to conscience.

7. Plato, *Republic* 352E–353A.

8. Richard Sorabji, "Function," *Philosophical Quarterly* 14, 1964, pp. 289–302.

9. Even in so brilliant an author as Elizabeth Anscombe, "Modern moral philosophy," *Philosophy* 33, 1958, pp. 1–19.

Butler, like Adam Smith after him, repeatedly takes the Stoics as model. In the preface, he attacks the Stoics' rivals, the Epicureans, and Hobbes as following Epicurus (35, 37, 41–42). He approves the Stoic view that virtue consists in following nature (13 ff.). As Cicero explains, the natural is not the easy, but what would be in accordance with our true nature, and that only when we have reached the years of adult maturity.[10]

In the preface (13 and 15) and the Third Sermon (2), Butler cites with approval a passage of Cicero, possibly influenced by the Stoic Panaetius, in which he says that stealing is more contrary to nature than death, poverty, or pain.[11] Sermon 3 explains that it is not contrary to our lower nature, but to the system of our nature taken as a whole.

When the preface (19) and the First Sermon (8) define the principle of reflection or conscience as an *approbation* of some principles or actions and *disapprobation* of others, the similarity has been pointed out to the phrasing of the Stoic Epictetus at the opening of his *Discourses* (1.1.1).[12] Butler is presumably like Epictetus in regarding approbation as a function of reason. But nonetheless Epictetus' faculty of approving or disapproving there is not conscience, but a faculty of distinguishing truth and falsehood, when something initially appears to us as beneficial or harmful, and a response appears appropriate or inappropriate. A reference to conscience could rather be found in Epictetus' claim that Zeus has installed within us a *daimonion* or guardian spirit—the term used also by Socrates—as a guard (*phulassein*), and it and he are both within us and see what we are doing.[13]

Although Butler enables us to see how we might make a case for conscience having authority, even if we did not, like him, invoke God's intention, his case for a further conclusion does rest on God, when he agrees with Paul that the law within is the rule of right. To find someone more clearly admitting that conscience draws on the opinions of other people, and yet rehabilitating conscience, we will need to consider Adam Smith.

Adam Smith, Conscience as Imagined Impartial Spectator

The two great books of Adam Smith (1723–1790), *The Theory of Moral Sentiments* and the better known *Wealth of Nations* were first published in 1749

10. Cicero, *On Ends* 3. 20–22.

11. Cicero, *On Duties* 3.5.21.

12. A. A. Long, "Stoicism in the philosophical tradition: Spinoza, Lipsius, Butler," in Jon Miller and Brad Inwood, eds., *Hellenistic and Early Modern Philosophy*, Cambridge University Press, Cambridge 2003, 22.

13. Epictetus, *Discourses* 1.14.11–15.

and 1776, respectively, but each went through many fresh editions. The second book with its famous "invisible hand" over the markets was not meant to replace the book on moral sentiments with its interest in moral conscience. Smith was professor of moral philosophy at Glasgow at the time his first book was published, and he revised it in later editions, of which I shall use the sixth and last of 1790, except where specified. Part 3 of the *Theory of Moral Sentiments* is concerned with duty, and he opens it by saying he is turning from moral judgments about others to moral judgments about oneself.[14] Insofar as his discussion is about conscience, this is faithful to the original Greek conception of conscience as a kind of self-awareness. And he is closer still when a little later he says that in assessing his own conduct he divides himself, as it were, into two persons, although he gives his own specifications, different from the ancient one, of the two persons as the examiner or judge and the examined or judged.[15] His idea of conscience as an imagined impartial spectator is announced almost at once: "We endeavour to examine our own conduct as we imagine any other fair or impartial spectator would examine it."[16] The conception of the imagined impartial spectator, though present in the first edition, was more fully explained in the second of 1761 (and later in the sixth), after Sir Gilbert Elliot responded to the first edition with a question about how conscience differed from a mere reflection of the attitudes of others. That, of course, was the description with which Montaigne and Locke had belittled conscience, or the typical conscience. And Smith answered it, by insisting that one needs to imagine not the ordinary spectators of one's acquaintance, but an *impartial* spectator.

However, it takes time to build up the image of such a spectator. At a first stage we imagine actual people, and "we begin, upon this account, to examine our own passions and conduct, and to consider how these must appear to them, by considering how they would appear to us if in their situation. . . . This is the only looking-glass by which we can, in some measure, with the eyes of other people, scrutinize the propriety of our own conduct."[17] The imagined spectator at this stage is not yet the impartial one. The progress from here to the imagined impartial spectator is analogous to a progress in

14. Adam Smith, *The Theory of Moral Sentiments*, pt. 3, ch. 1, sec. 1. I have used the modern edition of D. D. Raphael and A. L. Macfie, Oxford University Press 1976, which shows all the original versions, along with D. D. Raphael, *The Impartial Spectator: Adam Smith's Moral Philosophy*, Oxford University Press 2007.

15. Smith, *Theory of Moral Sentiments* 3.1.6.

16. Ibid., 3.1.2.

17. Ibid., 3.1. 5.

Greek philosophy from Plato's and Aristotle's idea of an actual other person as a looking glass or mirror in which one sees oneself, to the idea of Epicurus and the Stoics of an admired philosopher *imagined* as a watcher and as a model for one's own conduct. Adam Smith's *Theory of Moral Sentiments* includes a whole chapter on the Stoics. He would surely have known of their endorsement of the Epicurean imagined spectator, and this, I think, is a far more likely source of his own imagined spectator than the brief references to a spectator, not described as imagined, that have been noticed in Hume.[18]

To recall for a moment these Greek conceptions, the *First Alcibiades*, ascribed by the ancients, but not all moderns, to Plato, says that the eye sees itself best by seeing its reflection in the eyes of another, and this is applied to our self-knowledge in the sense of our knowing the rational character of human nature.[19] An application more relevant to the idea of conscience is made in (pseudo?)-Aristotle, *Magna Moralia*, where Aristotle's follower says that we cannot look at ourselves from our own perspective, as shown by our seeing the wrongdoing of others better than our own. So just as (in Plato's analogy) we use a mirror to look at our own faces, so we can achieve the pleasure of knowing ourselves only by looking at a friend.[20] The move from an *actual* friend as mirror to an *imagined* and admired spectator was outlined in chapter 1. It started in the next generation after Aristotle with Epicurus, and was later reported and endorsed by the Stoic Seneca. The idea was that we should imagine an admired philosopher watching our conduct, to avert us from wrong.[21] Seneca and his fellow Stoic Epictetus also suggested the variant of imagining an admired philosopher as a model (*exemplum*) to direct us aright. We should ask ourselves what our model would do.[22] In 7.2.1.15–47 of the sixth edition Adam Smith supplied an extensive account of Stoic moral philosophy, which covers twenty-two pages in the modern edition. At sections 44–45, he wrote virtually as if the "man within the breast," one of his descriptions of the impartial spectator, were Stoic.

18. D. D. Raphael, *The Impartial Spectator*, p. 30, cites David Hume, *A Treatise of Human Nature*, bk. 3, pt. 3, sec. 1 (paras. 14 and 30, ed. L. A. Selby-Bigge, Oxford University Press 1896, rev. P. H. Nidditch 1978, pp. 581, 591); David Hume, *An Enquiry Concerning the Principles of Morals* app. 1, paras. 10 and 5.1, para. 1 (in *Enquiries concerning Human Understanding and concerning the Principles of Morals*, ed. L. A. Selby-Bigge, Oxford University Press 1893, rev. P. H. Nidditch 1975, §§ 172, 239).

19. Plato, *First Alcibiades* 132C–133C.

20. Ps.?-Aristotle, *Magna Moralia* 2.15, 1113a13–26 on which ps? see Peter Simpson p. 23, n. 47 above.

21. Seneca, *Letters* 11.8–10, 25.5–6, 32.1, 83.1–2.

22. Seneca, *Letters* 11.9–10 (imagining both watcher and mentor); 95.72; 104.21–2; *On Leisure* 1.1; *On the Shortness of Life* 14.5; Epictetus, *Handbook* 33.12.

Adam Smith explains further the importance of the imagined spectator being *impartial*. Even if we know that the truth will never be discovered, we do not want to believe ourselves wrongly admired; rather, we want to believe ourselves *admirable*. Strikingly, he thinks the same is true about believing ourselves wrongly blamed. Even if never to be discovered, we dread more believing ourselves *blameworthy* than believing ourselves wrongly blamed. In order to believe ourselves admirable or not blameworthy, we need the endorsement not of public opinion, but of an *impartial* spectator.[23] This conception circumvents a charge leveled against Epicurus. Cicero and Seneca had ascribed to Epicurus a view of conscience as fear of public detection and punishment.[24] Cicero found this an unsettling form of conscience and complained that Epicurus rejected the steady conscience that he believed in.[25] Adam Smith would have restored that steady conscience, susceptible not to sudden detection, but to the impartial spectator.

The second edition had said more about the qualifications of the imagined impartial spectator. He would be candid and equitable, not a relative nor a friend either of the owner of the conscience or of those whose interests were affected by that owner's conduct.[26] In imagining the spectator, Adam Smith spoke of dividing himself, as it were, into two persons. This is virtually the original Greek metaphor of sharing knowledge with *oneself*. He went on to reintegrate the two persons, when he said that the man of real constancy and firmness almost becomes the impartial spectator.[27]

In one passage, Adam Smith unconsciously repeated Butler's evidence for conscience having authority, although it has been argued that he is likely to have encountered the Butlerian wording in the lectures of his own teacher, Francis Hutcheson.[28] There is a reference to God: certain principles were plainly intended to be the governing principles of human nature, and the rules they prescribe should be regarded as the commands and laws of the Deity. They are promulgated by the vicegerents of God, the imagined human spectators within us. The vicegerency had been explained earlier at 3.2.31. Humans have been taught by nature to be mortified by the disapproval of fellow humans whom God has appointed to be his vicegerents on earth, to superintend the behavior of his bretheren. Thus, like Butler,

23. Smith, *Theory of Moral Sentiments* 3.2.3, 3.2.5, 3.2.9, 3.2.32.

24. Seneca, *Letters* 97.15–16; Cicero, *On Ends* 2.16.53.

25. Cicero, *On Ends* 2.22.71.

26. Adam Smith, *The Theory of Moral Sentiments*, ed. D. D. Raphael and A. L. Macfie, p. 129, originally printed after what is in the 6th ed., 3.1.7.

27. Ibid., 3.3.25.

28. Ibid., 3.5.5–6, with comment in the edition of D. D. Raphael and A. L. Macfie, p. 11.

Adam Smith appeals to God. Nonetheless, his imagined spectator, being an imagined human, provides a slightly more secularized version of conscience than we might have found a little earlier. Moreover, as with Butler, his case about the value of a cultivated conscience would have force, even if he had not appealed in this way to the arrangements made by God.

Despite the very strong influence of the Stoics on Adam Smith's moral philosophy, he is not uncritical of them. While discussing the impartial spectator, he speaks of the importance of the *feelings* of parents for children and of people for the misfortunes of their friends and loved ones. In these cases, he thinks that literary descriptions of feelings are much better instructors than stoical apathy—in other words, the freedom from emotion of the great Stoics, Zeno, Chrysippus, and Epictetus. We may imagine, then, that when assessing one's own emotions, as well as those of others, the impartial spectator will not adopt a Stoic disapproval of emotion.

The reference to *sentiments* in the title of Smith's book follows the terminology of his teacher, Hutcheson, and the views of his friend Hume, even though he comes to reject the idea that there is a distinctive moral sense, and insists that a variety of sentiments are relevant, not some single peculiarly moral sentiment.[29] One of Smith's most authoritative interpreters treats him at one point as identifying conscience with the *approval and disapproval* of oneself engendered by the imagined spectator.[30] Approval and disapproval are good examples of *sentiments*. But Smith seems also to identify conscience with *other* aspects of imagining a spectator instead or as well. At one point, he puts conscience in a list of items as if they were equivalent: "Conscience, the inhabitant of the breast, the man within."[31] Another time, he speaks of the *tribunal* of their own consciences, referring to the spectator's *role*.[32] Elsewhere he says that conscience is our consciousness of having acted agreeably or contrary to the moral faculty by which we approve or disapprove.[33] Of these four accounts, three preserve the idea of a split, two refer to the idea of being in the wrong, and two keep the idea of self-awareness about that wrong.

Adam Smith criticizes the Stoics further for their acceptance in certain circumstances of suicide, and he even knew, and spoke critically of, the

29. Smith, *Theory of Moral Sentiments*, 6th ed., pt. 7, ed. D. D. Raphael, p. 326–27.

30. D.D. Raphael, *The Impartial Spectator*, p. 34: "According to Adam Smith, the approval and disapproval of oneself that we call conscience."

31. Smith, *Theory of Moral Sentiments* 2nd ed., 3.3.5, cited by D. D. Raphael, *The Impartial Spectator*, p. 40.

32. Ibid., 3.2.32.

33. Smith, *Theory of Moral Sentiments*, 6th ed., pt. 7, ed. D. D. Raphael, p. 326.

then practice in Bengal of suttee, the widow's being burned alive on her husband's funeral pyre.[34] There were widows who insisted on practicing suttee, long after it had been outlawed. For assessing *their* conduct, one would need to understand the quite alien beliefs and attitudes which at that time led them to that insistence.

One may have dealings with practices nearer home too that are hard to understand, and in assessing one's dealings with such practices, one would expect the imagined spectator would need to possess more than impartiality. He would need imaginative understanding of other points of view if he was to assess whether one had sufficiently tried to understand the practices one was dealing with. Smith did think that benevolence, whether or not conscience, could be stretched far afield. In the sixth edition of his work in 1791, writing not about conscience but "Of universal Benevolence," he described that love for all humans which the Stoics had argued to be natural. He mentions the Stoic Roman Emperor Marcus Aurelius, who took things even further. Marcus coped with the dangers he faced from conspirators by stressing that we are only parts of a larger universe.[35] Smith says correspondingly that our goodwill is "circumscribed by no boundary, but may embrace the immensity of the universe," and that "the wise and virtuous man should be willing to sacrifice the interest of his own particular society to the interest of that great society of all sensible and intelligent beings," and at this point he brings in God, since he thinks such an attitude impossible without the belief that these beings are under God's care and administration.[36]

Rousseau: Conscience a Source of Feeling that Guides the Pupil, if Shielded from Corrupt Society and the Doctrine of Authorities

In 1762, Adam Smith's Swiss contemporary Jean-Jacques Rousseau (1712–1778) published his treatise on education, *Émile,* in which he made two striking uses of the idea of conscience. The first is Rousseau's connecting conscience not so much with knowledge as with *sentiment* in French. This is clearer when Rousseau speaks in book 1 in his own person than it is in book 4, when the speaker is his mouthpiece, the Savoyard vicar, whom he elsewhere endorses. He allows the vicar to speak of conscience as a principle by which we *judge* (*juger*) actions good or evil, and which itself is a *judge* of

34. Ibid., 7.2.1.25–34, with reference to suttee at 33.

35. Usefully stressed by Julia Annas, *The Morality of Happiness,* Oxford University Press 1993, ch. 5, esp. pp. 175–76.

36. Adam Smith, *Theory of Moral Sentiments,* 6.2.3.1, ed. D. D. Raphael, 1976, pp 235–36.

good and evil.[37] But in book 1, by contrast, Rousseau said that it is *reason* that teaches us to *know* good and evil, whereas conscience makes us *love* the one and *hate* the other. He repeats the idea early in book 4 before the vicar takes over. Reason does not *motivate* us to do as we would be done by; it is conscience and *sentiment* that motivate. The vicar himself is represented as taking the same view. The activitities (*actes*) of conscience are not judgments, but *sentiments* by which we recognize (*connaître*) the fitness or unfitness of things in relation to ourselves and so seek or shun them. With echoes of Bonaventure's treatment of *synderesis*, he concludes that the knowledge of good is not innate, but when *reason* leads us to recognize good, conscience leads us to *love* it, and this *sentiment* is innate and manifested in primitive affections.[38]

The late onset of knowledge of good and evil is a second striking idea, which he needs in order to screen out the corrupting influences of society and Church teaching. He made conscience a paramount guide for his pupil, Émile, but only in book 4 at a late stage of his development after puberty had arrived and the age of reason, and only after an earlier education that sheltered Émile from the corruption of society, something of which the Stoics also complained.[39] Furthermore, the praise of conscience is put into the mouth of the Savoyard vicar, a Christian who rejects the authority of Church teaching. Conscience is a supreme guide to the pupil only if it is shielded from the doctrines of authorities as well as from the attitudes of society. The attempt to delay appeal to conscience as guide until the supposedly late age of reason would come as no surprise to early Christians, such as Origen and probably Augustine, who held that the law in our hearts is *naturally* so delayed. But it seems to contrast with the view of Freud, to be discussed in the next chapter. Freud treats conscience not as innate, but as an infantile development that cannot be delayed or shielded from paternal values.

The vicar has much more to say in favor of conscience. He may be defending it from Montaigne's account of conscience as due to custom, not nature, when, while avoiding direct mention of the creative role of God, he includes the *sentiments* which are the acts of conscience in the following Stoic-sounding statement: "Whatever may be the cause of our being, it has

37. Jean-Jacques Rousseau, *Émile*, paras. 1031; 1038 in the online French version at http://www.ilt.columbia.edu/pedagogies/rousseau/Contents2.html, pp. 252 and 254, in the Everyman English translation of Barbara Foxley, Dent, London 1911, repr. 1974.

38. Ibid., bk. 1, para. 165, Eng. p. 34; bk. 4, note to para. 835, Eng. Note to p. 196–97; para. 1035–36, Eng. pp. 253–54.

39. Chrysippus, discussed Richard Sorabji, *Emotion and Peace of Mind*, Oxford University Press 2000, p. 257.

provided for our preservation by giving us *sentiments* suited to our nature; and no one can deny that these at least are innate" (unlike the knowledge of good and evil). Conscience never deceives us (*tromper*). For to follow conscience is (and here he uses a Stoic term) to follow nature. He finishes his discussion of conscience with a paean to the superiority of conscience over philosophy, calling it an instinct: "Conscience, conscience! Divine instinct, immortal and celestial voice, sure guide (*guide assuré*), . . . infallible judge (*juge infaillible*) of good and evil, which makes man like God, . . . apart from you I feel nothing in myself that raises me above the beasts. . . . Thank heaven we are thus delivered from all this frightening show of philosophy."[40] What a contrast this represents with the satirization of moral sentiment in Sheridan's *School for Scandal* of 1777. He shows people taking disastrous moral decisions by relying on sentiment.

Rousseau's appeal to conscience as independent of authority is familiar from seventeenth-century Protestant England. But unusual in the Christian tradition is the claim of infallibility. Nonetheless, this feature was to recur, we shall see in chapter 10, in Gandhi. The last figure I shall consider in this chapter, Immanuel Kant, had taken Rousseau into account and like him gave to conscience a role different from judgment, but therefore, with greater consistency, regarded conscience not so much as infallible, but rather as not liable to any such thing as fallibility.

Kant

The views of Immanuel Kant (1724–1804) on how moral principles may be made reliable turn on his categorical syllogism in its three formulations. I have raised a question in chapter 7, not indeed about the truth of Kant's practical syllogism, but about its utility in the light of Stoic particularism. The Stoic example was that when Julius Caesar conquered the city of Utica, it was right for Cato to commit suicide, but not for anyone else in the same circumstances. But I will not return to the categorical syllogism here, because Kant gives rather unusual roles to conscience, which confirm its *utility*, but do not treat it in the traditional way as a *belief* about what has put, or would put, one in the wrong. This has the effect of *exempting* conscience from questions about its *reliability*. In the lecture notes taken by Vigilantius, we shall see, Kant says that conscience is not the sort of thing that is liable to error. The earlier lecture notes taken by Collins do allow erroneous conscience, but nonetheless say that questions of reliability concern our *understanding*,

40. Rousseau, *Émile*, bk. 4, paras. 1025; 1038–39, Eng. pp. 249–50, 254.

instead of our conscience. The question raised is whether conscience is a product of art and education rather than nature, and is inculcated simply by *habit*. But Kant refuses to connect this problem with *conscience*. He replies that it is *understanding* that needs to be cultivated, whereas conscience does not need to be, because it is *natural*.[41] This may seem surprising in view of the fact we shall see, that he connects conscience with attentiveness, and attentiveness needs to be *cultivated*. But the lecture on the Metaphysics of Morals confirms that there is no *artificial* conscience.[42] It was the notes on earlier lectures of 1762–1764 that had allowed some conscience to be artificial, while saying that the distinction was difficult to draw.[43]

Kant's interpretation of the nature of conscience, though different from the interpretations with which we started, nonetheless relates interestingly to them and reproduces some of their features, including the ideas of self-awareness and of a split person. Moreover, the central metaphor of an inner courtroom preserves the idea of being in the wrong. What is missing is the idea that conscience is a *belief* about one's being in the wrong, although it may deliver a judicial verdict to that effect and a judicial sentence. Moreover, as in St. Paul, it holds duty before us for our acquittal or condemnation, and it sets the law before us, applying it to our own case. But it plays other judicial roles as well.

In the *Metaphysics of Morals* of 1797, Kant tackles one issue, the apparent contradiction in the idea of a person being split, or what he calls the "doubled self," which we found in the original Greek concept, and introduces the imagined spectator, who can, he thinks, be thought of subjectively as God. The person is split again differently from the ancient way, in Kant's case into accused, judge, and prosecutor. To avoid contradiction, he assigns the roles of accuser and accused to different faculties. There is only one person, but as described in two different ways, he is specifically diverse. It is one's lower faculties that are accused. But conscience also needs to exaggerate the split and think of the judge as *other* than the human being as such. The judge may be thought of as an actual person or an ideal person. The ideal person may momentarily remind us of Adam Smith's impartial spectator, but Kant takes a different route. The ideal person must be thought of as imposing all obligation, and so as having all power to give effect to his laws. Only God

41. Collins's notes vol. 27, pp. 355–56, in the Berlin Academy edition of *Kant's Gesammelte Schriften*, translated in *Lectures on Ethics*, Cambridge University Press 1997.

42. Vigilantius' lecture notes on the *Metaphysics of Morals*, vol. 27, p. 617, translated in *Lectures on Ethics*, Cambridge 1997.

43. Notes by Herder, vol. 27, pp. 42–43, translated in *Lectures on Ethics*, Cambridge University Press 1997.

fits this description, but all the same, it does not follow that God actually exists outside oneself. For the idea is given subjectively by practical reason, not objectively by theoretical reason. We are merely to act in keeping with the idea and follow out the analogy of a lawgiver. It is rather as with Bayle, who said only that conscience is *interpreted* as the voice of God, rather than that it *is* such. Conscience must simply be thought of as the subjective principle of being accountable to God. Kant thus secularized conscience to the extent of making God no longer an *objective* feature of it.[44]

Kant's views on a *second* issue, the multiple *roles* of conscience, naturally changed between 1762 and his final statement in 1797, and some of his accounts come only from lectures recorded by students. Lecture notes taken by Vigilantius in 1793 assign to conscience the earliest type of role we found in the Greeks: conscience is consciousness of our self. In Kant's version, it is consciousness of what duty is for itself.[45] The final treatment in the *Metaphysics of Morals* (1797) uses the language of an inner court. Conscience in this passage is said to be awareness of the inner court.[46] But it is also more than awareness. It is a predisposition on the side of *feeling* for being affected by the concept of duty. Conscience holds duty before us for our acquittal or condemnation (as St. Paul said), and that is how it affects our moral feeling.[47] In a court there are many different roles, of which this is only one, and Kant is hard to follow because he ascribes some roles to judgment, reason, or understanding, and yet a large, overlapping set of roles to conscience. How can different faculties play the same role? The solution may be that conscience is not the name of any one faculty, but of the whole quasi-judicial process in the court.[48]

Kant says that the question whether a forbidden action has occurred is decided by judgment (*iudicium*), in German, *Urteilskraft*. The verdict (*Sentenz*), condemnation or acquittal, is decided by reason. But it turns out to be conscience that plays the role of acquitting or condemning, when Kant speaks of the verdict (*rechtkräftige Spruch*) of conscience as acquitting or condemning us.[49] The much earlier lectures from 1784 to 1785, recorded by Collins, agree about the two roles given to conscience in the *Metaphysics*

44. Kant *Metaphysics of Morals* in the Berlin Academy edition of *Kant's Gesammelte Schriften*, vol. 6, pp. 438–39, translated in *Practical Philosophy*, Cambridge University Press 1996.

45. Notes by Vigilantius on lectures of 1793, Academy vol. 27, pp. 613–14, translated in *Lectures on Ethics*, Cambridge University Press 1997.

46. Kant, *Metaphysics of Morals*, Academy vol. 6, p. 438.

47. Ibid., Academy vol. 6, pp. 399–400.

48. I thank Allen Wood for this suggestion.

49. Kant, *Metaphysics of Morals*, Academy vol. 6., p. 440.

of Morals, but add a third. Collins agrees with the later *Metaphysics of Morals* that conscience sets the laws before us (a traditional role) and obliges us to appear before the court.[50] He also denies that conscience is merely (*bloss*) a faculty of judgment (*Vermögen der Beurteilung*), because it *also*, like a magistrate (*Richter*), gives *force* to its judgments, which become a judicial verdict (*richterlich Ausspruch*) and a sentence (*Sentenz*). In adding a third role, Collins combines two ways of talking that may initially seem unexpected bedfellows, that conscience passes sentence (*Sentenz*) on us,[51] and that it compels *us* to pass sentence (*richten*) on ourselves. But the second is probably a reference to Kant's later stage at which conscience, having condemned, provokes in us remorse and a wish to make amends.[52] This last is yet another role of conscience. Different again are two works of 1793, which stress the role of ensuring that examination has been *thorough*. In *Religion within the Bounds of Reason*, book 4,[53] conscience is reason judging *itself* and calling the man to witness whether diligent appraisal of conduct by his reason has actually taken place. Also in 1793, Kant gave the lectures on the Metaphysics of Morals, recorded in the lecture notes of Vigilantius. The *understanding* (*Verstand*) was separated off, rather like *Urteil* in Collins, and given the duty of examining whether an action was right or wrong. The duty of conscience was different: to provide awareness of whether the examination was thorough.[54]

But if conscience plays so many roles, this might seem to exacerbate the difficulty of Kant's treatment of a *third* issue, his argument against the possibility of *erroneous* conscience. For if "conscience" is not the name of certain selected functions, but of the whole quasi-judicial process with all its possible errors, the claim of freedom from error becomes all the more surprising. Kant had earlier allowed, in Collins's lecture notes, that conscience could be in error about human law, and this error might or might not be culpable.[55] Still earlier, in notes taken by Herder from Kant's lectures of 1762–1764, and in other lecture notes edited by Paul Menzer from a manuscript now lost, Kant had also allowed for erroneous conscience.[56] But now in Vigilantius' lecture notes, he wants to say that conscience is not erroneous and he tries

50. Ibid., Academy vol. 27, pp. 297; 351.
51. Ibid., Academy vol. 27, pp. 351; 353.
52. Ibid., Academy vol. 27, p. 353.
53. Kant, *Religion within the Bounds of Reason*, Academy vol. 6, p. 186.
54. Kant, *Metaphysics of Morals*, Academy vol. 27, p. 619.
55. Ibid., Academy vol. 27, pp. 354–55.
56. Notes by Herder, Academy vol. 27, p. 42, translated in *Lectures on Ethics*, Cambridge University Press 1997; lecture notes edited by Paul Menzer and translated by Lewis Infield, London 1930, under the same title *Lectures in Ethics*, pp. 132–33.

to *explain* why it is immune from error.[57] He admits that errors are made by the judgment (*Beurteilung*) of understanding (*Verstand*), in examining whether an action was right or wrong. But *conscience*, he says, cannot be in error about whether the examination was thorough, because if conscience submitted conduct for examination, it must be aware of doing so. As Allen Wood has pointed out,[58] it is presupposed that if something *other* than conscience erroneously supposes that that conscience submitted conduct to examination, the error will not be that of conscience.

It is further admitted in Vigilantius' notes that error can occur because of lack of conscientious investigation, but again this is the product not of conscience, but of the *lack* of conscientiousness, a *want* of conscience and an urge to *dispense* with conscience. In the *Metaphysics of Morals*, Kant takes the denial of error further. An erring conscience is now an actual absurdity, for the old reason that I can be mistaken in my objective judgment as to whether something is a duty, but not in my subjective judgment as to whether I have submitted it to practical reason as judge. But the claim is now added that lack of conscientiousness is *not* lack of conscience—everyone has a conscience within him originally, and he hears it—his failure is not to *heed* its judgment. Hence it is not conscience that fails to warn, but we who fail to listen. One has a duty to cultivate conscience, sharpen attentiveness, and obtain a hearing for it,[59] but because it is correct, not because it may be in error. A surprising feature of his attempt to free conscience from error is that it focuses on a single one of the many roles of conscience: checking whether examination was thorough. It is important to Kant to free conscience from the charge of self-deception about having checked. But checking thoroughness is only one of the many roles he has listed; what about other errors connected with other roles?

One strategy he uses is to distinguish the judgment (*Beurteilung*) of understanding (*Verstand*) from the *judicial* force of conscience, assigning error only to the first.[60] It is true that we can distinguish in our minds the aspect of judicial force from the judgment of understanding. But the judicial force cannot actually *occur* without the judgment of understanding, and, moreover, the magistrate with whom conscience is compared would be *responsi-*

57. Notes by Vigilantius on lectures of 1793, Academy vol. 27, pp. 614–19, translated in *Lectures on Ethics*, Cambridge University Press 1997.

58. Allen Wood, *Kantian Ethics*, Cambridge University Press 2008, ch. 10, "Conscience." I am very grateful to him not only for showing me his chapter, but for answering my questions on Kant with superb clarity.

59. Kant, *Metaphysics of Morals*, Academy vol. 6, pp. 400–401; 438.

60. Collins, Academy vol. 27. 351; cf. Vigilantius, Academy vol. 27, pp. 614–19.

ble for the judgment of his understanding, and could not deny that failure to understand was a *judicial* failure. It seems, then, that failure to understand ought to have been classed as an error of *conscience*.

An alternative suggestion[61] is that with small changes, Kant's claim of freedom from error could be defended in the spirit that he intended. According to this suggestion, we should compare conscience not, as Kant does, with an accusing judge, nor should we assign to conscience all the fallible judicial roles he appears to assign. He was right when he assigned them to *Verstand*, or to other faculties. The role of conscience can be compared not with that of a judge, but with the supervisory role of the praetor in the Roman Republic, who is responsible for the proper conduct in the court of the roles of *other* officials. This would justify Kant's appealing only to one of the four roles, a supervisory role, in arguing for conscience's freedom from error. Conscience is expected only to make sure that it has submitted (or, perhaps, supervised the submission of) conduct for examination and that the examination (carried out by other, fallible entities) has been thorough. It is only a way of speaking to say that when it supervises the judicial activities of other fallible entities, it is carrying out their activities *itself*. If this captures the spirit of Kant's intention, the freedom from error will be a very limited one. Many types of error can occur in the internal court, and even a "supervisor" needs to learn his job, and discover what failures of procedure have serious consequences. If conscience is a supervisor of proceedings in the inner court, it will at first, and perhaps forever, be a trainee supervisor.

Kant thus provides a fourth attempt to justify conscience, but for its utility in roles *other* than that of constituting reliable belief, which had occupied Butler, Smith, and Rousseau. In the next chapter, we shall find a mixture of champions and critics.

61. I am grateful to John Wynne for this suggestion.

TEN

Critics and Champions of Conscience and Its Continuing Resecularization: Nineteenth to Twentieth Centuries

The biggest threat to the idea of conscience was, I believe, the question raised by Montaigne, Hobbes, and Locke about its reflecting mere custom and upbringing, rather than the law of God, and in general its being unreliable. We have seen that certain eighteenth-century thinkers, started to rehabilitate conscience, while nonetheless retrenching to some extent on the role of God. In the nineteenth and twentieth centuries, there were major defenders of conscience in the religious tradition, and I shall speak of Newman, Tolstoy, and Gandhi. But secularization continued, or rather, because of the secular origins of the concept of conscience, I shall call it a *resecularization*.

Continuing Resecularization of Conscience

The original idea of sharing knowledge with oneself of a defect, including moral defects, started off, it was argued in chapter 1, as a largely *secular* idea, until the time of the Stoics and Christians. In the seventeenth century Pierre Bayle described conscience only as being *interpreted* as the voice of God. In the eighteenth century, the idea of our moral sense of right and wrong was made by the Third Earl of Shaftesbury and Francis Hutcheson independent of our *knowledge* of God. Bishop Butler and Adam Smith, though not secularists themselves, use arguments that secularists could adopt. Immanuel Kant, building on Smith, is explicit that the subjective idea of God in conscience implies nothing about his objective existence. J. S. Mill's account of conscience as a usefully painful prod was more secular still. Another most important figure was the American Henry David Thoreau, whose *Civil Disobedience* was published in 1849. He advocated civil disobedience on the grounds of conscience, and his protests have been described as secular. In this chapter we shall see in one spirit Thoreau, and in a quite different spirit

Freud and Nietzsche taking secular positions on conscience, and in the next chapter we shall see conscientious objection to conscription bringing about a secular concept of conscience, quite early in Britain, but not in the US.

Thoreau: Conscientious Civil Disobedience, Not Freedom of Conscience

The American Henry David Thoreau (1817–1862) published his *Civil Disobedience* in 1849. Near the beginning, he based his protest on the need to follow *conscience*, rather than, like democratic legislators, await the views of the majority.[1] He objected to slavery and to the war on Mexico and his disobedience took the form of withholding his tax payments. A call for civil disobedience is not necessarily the same as a call for freedom of conscience. The conscientious use of disobedience for changing the law or government policy, though driven by conscience, need not demand freedom of conscience for oneself, let alone for the government. The freedom Thoreau wanted was physical freedom for slaves. If the law or policy stayed intact by granting his conscience freedom from tax, he would have to find a new way of opposing it. He had refused for the past six years to pay the poll tax. He described the night he spent in prison as a result. But it was not, he said, for any particular item in the tax bill that he refused to pay it. He thought the legislature should not have his allegiance. Another form of protest that he would have liked to see was the tax gatherer resigning his office, and, if the government said, "your money or your life," you should not protect your life. He did not base his appeal to conscience on God, and his convictions have been described, influentially, by Justice Warren Burger in 1972 as secular.[2] But this did not prevent him citing the Gospel of Matthew and regretting that legislators did not live by the New Testament.

Thoreau's civil disobedience was very unlike that of Gandhi, and Gandhi said that he took only the name "civil disobedience" from Thoreau, because he had invented the method independently in South Africa and Thoreau only gave him scientific confirmation of what he was doing.[3] Thoreau opposed particular things, and supported a return to nature, but Gandhi shared

1. Henry David Thoreau, *Civil Disobedience*, pt. 1, [4], 1849.

2. *Wisconsin v. Yoder*, 406 U.S. 405 (1972), cited by Amy Gutmann, *Identity in Democracy*, Princeton University Press 2003, 167.

3. Gandhi, "Letter to Kodanda Rao," September 10, 1935, electronic *Collected Works*, vol. 67, p. 400; "Letter to American friends," August 3, 1942, electronic *Collected Works*, vol. 83, p. 163.

only his value-laden conception of nature, not his isolationist retreat.[4] In that, he was more like those Hindus who go off into the forest in the fourth stage, or *ashrama*, of life and leave society behind in favor of spiritual reflection. Thoreau went into the woods and combined immersion in nature with spirituality. Gandhi, by contrast, claimed that he sought spiritual liberation (*moksha*) not by retreat from the world, but by immersing himself in the sufferings of the oppressed. He saw God in their faces.[5] Thoreau also differed in supporting John Brown's violent seizure of the federal armory at Harpers Ferry in 1859 with the intention of distributing its one hundred thousand rifles and muskets to create an armed slave rebellion in the South. Thoreau's *A Plea for Captain John Brown* was first delivered as a speech at Concord, Massachusetts, before Brown's execution later that year.

Nietzsche

Two criticisms of conscience were mounted in the nineteenth and twentieth centuries, both of them by secularists: Nietzsche and Freud. Friedrich Nietzsche (1844–1900) criticized conscience as part of his lifelong iconoclastic attack on morality as it was known not only in Christianity, but among the ethical thinkers of various other religions and cultures too. His attacks are scattered over most of his works,[6] but I shall focus mainly on the second of three essays in his *Genealogy of Morals: A Polemic* (1887), where his attack on conscience is most concentrated.

Starting with the topic of responsibility, he quickly introduces a different type of conscience which he elsewhere calls "intellectual conscience." This is the conscience of the sovereign individual, who has broken loose from the morality of custom and has become the autonomous individual beyond morality. With a sideswipe at Kant's autonomy as the adoption of the moral law as one's own, Nietzsche says that "autonomous" and "moral" are mutually exclusive terms. The sovereign individual is entitled to make promises, because he makes them like a sovereign, knowing that, with his unbreakable will, he is strong and dependable. He must be ready to kick the scrawny

4. For value-laden nature, see Bilgrami, p. 145n37; for differences, Ramin Jahanbegloo, *Gandhi, aux sources de la non-violence: Thoreau, Ruskin, Tolstoy*, Éditions du Félin Paris 1998, pp. 53–63.

5. References in Richard Sorabji, *Gandhi and the Stoics: Modern Experiments on Ancient Values*, Oxford University Press and University of Chicago Press 2012, 13, 16.

6. I am grateful to Ben Abelson for first alerting me to Nietzsche's views on conscience in a large number of works in a paper written for a seminar on conscience in the ancient world at the CUNY Graduate Center in 2007.

men, who make promises without being entitled. He alone is responsible in giving promises, and his proud knowledge of this responsibility has become an instinct, which is his conscience.[7] Nietzsche's view contrasts with that of the Stoic Epictetus, who would have considered such autonomy a hostage to fortune.[8]

By contrast, conscience as ordinarily understood was the cruel self-punishment of guilt (*Schuld*), originally derived from the cruelty inflicted by a creditor on a debtor because of his debts (*Schulden*). The relationship of creditor and debtor was a contractual one based on a promise to repay. In case of default, the repayment might take the form of flesh sliced out of the debtor, which rewarded the creditor with a kind of pleasure at being able to mistreat the debtor as an inferior. The possible pain of such punishment would help the debtor to remember his undertaking to repay.[9] Kant's moral law or categorical imperative, is attacked here as stinking of cruelty. Even before Christianity, gods were seen as liking the spectacle of cruelty.[10]

As regards law and punishment, the community took on the role of creditor for security provided. The lawbreaker came to be seen as a breaker of the contract to repay the advantages of membership. In anger, the community returned him to the state of outlaw. But the reactive emotion of revenge on him was less just than that of the aggressive, stronger, braver, nobler man. As the higher power, it was the nobler man who first introduced law. As a result, illegal acts were seen impersonally, as an outrage against the law of the higher power, rather than as occasions for the injured party to seek revenge. Punishment was introduced through his will to power. It was wrong to think it was introduced because of some useful function, and especially that its cruelty could introduce a sense of guilt for cruelty. The criminal could see that cruelty was esteemed by the punishers and his reaction was to become hard, cold, estranged, and resistant.[11]

Nietzsche elaborates his theory with a hypothesis about the origin of bad conscience. Humans had been happily adapted by their instincts to wilderness and war. Suddenly caged in by society and peace, they found that the State protected itself against their old instincts by punishments. Unable to exercise those instincts against others, they turned these instincts against themselves, in a form of sickness, scraping themselves against the bars of

7. Friedrich Nietzsche, *Genealogy of Morals*, C. G. Naumann, Leipzig 1887, 2.2.

8. As described in, e.g., Richard Sorabji, *Self: Ancient and Modern Insights about Individaulity, Life, and Death*, Oxford University Press and University of Chicago Press 2006, ch. 10.

9. Nietzsche, *Genealogy of Morals*, 2.3–5.

10. Nietzsche, *Genealogy of Morals*, 2.6–7.

11. Nietzsche, *Genealogy of Morals*, 2.9–14.

their cage, and inventing bad conscience as a new form of danger. The change was neither voluntary, nor produced by contract, but imposed by conquerors, who knew neither bad conscience, nor responsibility. Both the conquerors and the conquered were exercising their will to power, but the conquered against themselves.[12] Here, although there was no contract, and Nietzsche despised Rousseau,[13] there seems to be something in common with him, in that the formation of society is seen as a downward step.

The next step was the invention of God, which may have grown out of ancestor worship, but took its extreme form in Christianity. To the Christian God such debt is owed that it can never be paid, and therefore God paid the debt himself, leaving humans even more guilt-ridden in relation to God, the original ancestor. Nietzsche does not stop to consider Luther's opposite conclusion that the message relieves us joyfully of the burden of paying. The result, he continues, is illness: the will to inflict pain, blocked from its natural outlet, and turned on oneself.[14]

The Greek gods were very much better. They were reflections of nobler men with animal instincts. The Greeks were thus for a long time able to keep bad conscience at bay. Nietzsche's claim appears to overlook the treatment of conscience in the Greek playwrights, as described in chapter 1, when only Euripides has someone call it an illness. But Nietzsche admired Dionysus, god of wine and frenzy,[15] and felt very akin to Epicurus, who thought the gods were enjoying themselves too much to wish to interfere with us in any way.[16] Modern men, by contrast, inherit thousands of years of the vivisection of conscience, evidently longer than Christianity. Elsewhere, Nietzsche did indeed see this decline as starting earlier than Christianity with another of his bugbears, Socrates, if he considered the Socratic interest in dialectic, which he deplores, a form of vivisection.[17] Nietzsche finishes by looking forward with hope to the arrival of the Antichrist—after whom he named almost the last work he wrote the following year.

This deeply unhistorical account of heroes and villains treated conscience as a pathological attitude of hostility to oneself, ignoring the historical details of its character and functions. But the pathology had the merit of influencing one very important person, Sigmund Freud, who knew Nietzsche's

12. Nietzsche, *Genealogy of Morals*, 2.16–18.

13. Nietzsche, *Twilight of the Idols* (1889).

14. Nietzsche, *Genealogy of Morals* 2.19–22.

15. Nietzsche, *Twilight of the Idols*.

16. On his liking for Epicurus, see the notes of Walter Kaufmann on Nietzsche, *The Gay Science*, 45.

17. Nietzsche, *Twilight of the Idols*.

work, admired his insights into psychology, and also provided a secular treatment of conscience. At Christmas 1888, the last month before his final insanity, Nietzsche compiled out of many of his earlier writings going back to 1877 a very hostile attack on someone who had once been a father figure to him, Richard Wagner. He gave it a significant title, *Nietzsche contra Wagner: Out of the Files of a Psychologist,* and he said in the preface, "This is an essay for psychologists, but *not* for Germans," for whom he went on to express hatred. Freud's studies of pathological conscience repeatedly remind us of Nietzsche. Freud's term "id" (German: *es*) goes back eventually to him, and Freud himself said of Nietzsche, "His guesses and intuitions often agree in the most astonishing way with the laborious findings of psycho-analysis," although he insisted that his own findings had been made independently.[18]

Freud

Sigmund Freud (1856–1939) introduced his idea of the superego as the vehicle of conscience late in his career in 1923, and wrote further important studies of the superego over the next ten years.[19] His interest was not in our questions of how conscience had been conceived and how it might be made a more reliable guide. Rather, he was studying, but more empirically than Nietzsche, how a wrongly developed conscience could turn into illness, and he wanted to find, as a prerequisite of treatment, a mechanism in the mind under which conscience could be subsumed. The mechanism he postulated was the superego, which was split off from the rest of the personality in early childhood, another split of the person into parts. But the splitting off of the superego is not the same as the split of a person recognized by the original metaphor of sharing knowledge with oneself.

His hypothesis included the Oedipus complex, the idea that every male child wants to sleep with his mother and kill his father, or vice versa for female children. But the boy's fear of being castrated by his father leads him to avoid this fate by identifying instead at least normally with the father. Girls identify normally with the mother, but quite often with the father.

18. Freud, "An autobiographical study," in *Freud, Standard Edition,* ed. James Strachey, vol. 20, p. 60. For the possible influence of Nietzsche on Freud's theory of the unconscious, see Ken Gemes, "'We remain strangers to ourselves,' the key message of Nietzsche's *Genealogy*" in C. D. Acampora, *Nietzsche's* On the Genealogy of Morals: *Critical Essays,* Rowman and Littlefield 2006, pp. 191–208. I thank Adam Papaphilippopoulos for the reference.

19. Freud, *The Ego and the Id,* 1923, in Freud, *Standard Edition,* vol. 19; *The Question of Lay Analysis,* 1926, in *Standard Edition,* vol. 20, 1926; *New Introductory Lectures on Psycho-Analysis,* 1933, lecture 31, "The dissection of psychical personality," in *Standard Edition,* vol. 22.

The need to repress Oedipal feelings leads the ego to create a repressive agency within itself: the superego, an agency that retains the character of the father. The father may be absorbed not only as a repressive agency, but also as an ideal model, and later other authorities may take on the role of father figure.[20] It is this superego that is the vehicle of conscience. Mental health depends on its becoming sufficiently *impersonal* and distant from the father. In neurotics it fails to do so, and a need for self-punishment arises which takes the form of a need to be physically ill, and a resistance to anything that might provide a cure.[21] Another form of mental sickness is taken by melancholic attacks. Conscience and its treatment as an external observer are functions of the superego. In melancholic attacks the superego torments the ego with merciless threats of punishment out of all proportion to any possible wrongdoing. But in between attacks, the ego sometimes rushes to the opposite extreme of uninhibited satisfaction of its appetites. Freud's secularism is expressed in his comments that it is remarkable to see morality, which is supposed to have been given us by God, functioning in these patients as a merely periodic phenomenon. Moreover, he says, God has done an uneven and careless piece of work, for a large majority of men have very little conscience. He adds, "We are far from overlooking the portion of psychological truth that is contained in the assertion that conscience is of divine origin; but the thesis needs interpretation. Even if conscience is something 'within us,' yet it is not so from the first." Conscience, in other words, is not innate, given its development from a reaction to the father. But none of this would necessarily surprise St. Paul, who does not consider innate the *law* that God implanted in our hearts, much less the *conscience* which is fallible, nor Origen and Augustine for whom the law in our hearts is not heard or does not appear during childhood, and may not be read later. More important is to see whether conscience can retain its value when it has been secularized, a subject to which I shall return in the final chapter.

Freud has transformed public conceptions about the mind. But on the particular subject of conscience, doubts have been raised. I am not thinking so much of the cultural studies which have questioned not only Freud, but also non-Freudians, on whether the attitudes they adduced were universal across cultures. Rather, even Freud's followers have found that he left out many important influences on later adolescence other than the father. Subsequent work on adolescence, by Freudians, passes beyond his views on

20. Freud, *The Ego and the Id*, 1923, *Standard Edition*, vol. 19, pp. 32–37.

21. Freud, *The Question of Lay Analysis*, 1926, *Standard Edition*, vol. 20, pp. 223–24; "The dissection of psychical personality," *Standard Edition*, vol. 22, pp. 58–66.

infantile stages. Particularly important was Erik Erikson (1902–1994), who was psychoanalyzed by Freud's daughter, Anna Freud, and retained many of Freud's views in the background, but gave an account of adolescence that appears to fill a vacuum left by Freud. Erikson introduced his ideas in 1950 in his "eight stages of man."[22] He saw life as concerned with the successful or unsuccessful establishment of personal identity. He recognized the intense need of many adolescents for *peer* recognition, and the *rebellion* of adolescents against parents, and saw these as one stage in progress or lack of progress in forming self-identity. A successor, James Marcia, recognized as one scenario a situation called "foreclosure," in which identities are *passively* adopted on the basis of other people's views, and another called "moratorium" in which people oscillate among different identities and try them out. The different scenarios do not necessarily form a developmental sequence and only some people win through to a situation of identity achievement, and only for so long as further change is not required.[23]

I believe that the later Stoics of antiquity could have helped with successful identity achievement, because of their theory of *personae* introduced by Panaetius in the second century BCE and continued by Epictetus.[24] They held that in making decisions in life, we must consider who we are and who we want to be. In choosing a career, for example, one rational and decent wish is to follow our parents' careers. But we must consider our *persona*—who we are—and whether that is where our talent lies, or whether we would merely disgrace our parents.

The correction applied to Freud's theory so far is that the overwhelming stress on the father does not do justice to the later period of adolescent identity formation. Freud's account of conscience formation has been criticized by a philosopher, William Lyons, on a different issue, the formation not of identity, but of conscience itself.[25] In rejecting Freud's authoritarian account, he substitutes an optimistic view of how adolescents might form a reliable moral conscience for themselves, not passively through fear of the father, but through the *active* and *dynamic* process of questioning everything in dialogue with elders and with peers. He regards this trial and error as en-

22. Erik Erikson, "Eight stages of man," in his *Childhood and Society*, W. W. Norton 1950.

23. J. E. Marcia, "Identity in adolescence," in J. Adelson, ed., *Handbook of Adolescent Psychology*, Wiley 1980. A useful survey including these two views is provided in the later editions of Rolf E. Muuss, *Theories of Adolescence*, McGraw Hill, e.g. 6th ed., 1996, chs. 3–4.

24. Panaetius' theory is reported by Cicero, *On Duties*, bk. 1, 107–21, and continued by Epictetus, *Discourses*, bk. 1, 2.8–24, discussed in Richard Sorabji, *Self*, ch. 8.

25. William Lyons, "Conscience: An essay in moral psychology," *Philosophy* 84, 2009, pp. 477–94.

abling adolescents *deliberately* to distance themselves from the authority of external sources and to develop an objective moral point of view, which is morally reliable. He does not refer to James Marcia's warnings of alternative scenarios, such as passive acceptance, or endless search and oscillation. I believe that far more can be done to make conscience more reliable, but that it takes special efforts, and I shall make some different suggestions about what helps in the final chapter.

What all these accounts of adolescence have in common is that Freud's authoritarian father figure has receded into the background, and with it the focus on the self-tormenting conscience of both Nietzsche and Freud.

I turn now to three champions of conscience, none of whom took note of the criticisms of Nietzsche and Freud, and none of whom was secular. All of them retained the criticized association of conscience with God. The three champions were Newman, Tolstoy, and Gandhi.

Newman and Tolstoy

Cardinal Newman (1801–1890), the Catholic theologian, diverged from the core concept by treating conscience not only as feeling, but also as the voice of God and innate. He called it "the divine law," which may seem to collapse Paul's distinction of conscience and law. But he added the qualifications "as apprehended in the minds of individual men," that it claims to be a divine voice, but that it may be mistaken. Nonetheless, in view of its claim, it would always be wrong to go against it, and very occasionally it might conflict with the Pope, and then it is right to prefer conscience, as indeed it is for a heretic, although in both cases it is important to correct any errors. Newman did not have to defend freedom of religion. What he was defending was rather freedom of conscience within religion.[26]

For Leo Tolstoy (1828–1910), the concept of conscience was very important, as shown by his book *The Kingdom of God Is Within You* (1894), a book whose title Tolstoy had taken from scripture (Luke 17: 20–21). He there postulated that there were three stages, which he considered inevitable, in the history of mankind. At first each man was concerned only with himself. In the second stage concern spread to family, tribe, and even to one's country. There it halted until eighteen hundred years before Tolstoy wrote, Christ put forward the law of love, a new concern that did not stop at the artificial frontier of country. This was a doctrine of universal brotherhood, community

26. *John Henry Newman, Letter to the Duke of Norfolk, 1874, section 5,* §1. For feeling *see* 169n6.

of property, and not resisting evil by violence. National distinctions led to violence and should be eliminated. The transition from each stage to the next is slow and seems strange and impossible, until the old attitude becomes too uncomfortable to maintain. That time was already coming because there was an increasingly intolerable conflict between the old attitude of the second stage and our *consciences* which already contain the law of the brotherhood of men. It was evidenced by the thousands of suicides every year among military men in Europe who were required to go out and kill other people who had done them no harm.[27] There are well over fifty references in the work to conscience, mostly conscience about violence.

Gandhi

When Mahatma Gandhi (1869–1948) called Tolstoy the second greatest influence among men who had influenced his life, he was thinking particularly of this book.[28] His interest was chiefly in Tolstoy's view of nonviolence. But he also endorsed Tolstoy's view of the three stages of mankind. They are represented in a piece from 1922: "Some day we must extend the national law to the universe, even as we have extended the family law to form nations—a larger family."[29]

Gandhi wrote more extensively about conscience.[30] His concept shows affinities to the guardian spirit of Socrates, as much as it does to the concept of St. Paul. He had paraphrased in Gujarati Plato's *Apology*, which he first came across in 1907.[31] In that dialogue Socrates treats the warnings of his guardian spirit as indubitable and as coming from the child of a god. Gandhi sees the voice of conscience as the voice of God, and as indubitable, two views which go naturally together. Neither view is in St. Paul, who does not tie conscience so directly to God, but the relation to God is not all that far from Socrates, and the indubitability is Socrates' view. Gandhi's belief in the

27. Leo Tolstoy, *The Kingdom of God Is Within You*, ch. 5, translated from Russian by Aylmer Maude, Oxford University Press, pp. 130–37, 157–59; Constance Garnett, Dover 2006 republication of the 1894 translation, pp. 97–102, 115.

28. The first was Rajchandra: Gandhi, Speech of September 10, 1928, on Tolstoy's anniversary, *Navajivan*, September 16, 1928, repr. in R. Iyer, ed., *Moral and Political Writings of Mahatma Gandhi*, vol. 1, no. 59, Oxford University Press 1973, see pp. 115–19.

29. "Notes," *Young India* Mar 2 1922, reprinted in *Young India 1919–1922*, Madras 1924, p. 285.

30. I repeat here some of my findings in Richard Sorabji, *Gandhi and the Stoics*, ch. 8.

31. Rajmohan Gandhi, *Mohandas*, p. 130. D. G. Tendulkar *Mahatma* records Gandhi as having read *The Defence and Death of Socrates* (*The Apology* with another extract) translated by H. Cary, London 1905.

indubitability of the voice also connects with his attitude to the difference between faith and reason. Faith is fallible outside its own sphere. Intellect and faith must each be given their own provinces. But whereas reason is always fallible, because it is easily upset by superior logic,[32] faith in its own sphere can be infallible. The claim of infallibility was made in response to an Englishman who asked Gandhi to help him believe in God. He replied that when the felt presence of God rules the heart and conduct, not merely the intellect, that is when faith is infallible.[33]

Gandhi's unquestioning attitude toward his conscience is illustrated by the two occasions when his leading associate, Rajagopalachari, wrote, and in the second case crossed half of India, to warn Gandhi that his conscience had misinformed him in telling him to conduct a fast. One of these fasts was in 1924, the other in 1933. In 1924 Gandhi replied, "Somehow or other I *feel* the absolute correctness of the step even though I cannot demonstrate it to your satisfaction. I know how difficult it must be for you and others to accommodate yourselves to these sudden changes. But how shall I help myself? . . . Is it not better that I should do that rather than I should suppress the clear voice within?"[34]

After the second fast in 1933, Gandhi wrote: "I can say this—that not the unanimous verdict of the whole world against me could shake me from the belief that what I heard was the true voice of God. . . . For me the voice was more real than my own existence. It has never failed me, and, for that matter, anyone else."[35] The previous year he had written that the voice overrode intellect and reason.[36] This fitted with his not being able to argue his case convincingly to Rajagopalachari. Looking back in 1939 on Rajagopalachari's second intervention in 1933, Gandhi wrote: "When I took the 21 days' purificatory fast in the Yeravada jail in 1933 and proclaimed that it was in answer to a call from God, Rajagopalachari came all the way from Madras to dissuade me. He felt sure that I was deluding myself. . . . I continue to think that I fasted in answer to the still small voice within."[37]

32. Speech at Congress Workers' Conference, *Harijan,* March 31, 1946, *Collected Works* vol. 82, p. 368.

33. "God is," *Young India,* October 11, 1928, p. 368.

34. Letter to Rajagopalachari, September 15, 1924, repr. Iyer, *Moral and Political Writings of Mahatma Gandhi,* vol. 2, pp. 128–29.

35. Gandhi, *Harijan,* July 8, 1933, reprinted in Iyer, "All about the fast," *Moral and Political Writings of Mahatma Gandhi,* vol. 2, p. 132.

36. Gandhi Letter to Bhuskute, May 25, 1932, reprinted in Iyer, *Moral and Political Writings of Mahatma Gandhi,* vol. 2, p. 130.

37. Gandhi discussion with members of Oxford group, *Harijan,* October 7, 1939, reprinted in Iyer, *Moral and Political Writings of Mahatma Gandhi,* vol. 2, no. 101, p. 136.

But in self-defense he felt obliged to enter some qualifications after the 1933 fast, such as he had already hinted at as early as 1909, when he said, "No man can claim that he is absolutely in the right or that a particular thing is wrong because he thinks so."[38] But here the words, "because he thinks so" may be ruling out one ground for certainty, rather than ruling out certainty itself. In the reflection quoted from just after the 1933 fast, he added a clearer qualification: "And everyone who wills can hear the Voice. It is within everyone. But like everything else, it requires definite and previous preparation." In the retrospective passage of 1939, referring to Rajagopalachari's remonstrance, his warning was more emphatic: "I say this to warn you how unwise it may be to believe that you are always listening to God. . . . It is better that listening is also based on solid rock. This listening in presupposes the fitness to listen, and the fitness is acquired after constant and patient striving and waiting on God." There were other contexts too in which Gandhi entered caveats. Taken in sequence through the years 1924 to 1947, he said that conscience is not found in the young, nor in savages. It is acquired by laborious training and is the ripe fruit of strictest discipline. It can reside only in a delicately tuned breast.[39] It is not found in the cannibal. You need training and discipline to listen, and there are honest differences of opinion.[40] We may be deceived in thinking that we are listening to God.[41] Conscience needs to be awakened, and not everyone has done that.[42] Finally, speaking of truth and nonviolence, he entered the following caveat, which I have italicized, "*So far as I know my own conscience* I have myself striven through thought, word and deed to reach the ideal."[43]

Gandhi would have been perfectly consistent if he had thought that one must be wrong sometimes, while never thinking "I am wrong this time." But he has gone beyond that by suggesting how much preparation it takes to be sure that you are listening to the voice of God. This puts him in a much weaker position. For one thing, why is he so confident that his listening has

38. Gandhi, *Indian Home Rule* (*Hind Swaraj and Other Writings*, Cambridge University Press 1997, ed. Anthony J. Parel, ch. 17, p. 91).

39. Gandhi, *Young India*, August 21, 1924, reprinted in Iyer, "Under conscience's cover," *Moral and Political Writings of Mahatma Gandhi*, vol. 2, p. 125.

40. Gandhi, "Religion of volunteers," *Young India*, September 23, 1926, reprinted in Iyer, *Moral and Political Writings of Mahatma Gandhi*, vol. 2, p. 126.

41. Gandhi talk with Moral Rearmament visitors, September 28, 1939, in Gopalkrishna Gandhi, *The Oxford India Gandhi: Essential Writings*, New Delhi 2008, p. 444.

42. Gandhi note to Gope Gurbuxani, March 4, 1945, reprinted in Iyer, *Moral and Political Writings of Mahatma Gandhi*, vol. 2, p. 128.

43. Gandhi, talk with Englishmen at Patna, April 25, 1947, reprinted in Iyer, *Moral and Political Writings of Mahatma Gandhi*, vol. 2, p. 293.

been good enough? For another, how can be so confident in telling others that they should consult their conscience to decide what their personal duty calls for?[44]

Gandhi was on better ground on the subject not of conscience, but of the values on which his conscience drew.[45] He did not claim, like St. Paul, that the original source of his values was an inner law implanted by God. In fact, he said, in this respect more secular than Paul, that his belief in nonviolence was acquired by reading someone from a different culture and religion from that in which he had been brought up: Tolstoy. His practice provides a *corrective* to the worry illustrated above from the seventeenth and eighteenth centuries, that moral principles come from ill-informed humans.[46] Gandhi's case shows that even those who grant that our principles do not come from God do not have to leap to the opposite conclusion that they are inevitably unreliable. Concerning nonviolence, Gandhi's principles came to him initially from a reflective reading of Tolstoy in a context where he was, like Tolstoy, immersed in a culture of violence. He refined those principles through consultation with the members of his ashram when they had to decide whether to kill the snakes which threatened the cows on which they depended for milk, and what to do with monkeys which stole the crops on which they also depended. Finally, he refined his values further by public discussion with his *opponents*, publishing their criticisms and his answers in his own newspapers which were read throughout India and worldwide. We can see him refining his nonviolent values in the course of seven articles published in his newspapers from October to November 1926. In these articles he defended his decision to endorse the shooting of sixty stray dogs which were liable to spread rabies to each other and to humans.[47] He was not discussing conscience, but his decision on the dogs was a matter of conscience which in turn caused him to reflect on his *principles* in the light of outraged (and violent!) protests from believers in nonviolence.

We can see Gandhi refining his concept of nonviolence over the course of his seven articles. He finished by maintaining his decision, but with far greater insight into what nonviolence amounts to. He decided that killing, even killing to protect others, was violent, unless it was for the sake of the

44. I thank Mohamed Mehdi for these questions.

45. I am here drawing on my *Gandhi and the Stoics: Modern Experiments on Ancient Values*, University of Chicago Press and Oxford University Press 2012, chs. 4 and 11.

46. Ch. 9 above.

47. "Is this humanity?," seven articles, October–November 1926, translated from *Navajivan* October–November 1926, for *Young India* by Mahadev Desai and recorded with replies to objections in Desai, *Day to Day with Gandhi*, vol. 8, Varanasi 1973.

being killed, and he continued to hold that violence was always wrong. But where did this leave his decision about the dogs? It was only partly for their own sake, to protect them from starvation and possible rabies, that he advocated their being killed. It was largely to protect other dogs and humans, and to that extent the killing was violent. His answer was that although violence is always wrong, it is a counsel of perfection that we should avoid it. We cannot always live up to this counsel, but it raises our sights to try. In fact, believers in nonviolence may have taken on positions of responsibility for protecting others. Others again are not believers in nonviolence, and the better course for them is to follow their own beliefs. Although violence is always wrong, we have to consider whether something else is even worse. Violence may be less bad than abandoning the charges under one's care, or one's own beliefs. The basis on which Gandhi deepened his principles was not the voice of conscience, but reflection on a decision of conscience made in consultation with ashramite friends or outraged foes in public, very public, discussion.

In his stance on potentially rabid dogs, Gandhi displayed the important insight that one may be in a moral *double* bind. Killing a potentially rabid dog or, in another of Gandhi's examples, using tear gas to prevent rape or mayhem, puts one in a position of sinning, whether one acts or not. The solution in each case is that one sin is less bad than the other. The insight that either course of action may be wrong has not always been appreciated, despite the interest of philosophers and playwrights in moral dilemmas. But earlier recognitions were discussed in chapter 4, and the point is recognized by Gandhi.

Gandhi also recognized a different principle, endorsed by Thomas Aquinas, and in the preceding century by Abelard, that conscience is binding, even if it is mistaken.[48] He enunciated the principle in a passage just cited from 1909: "No man can claim that he is absolutely in the right or that a particular thing is wrong because he thinks so, but it is wrong for him so long as that is his deliberate judgment. It is therefore meet that he should not do what he knows to be wrong."[49] He repeated the idea when, to defend against Rajagopalachari his decision to fast, he said, "Is it not better that I should do that rather than I should suppress the clear voice within?" The bindingness of an erroneous conscience provides another way in which one can be in the wrong whichever course of action one takes.

48. Thomas Aquinas, *Summa theologiae* Ia IIae, question19, article 5; *On Truth*, question 17, article 4.

49. Gandhi, *Hind Swaraj* (*Indian Home Rule*), 1909, ed. A. Parel, ch. 17, p. 91.

I have said that conscience is not the original source of one's general values. It might be thought that this is because conscience speaks about the particular, not the general. It certainly addresses the individual about what he or she in particular should do. But Gandhi's career reveals a qualification to the idea that conscience never speaks about what others should do. He may have been writing in a compressed way when he appealed to *conscience* and "the inner voice of conscience," in arguing that Dalits (then called "Untouchables") should be allowed into temples closed to them.[50] He was here speaking as if his conscience had implications not only for himself, but for what others should allow. This could easily be justified by saying that his conscience told him that he should persuade others not to exclude the Dalits.

Given so much concern with the voice, it is not surprising that Gandhi shared the interest of ancient Platonists and Christians in how the voice communicated. Gandhi described that in his account of deciding to undertake his 1933 fast:

> For me the voice of God, of Conscience, of Truth, or the Inner Voice or the "still small Voice" mean one and the same thing. I saw no form. I have never tried, for I have always believed God to be without form. . . . What I did hear was like a Voice from afar and yet quite near. It was as unmistakable as some human voice definitely speaking to me, and irresistible. I was not dreaming at the time I heard the Voice. The hearing of the Voice was preceded by a terrific struggle within me. Suddenly the Voice came upon me. I listened, made certain that it was the Voice, and the struggle ceased. I was calm.[51]

Gandhi's conception of conscience connected with his individualism. He insisted, "There is no such thing therefore as mass conscience as distinguished from the consciences of individuals."[52] He would have rejected Hobbes's claim that the law is the public conscience and must be followed rather than private consciences, which are nothing but private opinions.[53] But Gandhi's own reasons are clear. He had just been describing how one needs training, discipline, and a delicately tuned breast to listen, and a child,

50. Rajmohan Gandhi, *Mohandas*, p. 309, citing Gandhi in the *Bombay Chronicle*, 16 September 1927, *Collected Works*, vol. 40, p. 105.

51. Gandhi, *Harijan*, July 8, 1933, reprinted in Iyer, "All about the fast," *Moral and Political Writings of Mahatma Gandhi*, vol. 2, pp. 131–32.

52. Gandhi, *Young India*, August 21, 1924, reprinted by Iyer, "Under conscience's cover," *Moral and Political Writings of Mahatma Gandhi*, vol. 2, p. 125.

53. Ch. 8 above.

in his view, would not be ready. It matters too that he thinks that conscience is the voice of God speaking to one about one's problems. There is something personal and direct about these communications. However, he should have allowed that making sure one is listening correctly would sometimes be a collective matter. We saw in chapter 7 that in the seventeenth century after the restoration of the English monarchy, the Quakers sought a compromise.[54] The policy of everyone following his or her own conscience had weakened such revolutionaries as the Levellers. But the Quakers would not go to the opposite extreme of accepting the authority of priests. The compromise was to follow the sense of small group meetings of Quakers.

From the nineteenth to twentieth centuries, I have looked at six treatments of conscience: three secular in Thoreau, Nietzsche, and Freud; and three religious in Tolstoy and Gandhi. A new impetus toward the continuing resecularization of conscience, at least in Britain, came from conscientious objection to military conscription, which I shall consider in the next chapter.

54.Christopher Hill, *The World Turned Upside Down: Radical Ideas during the English Revolution,* Maurice Temple Smith 1972 and Penguin 1975, 252, 256.

ELEVEN

Modern Issues about Conscientious Objection and Freedoms of Conscience, Religion, and Speech

Freedom of Conscience and of Religion Distinct

This chapter considers the need to balance the three freedoms of conscience, religion, and speech, and the different balances struck in different legislatures. The three freedoms are not the same. This was observed in chapter 8 and again with Cardinal Newman as regards freedom of conscience and of religion, which overlap, but do not coincide. Already in the seventeenth century appeals were discussed as matters of conscience independently of religion. This was true of freedom to divorce, freedom to publish, freedom for polygamy, and the recurrent appeal for freedom from military conscription. Freedom of conscience should therefore be recognized as a claim independent of freedom of religion. But equally freedom of religion needs independent recognition. For as Andrew Koppleman has pointed out,[1] claims for exemption based on religion do not always involve *conscience*. His examples include those who wished to take up the smoking of a dangerous drug, peyote, as a religious sacrament of their ethnic group. People might legitimately want a religious exemption for an outlawed practice that made them feel closer to God. Other religious people again had appealed to enlarge a religious building into a restricted area, or to avoid a logging road obliterating their only available place of worship. Religion could not easily be protected in these cases by an appeal to freedom of *conscience*.

Freedom of conscience and freedom of religion were both recognized as grounds for conscientious objection to military service in Britain in the First

1. I thank Andrew Koppleman for showing me his "Conscience, volitional necessity and religious exemptions," *Legal Theory* 15, 2009, 215–44; "The story of *Welsh v. United States*: Elliott Welsh's two religious tests," in Richard Garnett and Andrew Koppleman, eds, *First Amendment Stories*, Foundation Press, New York 2011, pp. 293–318.

World War of 1914–1918, and the recognition of conscientious, as opposed to religious, objection gave an impetus toward the continuing resecularization of conscience. But in the US only freedom of religion was recognized as late as 1965 and 1970, because of its constitution. In Canada there was controversy over the inclusion of freedom of conscience alongside freedom of religion in the 1982 Charter of Rights and Freedoms. One reason was that it is harder to determine a person's conscience than their religion,[2] and the inclusion has been limited in its application.

Secularization of Conscience in Conscientious Objection: Britain, 1916–1918

In the first World War, the British prime minister, Asquith, relied on volunteers to expand the army from 1914 until the start of 1916. This was not only because of his liberalism, but also because he wanted to avoid creating opposition, through compulsory conscription, to the war effort. According to a major study of conscientious objection in that war,[3] from 1660 to 1916, military service had been to a large extent based on a standing army and volunteers, and compulsion had been diluted with ballots, parish quotas, and numerous exemptions. The First World War started the same way. In the absence of military conscription, conscientious objection had first been recognized in 1898, in connection not with military service, but with compulsory vaccination. When military conscription started in 1916, the tribunals appointed to assess conscientious objectors recognized not only objections based on membership of a religious group that objected, but also the objections of individuals, whether on religious, *moral,* or *socialistic* grounds of political liberty. The secularization consisted of the recognition of conscientious grounds not based on religious belief or membership. Well over one thousand socialistic objectors were recorded, whether or not they gained exemptions. A committee appointed in 1916 to identify alternative work classified nearly half of the four thousand men referred to it as belonging to the Christadelphian sect, but the next largest number of nearly two hundred as having *moral* objections. Over ten thousand conscientious objectors gained exemption from some or all forms of service, against over four thousand refused. But nearly six thousand declined on conscientious grounds either to apply for exemption or to accept the tribunal's decision on exemption

2. Memoirs of Jean Chrétien, the then attorney general.
3. John Rae, *Conscience and Politics,* Oxford University Press 1970.

or the particular form of exemption offered, and upon refusal to serve, they were imprisoned in harsh conditions, although their cases were later reviewed. In the Second World War, which in Britain ran from 1939 to 1946, the kinds of alternative work offered were much better adjusted to the different grounds of conscientious objection.

A striking feature of the British experience is its treatment of *erroneous* conscience, a problem raised by twelfth- and thirteenth-century thinkers, as discussed in chapter 4. A majority thought in the First World War that conscientious objectors were *wrong* not to support the military, in many cases working neither for the war wounded, nor for civilian tasks that would directly help the war effort. But, recognizing that those who were sincere would also be wrong to go against their consciences, a large number supported the provisions for exemption. For them the difference of conscientious belief weighed more heavily than their own belief in the military duty of the moment.

Conscientious Objection as Quasi-Religious: US, 1965 and 1970

Recognition of conscientious objection to military conscription for nonreligious reasons came slower in the US, for reasons to do with its constitution based on its different history of accommodating citizens with very divergent religious beliefs. I have learned from more than one valuable account, and will again follow here that of Andrew Koppleman.[4] Conscientious objection to conscription had to be accommodated under the two clauses of Madison's First Amendment of 1791 to the constitution of 1787, which recognized religion, but not conscience in general. They read, "Congress shall make no law respecting an establishment of religion [the Establishment Clause], or preventing the free exercise thereof [the Free Exercise Clause]."

In the US in 1917, only well-recognized religious sects were exempted from military service. Rather than sect membership, in 1940, objection based on religious training and belief was allowed for, and in 1965 objection based on the Bible. Religious training and belief were tied in 1948 to belief in a Supreme Being, but in 1965 the reference to a Supreme Being was stretched to accommodate the objection of Daniel Seeger, who declared

4. I first learned about Welsh from the excellent account in Martha Nussbaum, *Liberty of Conscience*, Basic Books 2008, ch. 4, whom I thank for allowing me to see a prepublication version of her book. I have also learned from the two papers of Andrew Koppleman cited above.

himself agnostic about a Supreme Being. Belief in a Supreme Being was now understood as a sincere and meaningful belief that "occupies a place in the life of its possessor parallel to that filled by the orthodox belief in God of one who clearly qualifies for the exemption." So quasi-religious belief was protected. In 1970, the case was decided of Elliott Ashton Welsh, who had claimed exemption even from noncombatant service, while denying that his application was based on any religious belief at all. Interpretations by the Supreme Court of the freedom of religion clauses were to prove ambiguous. A ruling of 1947 had taken the Establishment Clause to mean that neither "a state nor the Federal Government can . . . pass laws which aid one religion, aid all religions, or prefer one religion over another." Another of 1968 had understood the clause as one that "mandates government neutrality between religion and religion, and between religion and nonreligion." The neutrality on nonreligion and ban on aiding all religions would seem to protect Welsh, who should not be disfavored for his nonreligion in comparison with all religions. But the Free Exercise Clause looked different, and in 1981, after Welsh's case, another Supreme Court ruling, not implausibly, understood it as a clause that "gives special protection to the exercise of religion."[5] The Supreme Court, ignoring the nonreligion plea, declared in 1970 that Welsh was exempt under the existing stretched understanding of belief in a Supreme Being. Exemption must be extended to "all those whose consciences, spurred by deeply held moral, ethical, or religious beliefs, would give them no rest or peace if they allowed themselves to become a part of an instrument of war." The effect was to treat Welsh's nonreligious belief as quasi-religious. Although there was a reference to consciences here, the First Amendment of 1791, passed under the heading of the Bill of Rights, was not taken to have offered freedom of conscience outside religious belief. We have seen that in England one of Oliver Cromwell's supporters argued against freedom of conscience on the grounds that it had been cited in favor of polygamy. But in America that difficulty would not have been avoided by sticking to freedom of religion, as emerged when polygamy was sought in the US Supreme Court in 1878 on *religious* grounds by a Mormon.[6]

5. Andrew Koppleman, "Conscience, volitional necessity and religious exemptions," p. 217, cites Everson v. Board of Educ. 330 U.S. 1.15 (1947), Epperson v. Arkansas, 393 U.S. 97.103–4 (1968), Thomas v. Review Bd., 450 U.S. 707.713 (1981).

6. The appeal was denied on the dubious ground that restriction of religious *practice* would not interfere with religious *belief*. See ch. 8 above.

Some have thought that the omission of freedom of conscience in the First Amendment should be redressed.[7] The difficulty of stretching the meaning of religious belief until it becomes quasi-religious has certainly supplied one good reason for redress.

Have Attempts to Restore Freedom of Conscience Appealed Instead to Quasi-Conscience?

Among those who advocate appeal to freedom of conscience, there has been disagreement about what gives *force* to an appeal to conscience. Suggestions have included the associated intensity of feeling, the role of conscience in constituting a person's identity, or its role in the rational capacity for self-direction of one's life.[8] I think that this looks to features more or less *correlated* with conscience, rather than at conscience itself, even though I agree that for those who feel the force of conscience *strongly*, the expression "I could not live with myself" displays the connection of a clear conscience with integrity. But the appeal to conscience has force, I believe, because, when it concerns the present or future, it represents a person's belief about what it would be *wrong* for them to do in an expected situation calling for decision. A person's sense of what it would be *wrong* for them to do has a special weight, and causes a degree of inhibition against overriding it. This is not to say that it trumps other considerations, and if rights are thought to trump, it will certainly *not* be a *right*. Appeals to conscience can be defeated—they are *defeasible*. But by contrast with the sense of what it would be wrong for one to do, the other considerations mentioned seem to me to be less directly connected to conscience, and also to be imperfectly correlated with it.

7. See Michael Sandel, *Democracy's Discontent*, Harvard University Press 1996; Amy Gutmann, *Identity in Democracy*, Princeton University Press 2003; Kwame Anthony Appiah, *The Ethics of Identity*, Princeton University Press 2005; Martha Nussbaum, *Liberty of Conscience*, as above.

8. For constitution of the person, see work cited in ch. 7, Michael Sandel, *Democracy's Discontent*, 67; Amy Gutmann, *Identity in Democracy*, 171; Kwame Anthony Appiah, *The Ethics of Identity*, 99; William Galston, *The Practice of Liberal Pluralism*, Cambridge University Press 2005, 67; cf. Jocelyn Maclure and Charles Taylor, *Secularism and Freedom of Conscience*, Harvard University Press 2011, 76, 89, 91, 108. For intensity of feeling, see Maclure and Taylor, *Secularism and Freedom of Conscience*, 97, and the report of Justice Harlan's advocacy in the case of Welsh, 1970, in Andrew Koppleman, "Conscience, volitional necessity and religious exemptions," as above, p. 224, and his critique at pp. 216, 221–22, 224, 225, 236–37. For rational capacity for self-direction, see David A. J. Richards, *Toleration and the Constitution*, Oxford University Press 1989, pp.71–80, 133–35, 144.

The issue arises not only in connection with the question what gives *force* to appeals to conscience, but also in connection with the further question what appeals have the *right force* to deserve protection under the law. In their important book, *Secularism and Freedom of Conscience*, based on their official report in 2007 to the government of Quebec in Canada on Accommodation Practices Related to Cultural Differences, two philosophers, Jocelyn Maclure and Charles Taylor, discussed secularism. They recommended a form of secularism as an attitude of government in a multicultural society toward diversity of beliefs, especially beliefs concerning religion, including atheism. They considered that freedom of conscience as well as freedom of religion needed special protection in some cases. In order to delineate the cases, they referred not to what I have taken to be the defining characteristics of conscience, but to all three of the correlated features. What needs protection, in their recommendation, is "core beliefs," and these are beliefs that "allow people to structure their moral identity and to exercise their faculty of judgment." Moreover, it is "the intensity of the person's commitment to a given conviction or practice that constitutes the similarity between religious convictions and secular convictions."[9] I am not sure that so far this is narrow enough to capture the idea of conscience, until reference is added to what I have taken to be its defining characteristics. One could imagine someone for whom making money satisfied all the criteria. His success in making money made him feel not merely good at moneymaking, but also like a good person (a "jolly good fellow"). Moneymaking allowed him to structure his identity, and if "good person" is a moral category, his *moral* identity. His belief in the need to make money might be intensely felt, and it would facilitate his rational capacity for directing his life. What is needed to make his belief and practice one of *conscience* is some reference to what it would be morally wrong for him to do or not to do. In the example imagined, the belief and practice of moneymaking would not need protection as a matter of conscience, since it is an agreed form of life in no danger from opposing viewpoints. But if for any reason it needed to be presented as a matter of conscience, that could easily be achieved by citing duties to family and shareholders, or, more admirably, by deliberately taking on duties to society.

The point is only that such a reference to what it would be wrong to neglect needs to be added, if a belief or practice is to be presented as one of conscience, however much it may already meet the three criteria cited.

9. Jocelyn Maclure and Charles Taylor, *Secularism and Freedom of Conscience*, 76 (cf. 89, 91, 108) and 97.

If that is so, the three criteria are not *sufficient* to constitute a case of conscience. I suspect that they are also not necessary. Too much reflection on conflicting demands of conscience might *impede* a conscientious person in structuring his or her moral identity. Alternatively, conscientious practice may admit of *lower* degrees of reflection or feeling, and of effect on personal identity, as well as higher. What is true is that someone who goes so far as sincerely to plead conscience in a court of law is likely to have reflected carefully, to have high intensity of feeling, and to have an identity partly structured by conscience. So what is being appealed to is not conscience itself, but conscience sincerely invoked under the pressure of court hearings. We might call this quasi-conscience by analogy with the quasi-religious belief invoked by the US courts, although that is rather a misnomer since it is a particularly strong example of conscience, not a bogus one, but the point is that it is not a standard one. This exemplary type of conscience is exactly what lawyers are right to consider. But that is not the same as a philosophical consideration of what conscience is in general.

Hate Speech: Impact of Freedom of Speech on Freedom of Religion

I now turn to the third freedom, freedom of speech. It has been emphasized not only in legal interpretations of the US First Amendment, but also, we have seen, in the arguments of Milton and Mill, who saw it as a route to truth.[10] But at a certain point, it can impact on freedom of religion. To follow Michael Sandel's account of interpretations of the US free speech clause,[11] the clause led in 1978 to a conflict with protection of the sensitivities of a religious ethnic group. A provocative Nazi demonstration was authorized in the village of Skokie, a suburb of Chicago, which included a Jewish community with survivors of Hitler's Nazi extermination camps. The demonstrators carried placards saying, "Hitler should have finished the job."[12] Interpretation of the free speech clause also led to striking down the local Skokie government's "racial slur" ordinance prohibiting the dissemination of materials promoting "hatred against persons by reason of their race, national origin, or religion."[13] The district court cited the Supreme

10. Ch. 8 above.

11. Michael Sandel, *Democracy's Discontent*, 72–75, 85–86, citing *Police Department of the City of Chicago v. Mosley* 48 U.S., 95–96.

12. The information on placards is supplied by Jeremy Waldron, *The Harm in Hate Speech*, Harvard University Press 2012, 34.

13. *Collin v. Smith*, 447F Supp. 676, 686–87 (1978) 578F. 2d 1197, 1202 (1978).

Court's earlier decision in 1972 that "the First Amendment means that government has no power to restrict expression because of its message, its ideas, its subject matter, or its content." This was parallel to interpretation of the freedom of religion clauses that religious beliefs were to be accommodated regardless of *content*. The only protection envisaged against the Nazi demonstration would have been if it had created a clear and present danger, for example of riot or crime. But the law-abiding Jewish community was not likely to riot. One might again wonder about this ruling whether an aggressive community likely to retaliate with riot or counterattack could have gained the protection from a Nazi demonstration that was denied to a law-abiding group. Further objections to the "racial slur" ordinance were that the harm expected by the Jewish residents was not physical, and that government might not punish defamation against groups, as opposed to individuals. This was in a certain way opposite to the interpretation of the religion clauses: groups were not exempt from defamation under the freedom of speech clause, but under the freedom of religion clauses it was for a long time *only* groups that were exempt from conscription. Could a rationale have been that there was not the same wish for individuals to be free to create new religions as to express new thoughts?

Certainly, there are reasons for giving considerable weight to freedom of speech, besides those of Milton and Mill. The US free speech decisions, according to one account,[14] sought to protect individuals from state interference. In a country which had accommodated from elsewhere groups with such a radical diversity of viewpoints, the government felt constrained to think of individuals as artificially divorced from affiliation to their competing groups, so as not favor one group over others. Moreover—and this would apply also to the freedom of religion clauses—it did not yet feel secure enough in 1791 to impose its own values concerning what would count as unacceptable speech, or as unacceptable religious belief. The authors of the Quebec report put it well when they advocated a view in their book close to the US view. A law allowing freedom of speech, however much some might be offended, protects liberal and democratic states from *stagnation* (the concern of Milton and Mill) and *authoritarianism* (the US concern).[15] There are other dangers too in seeking to protect religions from upsetting effects of freedom of speech. Laws or decrees against blasphemy

14. Robert C. Post, "Cultural heterogeneity and law: pornography, blasphemy and the First Amendment," *California Law Review*, vol. 76, 1988, 296–335, at 311–14.

15. Jocelyn Maclure and Charles Taylor, *Secularism and Freedom of Conscience*, 108.

can promote witch hunts against blasphemy. Luther has been accused of associating with blasphemy abandonment of the Apostles' Creed, absence from church and membership of the Catholics or Anabaptists, because the charge of blasphemy made it easier to punish divergence of belief.[16] The Ayatollah's fatwa decreed against the Muslim novelist Salman Rushdie called for his assassination without trial, and did so even though he was living under a nonreligious jurisdiction in Britain.

On the other hand, is any verbal attack on a religion to be allowed in any country, regardless of the historical context in that country? In some countries religions coexist that are far more diverse than the different persuasions of Christianity considered by the US founding fathers. So the likelihood of interfaith massacres in response to insult is correspondingly greater. Moreover, the harm in hate speech consists not only in the wounding of feelings. Jeremy Waldron has argued that the harm comes most of all from hate speech written in public places, whether in physical spaces, newspapers, or on the web. The persistence of such messages fosters the creation of groups of second-class citizens. A further problem concerns a country's *external* relations. Hate speech by a single uncontrolled person against religious groups *within* one's own country can trigger reprisals against citizens and property *across the globe,* in places where one has neither jurisdiction nor control. This kind of liability scarcely existed in 1791. Some symbolic attacks against a particular religion seem gratuitous. When cartoons were published in Denmark in 2005 ridiculing the Prophet, it seemed out of place to hear them defended on grounds of freedom of speech, when one recalls the personal risk against real oppression with which freedom of speech had been sought in the seventeenth century. The law, however, would not necessarily have provided the best corrective to that hate speech, and there was no prosecution in Denmark, although a prosecution was attempted when the cartoons were reprinted in France.

If it is reform of unjust or cruel religious practices that is sought, neither hate speech nor, on its own, legislation is likely to produce it, although legislation may be part of a wider program of support. There are cases in which legislation has had the merit of promulgating an ideal, without yet being enforceable. I have discussed elsewhere the religious practice of child marriage at an earlier time, when legislation against it would not have been

16. Roland H. Bainton, "The development and consistency of Luther's attitude to religious liberty," *Harvard Theological Review* 22, 1929, 107–49, at pp. 118–19 and 148, citing for abandonment of his preferred creed Luther's treatment of the 82nd Psalm (*Luthers Werke,* Weimar edition, vol. 31[1], p. 208).

enforceable in the absence of birth certificates. Moreover, the advantages of conformity would not have been appreciated without new education and new employment opportunities for women.[17]

Different Balances in Different Countries among the Three Freedoms

I think it is useful to see the different balances that have been struck in different countries between and within the three freedoms of speech, religion, and conscience. Taking up freedom of speech, without particularly addressing the other two freedoms, Jeremy Waldron has now impressively surveyed the regulation of hate speech in most European countries and Canada.[18] Hence I shall confine myself to taking some examples from a *different* country, India. I believe these show a much greater variety of considerations to be relevant to balance than I have so far discussed.

India's Freedom of Speech and the "Deliberate Malice" Safeguard

To start with freedom of speech, I think the Indian penal code seems to have attempted a more satisfactory balance. It included provisions (153-A and 295-A) against causing hatred of, or fear in, other groups, and against outraging or wounding religious feelings. But the religious feeling laws were hedged by a very salutary requirement that *deliberate and malicious intention* must be proved.[19] Moreover, the penalties under both laws were comparatively *light*. Both provisions ought to have made it difficult to use the law as a vehicle for anti-blasphemy witch hunts. No need arose to define what would count as *reasonable* outrage, not because the law invoked Waldron's idea of second-class citizenship. Rather, the need to prove deliberate and malicious intention bypassed the question of whether outrage was reasonable.

I have to admit that the laudable attempt at balance is not always easy to apply. But sometimes it is not the original law at fault, but *implementation* of that law. Of course if the original law is not implemented, it will be no good

17. Richard Sorabji, *Opening Doors: The Untold Story of Cornelia Sorabji, Reformer, Lawyer and Champion of Women's Rights in India*, Penguin India, I. B. Tauris 2010.

18. Jeremy Waldron, *The Harm in Hate Speech*.

19. Since 2006, a comparable appeal to intention has been adopted in the UK Racial and Religious Hatred Act, which makes it an offense to use "threatening words or behaviour, or display any written material which is threatening, . . . if he intends thereby to stir up religious hatred."

introducing a law requiring implementation. But other laws can be used to counter nonimplementation. India has introduced the Right to Information and Public Interest Litigation. The first can reveal how implementation is being blocked, the second permits litigation on noncompliance. Both of these can strengthen a wide range of rights, the right to freedom of expression among others. But the problem remains that these further laws themselves need to be implemented so that even good legislation requires unending vigilance.

India: Protecting Diversity of Religious Practice versus Protecting Individuals from Religious Practices

Indian legislation considered not only freedom of speech and its restriction. Article 25 (1) of the Indian Constitution called also for freedom of *conscience* and freedom to practice, profess, and propagate *religion*. I take much of my account from a recent subtle treatment that brings out some of the incompatibilities between different considerations.[20] The unexpected inclusion of *propagation*, which might reasonably have been considered inflammatory in a society of many religions, was a requirement secured by the Christian community. The multireligion situation of India had to give much more radical thought to the need for balance, and it provides entirely different reasons why it may be impossible to secure one freedom without sacrificing another. India's constitution was called secular, and secularism was in 1973 declared to be an unemendable feature of the constitution. But secularism is not in itself a very clarifying notion, because it allows for incompatible interpretations. The constitution inherited provisions from the Indian Penal Code written by the British under the chairmanship of Lord Macaulay, and introduced in 1860. Thus India continued different civil law for Muslims, allowing, for example, polygamy to them, but not to other religions. The approach that was thus continued had already been begun by the British East India Company in the eighteenth century. But in 1860, the British motivation included an urgent new consideration. After the Indian uprising of 1857, the British were anxious, among other things, to secure colonial government by not interfering provocatively with religion. This policy favored the rights of religious groups rather than of subgroups within

20. Rochana Bajpai, "The conceptual vocabularies of secularism and minority rights in India" *Journal of Political Ideologies* 7, 2002, 179–97; and *Debating Difference: Group Rights and Liberal Democracy in India*, Oxford University Press 2011.

them like women, or of individuals. Independent India retained different civil laws for Muslims for their own reasons.

It has been argued that in the Indian Constituent Assembly debates in the newly independent India of 1946–1949, the need for national unity was prominent, and this transferred attention to the rights of the individual citizen and away from the rights of potentially fissiparous religious groups. The idea grew that religious laws about personal life should not be protected if they denied equal rights to all citizens regardless of religious affiliation.[21] This addressed Waldron's more recent concern with not creating second-class citizens. But the difference was that this threat arose not from permitting free *speech*, but from the danger of overindulgence to practice in religious groups. In line with this policy, 25 (2) of the Indian Constitution allowed for the *reform* of aspects of Hindu law and mentioned particularly certain religious institutions of the Hindu majority. In 1956, Parliament passed four Hindu Code bills, modified in the light of opposition, that somewhat improved the position of Hindu women as regards divorce and inheritance.

But, unexpectedly, the same kind of issue arose with the Muslim minority as well. In 1986, the Indian Supreme Court rejected the plea of a Muslim that Muslim personal law allowed him to restrict maintenance payments to Shah Bano, his divorced wife, to a three-month period. The court invoked the *criminal* code, applicable to all irrespective of religion, and declared that it overrode the Muslim personal laws. It further declared that the *civil* code ought also to have been made the same for all citizens. Thus it was prepared to override beliefs of conscience—in this case what conscience permitted, not what it required—and beliefs of religion, in order to gain equal treatment for all citizens, regardless of religious affiliation. The rival desires in this case, the desire to reform for the sake of equal rights for individuals regardless of their religion, and the desire to respect the different personal laws of different religions might both be seen as worthy. The first was avowedly secular, the second was secular to the extent of not privileging the majority religion, but tolerating all religions.[22] But in this case the two desires proved incompatible: protecting diversity of religious practice and protecting individuals from unfair religious practice. In India, where most people have religious adherences, the politicians in the Shah

21. Rochana Bajpai, *Debating Difference* 2011, 88–96, 103–107, 193.

22. For a related ambiguity in Indian ideas of the secular, see Ashis Nandy and Ramin Jehanbegloo, *Talking India: Ashis Nandy in Conversation with Ramin Jehanbegloo*, Oxford University Press 2006, p. 97.

Bano case upheld religious diversity, whereas the courts had tried to protect individuals.

Another interesting feature in the Supreme Court's decision was that it went further, and looked at the actual *content* of Muslim law and the Koran, in a way that would not have been allowed in US courts, to argue that Islamic law was compatible with the maintenance provisions of the criminal code. Concern with the *content* of religious belief arose not only in relation to Muslims, but also in relation to Hindus in connection with a Bombay law that Hindu temples must be open to all Hindus. In 1966, a Hindu sect called the Satsangis claimed exemption from this law by claiming that they were not Hindus. The courts looked at the *content* of Hinduism to provide a definition of it, and argued that the Satsangis were Hindus, and so must comply.[23]

The Supreme Court decision in the case of Shah Bano, however, was reversed by Parliament. Alarmed by the strength of Muslim protests, it reversed the Supreme Court's decision by introducing a new law restoring force to the Muslim personal law on maintenance of divorced wives. It thus protected Muslim personal law, not because it approved its content, but without regard to its content, in the manner that US courts would approve, just because it was Muslim law. It overrode progressive Muslims among its own members on the supposition that they would form a minority in the Muslim population at large. Moreover, the protection was at the cost of equal treatment for divorced Indian women regardless of their religious affiliation. In this case, not only had the criminal law favored the opposite result, but its implementation was going to be enforced. The reversal of the law was introduced for different political reasons.

Overview and Conclusion

A number of reasons have been considered why the law should allow freedom of speech against groups. Free speech is a route to truth. It prevents stagnation holding us to one point of view, and it opposes authoritarianism on the part of the State. But reasons have also been considered why it needs some restriction, because hate speech can create second-class citizens, disturb the peace, and endanger life and property at home and abroad; and the outraging or wounding of sentiment causes distress often to no good purpose. But limits on freedom of speech against groups need

23. Matthew John, "Indian exceptionalism?," Asia Research Centre Working Paper 17, London School of Economics, http://eprints.lse.ac.uk/25192/.

severe restrictions, so as to avoid encouraging witch hunts and accusations of blasphemy.

In a society with a plurality of religions, there may be an incompatibility between protecting the practices of religious groups and protecting individual or sub-groups within those groups—for example, women—if those groups discriminate against them.

I would draw two further conclusions. Firstly, no balance between different desiderata can satisfy all requirements, although some balances may be better than others for a given historical moment and context. Secondly, there is no such thing as a balance that would be good for all countries independently of historical context. The need to protect religious groups was rather strong in seventeenth-century England, where they were often persecuted. In newly independent India, the need for national unity was more important.

In the next chapter, I shall consider again the nature of conscience, whether the resecularization of conscience has been a help or a hindrance, the value of conscience, and how the challenge of unreliability can be met. The last will bring us back to the value of free discussion.

TWELVE

Retrospect: Nature and Value of Conscience

Nature of Conscience: Two Prolonged Deviations, Individual Variations, and Two Violations

It proved possible to sketch a preliminary account of what conscience is at the end of chapter 1. The various interpretations that have been encountered since then, or the recent resecularization of conscience, do not necessarily require all that many revisions to the general picture. The two most prolonged deviations encountered did not last indefinitely. One was the need to accomodate *synderesis* alongside conscience, which made one difference if *synderesis* took over the motivational role from conscience, or another difference if it relegated conscience to the act of drawing a conclusion rather than holding a belief. A second deviation was the idea that conscience was a *sentiment* of approval or disapproval, or even a sensation of pain, rather than a *belief* or capacity for belief about what conduct or attitude was or would be wrong for one, a belief that might *cause* sentiments or pain.

There have been other variations in the idea of conscience, and I have tried to note them as we went along. But the concept of St. Paul, building on the Greek concept, had some authority in the Christian tradition. Moreover, it explains why some alternative accounts proved tempting, such as the last-mentioned idea that conscience is a sentiment of disapproval or a pain, features which are *caused* by its being a belief about being in the wrong. Again it supplies a framework against which it is possible to see the continuity and make sense of the variations in those who introduced them. The definition cited from Calvin drew from St. Paul only the Day of Judgment function of conscience. Pierre Bayle included a Pauline idea of conscience, but expanded his idea to include also *doctrines* that were matters of conscience, both doctrines about God and doctrines about general principles. Adam Smith's idea of conscience as an imagined impartial spectator drew on the Stoics, and retained a version of the original idea of a split person, along with the idea of being in the wrong and self-awareness of that wrong, even though he did not settle on one rather than another aspect of the spectator situation as his official definition of "conscience," but appealed to that situation as a whole. Such variability was even more marked in Kant. He retained the ideas of a split person, of being in the wrong and of self-awareness. But in developing the idea of being in the wrong he gave to conscience an increasing variety of *judicial* roles, while assigning to other agencies, such as understanding, the original idea of it as a certain kind of *belief*. Rousseau's vicar and Gandhi both differed from St. Paul in speaking of conscience as the voice of God. But Bayle, more cautiously, confined himself to saying that it was *interpreted* as the voice of God and Newman fell back on a similar position.

In contrast with these intelligible variations, a few people violated the original spirit of the idea of moral conscience, but they were acting as enemies of conscience as ordinarily understood and were making a case. Thomas Hobbes and on one occasion Oliver Cromwell, I believe, refused to recognize that conscience was not any old kind of belief, but a belief about what *actions* would be wrong for one, when they claimed that in suppressing action, they were not suppressing conscience. Admittedly, conscience was (later) expanded by Bayle to include doctrines, but these doctrines were expected to have implications for action, and in any case they did not supplant the traditional inclusion in conscience of beliefs about what actions would be wrong for one. Hobbes and (once) Cromwell differed in that they justified extensive interference with action only by closing their eyes to the connection of conscience with an individual's beliefs about how it would be wrong for that individual to act. Nietzsche's attack on conscience sought to reinterpret it as a dysfunctional attitude of hostility to oneself and ignored the historical details of the core concept. Whether or not these deviations were willful, even in their case, the concept developed by the Greeks and St. Paul still provides a useful framework. For it helps to make clear what the violations are and why they are violations.

In order to recapitulate, I attempt to describe the core concept against which intelligible deviations, variations, or violations occurred.

The Core Concept

The core conception of conscience which I have found to be most influential contains the following ideas:

1 It is a person's *belief* about what actions or attitudes had been in the past, or would be in the future, wrong or not wrong for him to adopt or not adopt in a particular situation. It could also be the *capacity* for such beliefs. The beliefs may be the things believed or the believing of them.
2 The beliefs require *personal* self-awareness and are in the first instance beliefs about what would be wrong for *oneself*.
3 Conscience is *motivating* because it is a *value* belief about what was or would be wrong for oneself. It can therefore cause both sentiments of approval or disapproval and painful or comforting sensations.
4 This connection with being in the *wrong* accounts for the *force* of, and respect for, conscience of others, for no one wants to be in the wrong. We do not have to look for something contingently and variably connected, such as its sometimes being central to people's identity, or causing intensity of feeling, or contributing to self-direction.
5 Conscience is acquired, not innate, nor present from birth.
6 It draws on values which need not take the form of laws, but which are in danger of reflecting merely local convention, and therefore require constant reflection and awareness of other values.
7 It is not the voice of God, and its value does not depend on whether the values derive from God.
8 It is not infallible.
9 Conscience creates an obligation, but not always an overriding obligation, since there can be counter-obligations, so that one is in a double bind, wrong if one does follow conscience and wrong if one does not.
10 Freedom of conscience is the absence, within limits, of forcible constraint by authority not only on one's value beliefs, but also on the *actions* which those value beliefs forbid or require.
11 Freedom of conscience is a narrower term than toleration. Toleration can be recommended on many grounds besides the desirability of freedom of conscience, such as the need for peace.
12 Freedom of religion is not the same as freedom of conscience, but the two overlap and many of the same arguments can be given for both. Conscience, however, can be secular, and there are some advantages in its being so.
13 Freedom of conscience has different meanings.

The Relation between Conscience and Values

It was very useful that Paul distinguished conscience from the values which conscience applied to one's own case. Although Paul had good reason for speaking of these values as a general *law*, I would prefer to speak of general *values*. If laws are thought of as rules, then it is quite difficult to find many as specific and instructive as the Ten Commandments, and even these do not cover all the moral decisions in life, nor command agreement among all humans alike. The Stoics' favorite example of a moral law was not specific, but, as seen in chapter 1, simply told us not to break the bonds of human society. They thought that specific moral rules tended to have endless exceptions, and they had a belief, which I have found also in Gandhi, that different people in the same circumstances have different individual duties (in Gandhi a different *svadharma*), because of their different individual *personae*.[1] What *is* needed, on this view, for moral decisions is not rules with their exceptions, but a sense of the values that matter in a human life and in an individual's life. This sense of values that matter, not being infallible or agreed, requires continuing reflection.

It is not conscience (at least not conscience in the core sense) that has to *supply* our values in the first place. St. Paul ascribes the inner law to God; a secular view should agree that conscience is never the original source of our values, even though particular decisions of conscience can lead to new reflection on general values, without being their original source. Conscience rather *applies* values to the conduct and thoughts of the individual. It became particularly clear in the case of Gandhi that the source of his original views on nonviolence was his reading of Tolstoy, but his conscience had to be brought to bear on how to *apply* those values to the case of shooting potentially rabid dogs, and this reflection in turn enriched and modified his values.

Benefits of Resecularization of Conscience, Including for Religion

I argued that the original idea of sharing knowledge with oneself of a defect started off secular in the fifth-century BCE playwrights, in Plato and above all in Epicurus. So the process of gradual secularization in the eighteenth to twentieth centuries is best seen as a process of *resecularization*. If I am right that the concept started off secular among the Greeks, where it performed a useful function, we should not think that the changes brought about by re-

1. Richard Sorabji, *Self: Ancient and Modern Insights about Individuality, Life, and Death*, Oxford University Press and University of Chicago Press 2006, ch. 8; *Gandhi and the Stoics: Modern Experiments on Ancient Values*, Oxford University Press and University of Chicago Press 2012, chs. 6 and 7.

secularization would necessarily rob it of value. I believe it actually involves some benefits, not least for religion itself.

One possible benefit of resecularization is that it may reduce dogmatism about one's own values, if we do not believe in a God-given law in our hearts, and it may encourage us to revise mistaken values. But there is something more positive that needs to be said. If a constitution offers to protect freedom of conscience, it needs a concept of conscience that is itself secular enough to be open between different religious beliefs, and other concepts need secularization too. The concept of *conviction or faith* (*pistis*) in Origen was so *unsecularized* that heretical belief was called credulity rather than conviction. An advantage of a secular concept of conscience is that it can be used in considering claims for protection independently of any particular religious views, as has happened in England with objections to military service. But at the same time it need not commit itself to protecting every sincere belief, however disruptive.

Limits to Freedom of Conscience, and the Appeal to Toleration

We saw that there were limits to freedom of conscience, arising from *erroneous* conscience. Problems were raised by Origen about whether freedom of conscience excused heresy, and by Abelard and Thomas Aquinas about consciences that called for killing the apostles or crucifying Christ. They were raised against the Levellers about consciences that called for polygamy. Protection for conscience has been claimed in other controversial areas, such as the refusal of blood transfusions for a family's children, or objection to military service based on anarchistic belief. On the other hand, we rightly feel some inhibition against overriding consciences, partly because of the point made above that conscience involves the idea of being in the *wrong*, and we appreciate that no one wants to be in the wrong.

The question was brought to a head particularly by Pierre Bayle, who started off by saying that erroneous conscience should be allowed freedom as much as correct conscience. His argument was shown to lead to a paradox by licensing *persecution* by erroneous consciences of beliefs held as matters of conscience by others. The persecutors would then, in the name of freedom of conscience, end up by *denying* freedom of conscience to those whom they persecuted. Instead, Bayle finished up relying on the need to tolerate incorrect doctrine, but within limits and for reasons *other* than freedom of conscience, namely keeping the peace. There were many other motives too for toleration and it was seen that Augustine's motives included love of one's neighbor, awaiting God's judgment, and the hope that toleration would unite the Church. Toleration, then, is a more wide-ranging source of protection than freedom of conscience. The US Constitution allowed freedom of religion, but not of conscience, while the Constitution of Canada has only recently added freedom of conscience to freedom of religion.

The issue of limits to freedom of conscience has an analogue in the question of limits to freedom of religious practice. Polygamy has indeed been allowed for Muslims in India's civil law, we saw in chapter 11, while being denied to other Indian faiths. So freedom of religion has there allowed a considerable degree of diversity. That is not to say that the law would transplant into societies with a higher rate of interfaith marriage or different laws of inheritance or of State welfare provision for children.

Value and Improving the Value of Conscience

Regarding the value of conscience, its role in averting from wrongdoing, or reforming was noticed very early. Both functions are ascribed to Epicurus, and in the fifth century BCE, writing not of sharing knowledge with oneself, but of a good kind of shame, the playwright Euripides saw the merit of such shame in its averting one's wrongdoing.

The most important criticism of conscience, I believe, was that it was derived from custom or superstition. In answering this criticism, we need to distinguish between the human *capacity* for making judgments of right and wrong and the actual content of the values applied in those judgments. The case of a certain rare form of autism in which its victims show no sense of right and wrong reminds us how alien that would be to normal human life. In 1945, there was a study of a patient called "L."[2] He did not react emotionally when other children removed his toys, evidently not seeing them as *his* in a sense that carried its normal emotional implications. Asked what would happen if he shot someone, he made no reference to his own responsibility, but replied that *he* (the victim) would go to hospital.[3] When we consider such an absence of the capacity to make judgments of right and wrong in relation to himself or others, we can hardly doubt that it is a desirable capacity for humans.

2. M. Scheerer, E. Rothmann, and K.Goldstein, "A case of 'idiot savant': An experimental study of personality organisation," *Psychological Monographs* 58, 4, 269, 1945, 1–63.

3. Simon Baron-Cohen, H. Tager-Flusberg, and D. Cohen, eds., *Understanding Other Minds: Perspectives from Autism*, Oxford University Press 1993; Simon Baron-Cohen, "Precursors to a theory of mind: understanding attention in others," in A. Whiten, ed., *Natural Theories of Mind. Evolution, Development and Simulation of Everyday Mindreading*, Blackwell 1991; Peter Hobson, *The Cradle of Thought: Exploring the Origins of Thinking*, Oxford University Press 2002, chs. 7 and 8.

But the criticism about custom or superstition concerned something different from capacity, namely the *content* of the values applied, which may be woefully mistaken. However, it should be the job of a philosopher to consider how that defect might be corrected. It is not only thinking that can help to correct the defect, but also art, because imagination is needed to expand the beliefs on which conscience draws, perhaps even more than thought. *Uncle Tom's Cabin* may have had more effect than philosophical discussion on attitudes to slavery. But I shall consider thinkers. We have already encountered many contributions, but the one which I believe looked in the wrong direction was John Locke's idea that we might find moral principles of mathematical certainty and universality.

Among the positive contributions to increasing reliability, some focused on making conscience more reliable at applying values rather than on making the values themselves more reliable. But rethinking applications can sometimes result in refining the values themselves. St. Paul, who thought that moral laws were written in our hearts by God, was aware that conscience was fallible in applying these laws, and he uttered some correctives himself. Bonaventure's contribution to reliability in the thirteenth century was to say that erroneous conscience does not bind us to act or not to act, but to *get rid* of the error. Pierre Bayle in requiring us to examine the moral and theological doctrines by which we lived as matters of conscience, suggested an exercise of imagining their importation into a new country. He also considered a huge number of objections to his initial plea for freedom of erroneous conscience and moved to the idea of toleration to keep the peace. Further, though himself a victim of Catholic persecution by the French king, he proposed restrictions on Protestant freedom to persecute Catholics in a way that would have been unusual in England at the time, although it had been the position of the early seventeenth-century English Baptists and was to be that of William Penn. Kant insisted that conscience needs to be repeatedly awakened, with frequent evocation of consciousness of one's deeds. One must also sharpen attentiveness to the voice of conscience and use every means to obtain a hearing for it. Adam Smith had gone further, with his insistence that what is needed is a conscience that serves not just as an imagined spectator, but as an imagined *impartial* spectator. But even impartiality may not be enough if it is impartiality within the background of assumptions with which one first grew up.

I come finally to the contributions of J. S.Mill and Mahatma Gandhi. Gandhi, despite his view that conscience was the indubitable voice of God, provided a very good example of how we can develop the *values* on which conscience *draws*. He favored the view that only partial perspectives on the truth are available to any one person.[4] This was a reason for learning from other cultures, but not for wholesale conversion from one partial perspective to another. Gandhi himself rejected the Jain view of nonviolence that he had learned at home, but found his assumptions changed when he was converted to nonviolence by reading someone from another culture, Tolstoy.[5] He learned about many of his favorite books, even about his beloved Indian scripture, the *Bhagavadgita*, from that culture, reading it first in English translation when introduced by English friends.

Gandhi learned not only from friends, but, as we saw in the case of the potentially rabid dogs, from opponents. The seven articles of 1926 about its being right to shoot the dogs made Gandhi's reflections on what was right a cooperative process and, thanks to his weekly newspapers, a nationwide and even worldwide process. He finished with a greatly enriched view of nonviolence. All killing was violent, unless carried out for the sake of the killed, as in euthanasia. Even killing to protect others was violent. Moreover, violence was always wrong, without exception. But failure to protect against rabid dogs or snakes could be even more wrong, a *double* bind. It remained preferable, as he first said, for the municipality to shoot the potentially rabid dogs. But even though that showed nonviolence not to be morally possible in this case, it was still best to adhere to it as a counsel of perfection, not always achievable, because that helped one to raise one's aspirations and aim high. Gandhi was enriching his understanding (and ours) of his conscientious belief in nonviolence.

The best *verbal* account of how to strengthen the values which one's conscience applies was the one described in chapter 8 from Mill in his treatment of liberty, although he did not even mention conscience, thinking it a mere pain that did not entertain knowledge or belief. But he was developing a view of John Milton, who did discuss conscience, when he advocated free discussion of rival beliefs as the best route to truth. Like Gandhi after him, Mill was recommending learning, not wholesale conversion. To recall, he held that one did not know one's own case until one knew one's opponent's. Even Newton's views would seem uncertain if it were forbidden to question them. Without free discussion, even true opinions are *superstition*. Here Mill uses Locke's word. One could not see the grounds for one's own

4. Letter to Devdas Gandhi, March 5, 1922, eCW, vol. 26, p. 287; Letter to Mathuradas Trikumji, March 6, 1922, eCW, p. 288; "Three vital questions," *Young India*, January 21, 1926, eCW, vol. 33, pp. 408–11; Letter to D. B. Kalelkar, July 2, 1926, eCW, vol. 35, pp. 454–56; Discussion with Dharmadev, eCW, vol. 59, pp. 494–97. Compare the idea that there is more than one road to God in Themistius, Symmachus, and Bayle.

5. Gandhi is discussed on these issues in Richard Sorabji, *Gandhi and the Stoics*.

case, or even take in its full meaning, without facing up to its rivals. One's beliefs could not have the same regulative force in one's life if the rival views had not been confronted. One might supplement one's views with those of others. But even if one kept the same views, one would have transformed one's understanding of them. Mill's prescription is secular. It certainly does not depend on the idea that there is a God-given inner law. But it can be used by those who believe there is, so long as they do not think that they know it all already. It moves them from looking only at their own tradition, to comparing themselves with others, and with dissenting others. These recommendations are a world away from Locke's brief sketch of an imaginary demonstrative system providing mathematical certainty cited in chapter 8.

Gandhi differed from Mill in that he provided a *living* example of what Mill advocated. Moreover, his discussions were on a nationwide and worldwide scale that Mill could scarcely have imagined. This is the direction in which the criticism should be answered, that one's moral principles can depend on custom or superstition: it is up to us whether they do or not.

SELECT BIBLIOGRAPHY

GENERAL TREATMENTS OF MORAL CONSCIENCE

Edward G. Andrew, *Conscience and Its Critics*, University of Toronto 2001.

James F. Childress, "Appeals to conscience," *Ethics* 89, 1979, 315–35.

C. S. Lewis, "Conscience and conscious," in his *Studies in Words*, 2nd ed., Cambridge University Press 1967, ch. 8.

Ian Shapiro and Robert Adams, eds., *Integrity and Conscience, Nomos* 40, New York University Press 1998.

Paul Strohm, *Conscience: A Very Short Introduction*, Oxford University Press 2011.

ANTIQUITY FROM THE FIFTH CENTURY BCE AND THE CHRISTIAN RESPONSE

G. E. M. Anscombe, "Modern moral philosophy," *Philosophy* 33, 1958, 1–19.

Jed W. Atkins, "Euripides' *Orestes* and the concept of conscience in Greek philosophy," *Journal of the History of Ideas* 75, 2014, 1–22.

Shadi Bartsch, *The Mirror of the Self: Sexuality, Self-Knowledge, and the Gaze in the Early Roman Empire*, University of Chicago Press 2006.

Henry Chadwick, "Conscience in ancient thought," reprinted as ch. 20 in his *Studies in Ancient Christianity*, Ashgate 2006. English original with revisions of the German of 1978.

Michel Foucault gave six lectures at University of California–Berkeley in 1983. The fifth, "Techniques of Parrhesia," at www.foucault.info/documents/parrhesia/.

Michel Foucault, "Technologies of the Self": a seminar with Michel Foucault, ed. L. H. Martin et al., London 1988, pp. 16–49, amended with footnotes in *Essential Works of Foucault, 1954–1984*, vol. 1, ed. Paul Rabinow, *Ethics*; Penguin 1997, and without footnotes: http://foucault.info/documents/foucault.technologiesofself.en.htm.

J. Hebing, "Ueber conscientia und conservatio im philosophischen Sinne bei den Römern von Cicero bis Hieronymus," *Philosophisches Jahrbuch* 35, 1922, 136–52, 215–31, 298–326.

Rachana Kamtekar, "Aidôs in Epictetus," *Classical Philology* 93, 1998, 136–60.

David Konstan, *Before Forgiveness*, Cambridge University Press 2010.

C. A. Pierce, *Conscience in the New Testament*, SCM Press, London 1955.

Richard Sorabji, "Graeco-Roman origins of the idea of moral conscience," in *Studia Patristica* 44, 2010, 361–83.

Richard Sorabji, "Moral conscience: contributions to the idea in Plato and Platonism," in Vassilis Karasmanis and Eliza Tutellier, eds., *Presocratics and Plato: A Festschrift in Honor of Charles Kahn*, Parmenides Publishing, Las Vegas 2012; also in Richard Sorabji, *Perception, Conscience and Will*, Ashgate 2013.

Bernard Williams, *Shame and Necessity*, University of California Press 1993.

PAGAN RELIGIOUS PRACTICE

Angelos Chaniotis, "Under the watchful eyes of the gods: divine justice in Hellenistic and Roman Asia Minor," in *The Greco-Roman East*, vol. 31, 2007, pp. 1–41.

FREEDOM OF RELIGION IN EARLY CHRISTIANITY

Roland H. Bainton, *Concerning Heretics Attributed to Sebastian Castellio*, Columbia University Press 1935; repr. Octagon Books, New York 1979.

Roland H. Bainton, "The parable of the tares as the proof text for religious liberty to the end of the seventeenth century," *Church History*, vol. 1, 1932, pp. 67–89.

Peter Brown, *Augustine of Hippo*, University of California Press, 1967, 2nd ed. 2000.

Henry Chadwick, *The Early Church*, Pelican 1967.

Rainer Forst, *Toleranz in Konflikt*, Suhrkamp, Frankfurt 2003.

Peter Garnsey, "Religious toleration in classical antiquity," in W. J. Sheils, ed., *Persecution and Toleration*, Blackwell 1984, pp. 1–27.

Peter Heather and David Moncur, *Politics, Philosophy and Empire in the Fourth Century: Select Orations of Themistius*, Liverpool University Press 2001.

SYNDERESIS AND MORAL DOUBLE BIND IN MEDIEVAL THOUGHT

Jacques de Blic, "Conscience ou syndérèse?," *Revue d'ascétique et de mystique* 25, 1949, 146–57.

Robert A. Greene, "Instinct of nature: natural law, synderesis and the moral sense," *Journal of the History of Ideas* 58, 1997, 173–98.

Robert A. Greene, "Synderesis, the spark of conscience in the English Renaissance," *Journal of the History of Ideas* 52, 1991, 195–219.

O. Lottin, "Synderèse et conscience," in *Psychologie et morale aux XIIe et XIIIe siècles*, 5 vols., Louvain 1942–1960; vol. 2, pp. 103–349.

Timothy Potts, "Conscience," in N. Kretzmann, Anthony Kenny, and Jan Pinborg, eds., *The Cambridge History of Later Medieval Philosophy*, Cambridge University Press 1982, pp. 687–704.

Timothy Potts, *Conscience in Medieval Philosophy*, Cambridge University Press 1980.

M. Waldemann, "Synteresis oder syneidesis?," *Theologische Quartalschrift* 119, 1938, 332–71.

SYSTEMS OF PENITENCE FROM ANTIQUITY TO THE MIDDLE AGES

Mark Boda and Gordon Smith, eds, *Repentance in Christian Theology*, Liturgical Press, St. John's Abbey, Collegeville, MN 2006.

Peter Brown, "A tale of two bishops and a brilliant saint," *New York Review of Books*, vol. 59, March 8, 2012, p. 30.

W. H. C. Frend, *The Donatist Church*, Oxford University Press, 1952, ch. 15, "St Augustine and the Donatists."

Caroline Humfress, "Bishops and lawcourts in late antiquity: how not to make sense of the legal evidence," *Journal of Early Christian Studies*, special issue, ed. Kate Cooper, 2011.

Neil McLynn, *Ambrose of Milan*, University of California Press 1994.
Isabel Moreira, *Heaven's Purge: Purgatory in Late Antiquity*, Oxford University Press 2010.
"Pénitence," in *Dictionnaire de théologie catholique*, vol. 12, first twelve centuries by E. Amman, cols. 722–945; 1215 to sixteenth century by A. Michel, cols. 948ff.
Ronald Rittgers, *The Reformation of the Keys*, Harvard University Press 2004.
Thomas Tentler, *Sin and Confession on the Eve of the Reformation*, Princeton University Press 1977.
Alexis Torrence, *Repentance in Late Antiquity*, Oxford University Press 2013.
Kallistos Ware, Metropolitan of Diokleia, *The Orthodox Church*, Penguin 1963, revised 1993.
Oscar D. Watkins, *A History of Penance*, Longman, Green and Co., London 1920, in two volumes and 775 pages, with original texts and English translations. Vol. 1, which reaches 450 CE in 496 pages, is out of print. The scanned 2009 reprint by General Books covers only the shorter vol. 2, which goes up to 1215 CE.

PROTESTS AND PROTESTANTS

Roland H. Bainton, *Concerning Heretics Attributed to Sebastian Castellio*, Columbia University Press 1935; repr. Octagon Books, New York 1979.
Roland H. Bainton, "The development and consistency of Luther's attitude to religious liberty," *Harvard Theological Review* 22, 1929, 107–49.
Michael G. Baylor, *Action and Person: Conscience in Late Scholasticism and the Young Luther*, Brill 1977.
Sarah Coakley, "On the Fearfulness of Forgiveness," in A. Andreopoulos et al., eds., *Meditations of the Heart*, Turnhout 2011, 33–51.
A. Gewirth, *Marsilius of Padua, the Defender of Peace*, 2 vols. Columbia University Press 1951–56.
Harro Höpfl, *Luther and Calvin on Secular Authority*, Cambridge University Press 1991, provides a translation of Luther's *On Secular Authority* (also translated in *Luther's Works* vol. 45) with Calvin's *On Civil Government*.
Introductions to translations in *Luther's Works*, ed. J. Pelikan and Helmut T. Lehmann, 55 vols. (vols. 25, 29, 31, 32, 39, 40, 44, 45) and in *Works of Martin Luther*, in the Philadelphia edition, only partly overlapping, 8 vols.
A. J. P. Kenny, *Wyclif*, Past Masters series, Oxford University Press 1985.
Gordon Leff, *Heresy in the Later Middle Ages*, 2 vols., Manchester University Press 1967 (includes Jan Hus in a very large survey of other protesters).

CASUISTRY

Harold J. Berman, *Law and Revolution: The Formation of the Western Legal Tradition*, Harvard University Press 1983, ch. 5.
Albert R. Jonsen and Stephen Toulmin, *The Abuse of Casuistry*, University of California Press 1988.
Keith Thomas, "Cases of conscience in seventeenth-century England," in John Morrill, Paul Slack, and Daniel Woolf, eds., *Public Duty and Private Conscience in Seventeenth Century England*, Oxford University Press 1993.

FREEDOM OF CONSCIENCE IN THE SEVENTEENTH CENTURY

H. N. Brailsford, *The Levellers and the English Revolution*, Cresset Press, London 1961.
Jeffrey Collins, *The Allegiance of Thomas Hobbes*, Oxford University Press 2005.
Rainer Forst, "Pierre Bayle's reflexive theory of toleration" (compares with Locke),

in Melissa S. Williams and Jeremy Waldron, eds., *Toleration and Its Limits,* New York University Press 2008 (*Nomos* 48), www.uni-konstanz.de/FuF/sfb485/pdf/Diskussionsgrundlage_FORST.pdf.

Rainer Forst, *Toleranz in Konflikt,* Suhrkamp, Frankfurt 2003.

Rainer Forst, "Toleration," *Stanford Encyclopaedia of Philosophy,* online at http://plato.stanford.edu.

Mark Hanin, "Thomas Hobbes' theory of conscience," *History of Political Thought,* vol. 33, 2012, pp. 55–85.

Michael Hickson, "The message of Bayle's last title: providence and toleration in the *Entretiens de Maxime et de Thémiste,*" *Journal of the History of Ideas* 71, 2009, 547–67.

Michael Hickson, "Reductio ad malum: Bayle's early skepticism about theodicy," *Modern Schoolman* 88, 2012, 201–21.

Michael Hickson, "Theodicy and toleration in Bayle's dictionary," *Journal of the History of Philosophy* 51, 2013, 49–73.

Christopher Hill, *Milton and the English Revolution,* Faber and Faber, London 1977.

Christopher Hill, *A Turbulent Seditious and Factious People: John Bunyan and His Church,* Oxford Paperbacks 1988, ch. 7, published under the title *A Tinker and a Poor Man: John Bunyan and His Church, 1628–1688,* Knopf 1989.

Christopher Hill, *The World Turned Upside Down: Radical Ideas during the English Revolution,* Maurice Temple Smith 1972; Penguin 1975.

John Horton and Susan Mendus, eds., *John Locke, "A Letter Concerning Toleration" in Focus,* Routledge 1991, which includes the paper by Jeremy Waldron, "Locke: toleration and the rationality of persecution," reprinted also in his *Liberal Rights,* Cambridge 1993.

Jonathan Israel, *Radical Enlightenment: Philosophy and the Making of Modernity, 1650–1750,* Oxford University Press 2001, esp. on Spinoza.

H. Leon McBeth, *English Baptist Literature on Religious Liberty to 1689,* Arno Press, New York 1980.

Martha Nussbaum, *Liberty of Conscience,* Basic Books 2008.

George H. Sabine, ed., *The Works of Gerrard Winstanley with an Appendix of Documents,* Russell and Russell 1941.

Quentin Skinner, *Hobbes and Republican Liberty,* Cambridge University Press 2008.

Edward Bean Underhill, ed., *Tracts on Liberty of Conscience and Persecution, 1614–1661,* London 1846.

Richard Vernon, *Locke on Toleration,* Cambridge University Press 2010.

Jeremy Waldron, *The Harm in Hate Speech,* Harvard University Press 2012, ch. 8 (on Locke, Bayle, and Enlightenment).

Jeremy Waldron, "Locke: Toleration and the rationality of persecution," in Horton and Mendus above, reprinted in his *Liberal Rights,* Cambridge University Press 1993.

A. S. P. Woodhouse, *Puritanism and Liberty: Being the Army Debates (1647–9) from the Clarke Manuscripts,* Dent and Sons, London, last available of three eds., 1938/1986.

Blair Worden, *God's Instruments: Political Conduct in the England of Oliver Cromwell,* Oxford University Press 2012.

EIGHTEENTH-CENTURY CONSCIENCE: HOW FAR BASED ON HUMAN OPINION, HOW FAR ON GOD?

Fonna Forman-Barzilai, *Adam Smith and the Circles of Sympathy,* Cambridge University Press 2010.

Immanuel Kant, *Lectures on Ethics,* edited by Peter Heath and J. B. Schneewind, and translated by Peter Heath, Cambridge University Press 1997.

Immanuel Kant, *Practical Philosophy*, Cambridge University Press 1996.

A. A. Long, "Stoicism in the philosophical tradition: Spinoza, Lipsius, Butler," on Butler in Jon Miller and Brad Inwood, eds., *Hellenistic and Early Modern Philosophy*, Cambridge University Press 2003.

D. D. Raphael, *The Impartial Spectator: Adam Smith's Moral Philosophy*, Oxford University Press 2007.

D. D. Raphael, "Moral sense," *Dictionary of the History of Ideas*, University of Virginia Library online, 6; original print edition vol. 3, 230–35.

Jerome B. Schneewind, *The Invention of Autonomy*, Cambridge University Press 1998, esp. for Rousseau.

L. A. Selby-Bigge, *British Moralists*, Oxford University Press 1897.

Allen Wood, *Kantian Ethics*, Cambridge University Press 2008, ch. 10, "Conscience."

NINETEENTH- TO TWENTIETH-CENTURY CRITICS

Erik Erikson, "Eight stages of man," in his *Childhood and Society*, W. W. Norton 1950.

S. Freud, *An Outline of Psychoanalysis*, 1938/1940 standard edition, vol. 23, pp. 205–9.

S. Freud, *The Standard Edition of the Complete Works of Sigmund Freud*, ed. James Strachey, 1956–1974, vols. 19, 20, 22.

Ramin Jahanbegloo, *Gandhi, aux sources de la non-violence: Thoreau, Ruskin, Tolstoy*, Éditions du Félin 1998.

William Lyons, "Conscience: an essay in moral psychology," *Philosophy* 84, 2009, 477–94.

J. E. Marcia, "Identity in adolescence," in J. Adelson, ed., *Handbook of Adolescent Psychology*, Wiley 1980.

Rolf E. Muuss, *Theories of Adolescence*, McGraw Hill; later eds., e.g. 6th, 1996; chs. 3–4 provides a useful survey including the last two views.

Friedrich Nietzsche, *Genealogy of Morals*, C. G. Naumann, Leipzig 1887.

Friedrich Nietzsche, *The Portable Nietzsche*, ed. Walter Kaufmann, Viking Penguin 1982.

Gilbert Ryle, "Conscience and moral convictions," *Analysis* 7, 1940, 31–39.

NINETEENTH- TO TWENTIETH-CENTURY CHAMPIONS

M. K. Gandhi, *An Autobiography*, or *The Story of My Experiments with Truth*, Penguin 1982; or other edition.

Raghavan Iyer, ed., *Essential Writings of Mahatma Gandhi*, Oxford University Press 1990, ch. 9, "Conscience, heroism and humility," version reduced from same section in

Raghavan Iyer, *Moral and Political Writings of Mahatma Gandhi*, vol. 2 of 3 vols., Oxford University Press 1973.

Richard Sorabji, *Gandhi and the Stoics: Modern Experiments on Ancient Values*, University of Chicago Press and Oxford University Press 2012, ch. 8.

Henry David Thoreau, *Civil Disobedience*, 1849.

Leo Tolstoy, *The Kingdom of God Is Within You*, 1893, translated from Russian by Aylmer Maude, Oxford University Press 1935, World Classics ed. 1936; and by Constance Garnett, Cassell, New York 1894, reprinted Dover, Mineola, NY, 2006.

Jeremy Waldron, *The Harm in Hate Speech*, Harvard University Press, 2012; ch. 8 (on Mill).

TWENTIETH-CENTURY CONSCIENTIOUS OBJECTION TO WAR

Andrew Koppleman, "Conscience, volitional necessity and religious exemptions," *Legal Theory* 15, 2009, 215–44.

Andrew Koppleman, "The story of *Welsh v. United States*: Elliott Welsh's two religious tests," in Richard Garnett and Andrew Koppleman, eds., *First Amendment Stories*, Foundation Press, New York 2011, pp. 293–318.
Martha Nussbaum, *Liberty of Conscience: In Defense of America's Tradition of Religious Equality*, Basic Books 2008, ch. 4.
John Rae, *Conscience and Politics*, Oxford University Press 1970 (on objection to military conscription in First World War).
Michael Walzer, "Conscientious objection," in his *Obligations: Essays on Disobedience, War, and Citizenship*, Harvard University Press 1970.

FREEDOM OF CONSCIENCE, RELIGION, AND SPEECH IN DIFFERENT COUNTRIES

Kwame Anthony Appiah, *The Ethics of Identity*, Princeton University Press 2004.
Rochana Bajpai, "The conceptual vocabularies of secularism and minority rights in India," *Journal of Political Ideologies* 7, 2002, 179–97.
Rochana Bajpai, *Debating Difference: Group Rights and Liberal Democracy in India*, Oxford University Press 2011.
William Galston, *The Practice of Liberal Pluralism*, Cambridge University Press 2005.
Amy Gutmann, *Identity in Democracy*, Princeton University Press 2003.
Andrew Koppleman, "Conscience, volitional necessity and religious exemptions," *Legal Theory* 15, 2009, 215–44.
Andrew Koppleman, "The story of *Welsh v. United States*: Elliott Welsh's two religious tests," in Richard Garnett and Andrew Koppleman, eds., *First Amendment Stories*, Foundation Press, New York 2011, pp. 293–318.
Jocelyn Maclure and Charles Taylor, *Secularism and Freedom of Conscience*, Harvard University Press 2011.
Martha Nussbaum, *Liberty of Conscience: In Defense of America's Tradition of Religious Equality*, Basic Books 2008.
Robert C. Post, "Cultural heterogeneity and law: pornography, blasphemy and the First Amendment," *California Law Review* 76, 1988, 296–335.
David A. J. Richards, *Toleration and the Constitution*, Oxford University Press 1989.
Michael Sandel, *Democracy's Discontent*, Harvard University Press 1996.
Jeremy Waldron, *The Harm in Hate Speech*, Harvard University Press 2012.

TABLE OF MAIN THINKERS AND WRITERS

Greek Playwrights, Fifth Century BCE

Sophocles, 496–406
Euripides, ca. 480–406
Aristophanes, ca. 448–ca. 380

Pre-Socratic Philosophers BCE

Heraclitus wrote 499–478
Democritus, b. ca. 460; fl. ca. 430
Empedocles, 495–435

Platonic Tradition

Socrates, 469–399 BCE
Plato, 427–348 BCE
Cicero, statesman, lawyer, philosophical historian (Latin), sympathetic also to Stoics, 106–143 BCE
Plutarch of Chaeronea, 46–120 CE
Apuleius, b. ca. 123 (Latin)
Calcidius, fourth–fifth century (Latin)

Aristotle: 384–22 BCE

Epicurean School BCE

Epicurus founded school in Athens in 307
Philodemus, ca. 100, moved from Athens to Italy
Lucretius (Latin), ca. 94–55/51

Stoic School

Zeno of Citium founded school in Athens in 307
Panaetius, ca. 185–ca. 110
Antipater, head in Athens, ca. 152–129
Seneca (Latin), 4 BCE–65 CE
Epictetus, ca. 50–ca.125
Marcus Aurelius, Roman Emperor, 161–180

Latin Playwrights

Plautus, 254–184
Terence, 195/185–159

Early Christian Writers and Writings in Greek CE

Paul, Saint, 5–67
The Shepherd of Hermas, ca. 100, before 140
Hippolytus, ca. 160–236
Clement of Alexandria, d. before 215
Origen, ca. 185–253/254
Hippolytus, ca. 160–236
Gregory Thaumaturgus, ca. 210–70
John Chrysostom of Antioch, 347/349–407

Ancient Christians Writing in Latin

Tertullian, ca. 160–220
Lactantius, ca. 240–320
Cyprian, bishop of Carthage, 248–58
Constantine, first Christian emperor from 312
Ambrose, 330s–397
Jerome, ca. 347–419/420
Augustine, St., of Hippo, 354–430
Gregory, Pope, the Great, 540–604

Pagan Thinkers Writing in Greek

Galen, ca. 129–99
Themistius, 317–ca. 390
Symmachus wrote plea of 384

Neoplatonists Writing in Greek

Iamblichus, ca. 250–before 325
Damascius, head of Athenian school when closed in 529
Simplicius, writing after 529
Olympiodorus, 495/505–after 565

Church in British Isles and West

St. Finian founded monastery of Clonard, Ireland, ca. 530
St. Columban, mission to England and Gaul, ca. 543–615
Augustine (not of Hippo) appointed first Archbishop of Canterbury in 597, by Pope Gregory the Great
Theodore of Tarsus, 602–690, appointed Archbishop of Canterbury by Pope from 668
Bede, Venerable, scholar and monk, ca. 673–735

Charlemagne crowned Holy Roman Emperor by Pope, 800–814

Split of Roman and Greek churches, 1054

Christian Writers in Medieval Latin

Gratian, *Decretum*, legal compendium, ca. 1150
Abelard, Peter, 1079–1172
Alain of Lille, ca. 1128–1202
Albert the Great, ca. 1200–1280
Bonaventure, ca. 1217–1274
Thomas Aquinas, ca. 1225–1274

Fourth Lateran Council in 1215 introduces annual confession

Fourteenth- and Sixteenth-Century Protesters

Marsilius of Padua, 1275/1280–ca. 1342
Wyclif, John, 1330–1384
Hus, Jan, 1371–1415
Luther, Martin, 1483–1546
Calvin, John, 1509–1564
Castellio, Sebastian, 1515–1563
Council of Trent, 1545–1563, response to Protestant Reformation

Sixteenth–Seventeenth Century

Montaigne, Michel de, 1533–1592
Jesuit order founded by Ignatius Loyola in 1540

English Casuists

Perkins, William, writing 1558–1602
Ames, William, 1576–1633
Baxter, Richard, published 1673
Sanderson, Robert, published 1660
Taylor, Jeremy, 1613–1667
Pascale, Blaise, attack on casuistry, 1656

Seventeenth-Century Thinkers from before the English Civil Wars and Execution of King Charles I up to 1660

Baptists
- Smyth, John, ca. 1570–1612
- Helwys, Thomas, ca. 1575–ca. 1616
- Busher, Leonard, published 1614; in Holland, 1640s
- Murton, John, 1585–ca. 1626

Roger Williams, Anglican, converting to Baptist, 1603–1684
Hobbes, Thomas, 1588–1679
Cromwell, Oliver, 1599–1658
Milton, John, 1608–1674
Levellers, 1644–1649
- Walwyn, William, 1600–1681
- Lillburne, John, later a Quaker, ca. 1615–1657
- Overton, Richard, fl. 1640–1663

Quakers: Nayler, James, ca. 1617–1660
- Fox, George, 1624–1691
- Penn, William, 1644–1718

Diggers: Winstanley, Gerrard, 1609–1676

Seventeenth-Century Thinkers after the Restoration of the English Monarchy in 1660

Locke, John, 1632–1704
Bayle, Pierre, 1647–1706
Spinoza, Benedict, 1632–1677
More, Henre, 1614–1687

Eigteenth-Century Thinkers

Cooper, Anthony Ashley, Third Earl of Shaftesbury, 1671–1713
Hutcheson, Francis, 1694–1746
Butler, Joseph, Bishop, 1692–1752
Hume, David, 1711–1776
Rousseau, Jean-Jacques, 1712–1789
Smith, Adam, 1723–1790
Kant, Immanuel, 1724–1804

Nineteenth–Twentieth Centuries

Mill, John Stuart, 1806–1873
Newman, John Henry, Cardinal, 1801–1890
Thoreau, Henry David, 1817–1862
Tolstoy, Leo, 1828–1910
Nietzsche, Friedrich, 1844–1900
Freud, Sigmund, 1856–1939
Gandhi, Mahatma, 1869–1948

GENERAL INDEX

INDEX LOCORUM

Compiled by David Robertson

Made in the USA
Middletown, DE
16 September 2021